Winners Take All

The Elite Charade of Changing the World

Anand Giridharadas

ALLEN LANE
an imprint of
PENGUIN BOOKS

ALLEN LANE

UK | USA | Canada | Ireland | Australia
India | New Zealand | South Africa

Penguin Books is part of the Penguin Random House group of companies
whose addresses can be found at global.penguinrandomhouse.com.

First published in the United States of America by Alfred A. Knopf,
a division of Penguin Random House LLC, 2019
First published in Great Britain by Allen Lane 2019
001

Printed and bound in Great Britain by Clays Ltd, Elcograf S.p.A.

A CIP catalogue record for this book is available from the British Library

ISBN: 978-0-241-40072-2

www.greenpenguin.co.uk

MIX
Paper from
responsible sources
FSC
www.fsc.org   FSC® C018179

Penguin Random House is committed to a
sustainable future for our business, our readers
and our planet. This book is made from Forest
Stewardship Council® certified paper.

For Orion and Zora,

and the more than 300,000 children born today,
with hope that you will see through our illusions

I sit on a man's back choking him and making him carry me, and yet assure myself and others that I am sorry for him and wish to lighten his load by all means possible . . . except by getting off his back.

—LEO TOLSTOY, *WRITINGS ON CIVIL DISOBEDIENCE AND NONVIOLENCE*

Social change is not a project that one group of people carries out for the benefit of another.

—LETTER TO BAHÁ'Í FROM THE UNIVERSAL HOUSE OF JUSTICE IN HAIFA, ISRAEL

CONTENTS

Winners Take All

PROLOGUE

All around us in America is the clank-clank-clank of the new—in our companies and economy, our neighborhoods and schools, our technologies and social fabric. But these novelties have failed to translate into broadly shared progress and the betterment of our overall civilization. American scientists make the most important discoveries in medicine and genetics and publish more biomedical research than those of any other country—but the average American's health remains worse and slower-improving than that of peers in other rich countries, and in certain years life expectancy actually declines. American inventors create astonishing new ways to learn thanks to the power of video and the Internet, many of them free of charge—but the average twelfth grader tests more poorly in reading today than in 1992. The country has had a "culinary renaissance," as one publication puts it, one farmers' market and Whole Foods at a time—but it has failed to improve the nutrition of most people, with the incidence of obesity and related conditions rising over time. The tools for becoming an entrepreneur appear to be more accessible than ever, for the student who learns coding online or the Uber driver—but the share of young people who own a business has fallen by two-thirds since the 1980s. America has birthed a wildly successful online book superstore called Amazon, and another company, Google, has scanned more than twenty-five million books for public use—but illiteracy has remained stubbornly in place and the fraction of Americans who read at least one work of literature a year has dropped by almost a quarter in recent decades. The government has more data at its disposal and more ways of talking and listening to citizens—but only one-quarter as many people find it trustworthy as did in the tempestuous 1960s.

A successful society is a progress machine. It takes in the raw material of innovations and produces broad human advancement. America's machine is broken. When the fruits of change have fallen on the United States in recent decades, the very fortunate have basketed almost all of them. For instance, the average pretax income of the top tenth of Americans has doubled since 1980, that of the top 1 percent has more than tripled, and that of the top 0.001 percent has risen more than sevenfold—even as the average pretax income of the bottom half of Americans has stayed almost precisely the same. These familiar figures amount to three and a half decades' worth of wondrous, head-spinning change with zero impact on the average pay of 117 million Americans. Meanwhile, the opportunity to get ahead has been transformed from a shared reality to a perquisite of already being ahead. Among Americans born in 1940, those raised at the top of the upper middle class and the bottom of the lower middle class shared a roughly 90 percent chance of realizing the so-called American dream of ending up better off than their parents. Among Americans born in 1984 and maturing into adulthood today, the new reality is split-screen. Those raised near the top of the income ladder now have a 70 percent chance of realizing the dream. Meanwhile, those close to the bottom, more in need of elevation, have a 35 percent chance of climbing above their parents' station. And it is not only progress and money that the fortunate monopolize: Rich American men, who tend to live longer than the average citizens of any other country, now live fifteen years longer than poor American men, who endure only as long as men in Sudan and Pakistan.

Thus many millions of Americans, on the left and right, feel one thing in common: that the game is rigged against people like them. Perhaps this is why we hear constant condemnation of "the system," for it is the system that people expect to turn fortuitous developments into societal progress. Instead, the system—in America and around the world—has been organized to siphon the gains from innovation upward, such that the fortunes of the world's billionaires now grow at more than double the pace of everyone else's, and the top 10 percent of humanity have come to hold 90 percent of the planet's wealth. It is no wonder that the American voting public—like other publics around the world—has turned more resentful and suspicious in recent years, embracing populist movements on the left and right, bringing socialism and nationalism into the center of political life in a way that once seemed unthinkable, and succumbing to all manner of conspiracy theory and fake news. There is a spreading recognition, on both sides of the ideological divide, that the system is broken and has to change.

Some elites faced with this kind of gathering anger have hidden behind walls and gates and on landed estates, emerging only to try to seize even greater political power to protect themselves against the mob. But in recent years a great many fortunate people have also tried something else, something both laudable and self-serving: They have tried to help by taking ownership of the problem.

All around us, the winners in our highly inequitable status quo declare themselves partisans of change. They know the problem, and they want to be part of the solution. Actually, they want to lead the search for solutions. They believe that their solutions deserve to be at the forefront of social change. They may join or support movements initiated by ordinary people looking to fix aspects of their society. More often, though, these elites start initiatives of their own, taking on social change as though it were just another stock in their portfolio or corporation to restructure. Because they are in charge of these attempts at social change, the attempts naturally reflect their biases.

The initiatives mostly aren't democratic, nor do they reflect collective problem-solving or universal solutions. Rather, they favor the use of the private sector and its charitable spoils, the market way of looking at things, and the bypassing of government. They reflect a highly influential view that the winners of an unjust status quo—and the tools and mentalities and values that helped them win—are the secret to redressing the injustices. Those at greatest risk of being resented in an age of inequality are thereby recast as our saviors from an age of inequality. Socially minded financiers at Goldman Sachs seek to change the world through "win-win" initiatives like "green bonds" and "impact investing." Tech companies like Uber and Airbnb cast themselves as empowering the poor by allowing them to chauffeur people around or rent out spare rooms. Management consultants and Wall Street brains seek to convince the social sector that they should guide its pursuit of greater equality by assuming board seats and leadership positions. Conferences and idea festivals sponsored by plutocrats and big business host panels on injustice and promote "thought leaders" who are willing to confine their thinking to improving lives within the faulty system rather than tackling the faults. Profitable companies built in questionable ways and employing reckless means engage in corporate social responsibility, and some rich people make a splash by "giving back"—regardless of the fact that they may have caused serious societal problems as they built their fortunes. Elite networking forums like the Aspen Institute and the Clinton Global Initiative groom the rich to be self-appointed leaders of social change, taking on the problems people like them have been instrumental in creating or sustaining. A new breed of community-minded so-called B Corporations has been born, reflecting a faith that more enlightened corporate self-interest—rather than, say, public regulation—is the surest guarantor of the public welfare. A pair of Silicon Valley billionaires fund an initiative to rethink the Democratic Party, and one of them can claim, without a hint of irony, that their goals are to amplify the voices of the powerless and reduce the political influence of rich people like them.

The elites behind efforts like these often speak in a language of "changing the world" and "making the world a better place" more typically associated with barricades than ski resorts. Yet we are left with the inescapable fact that in the very era in which these elites have done so much to help, they have continued to hoard the overwhelming share of progress, the average American's life has scarcely improved, and virtually all of the nation's institutions, with the exception of the military, have lost the public's trust.

Are we ready to hand over our future to the elite, one supposedly world-changing initiative at a time? Are we ready to call participatory democracy a failure, and to declare these other, private forms of change-making the new way forward? Is the decrepit state of American self-government an excuse to work around it and let it further atrophy? Or is meaningful democracy, in which we all potentially have a voice, worth fighting for?

There is no denying that today's elite may be among the more socially concerned elites in history. But it is also, by the cold logic of numbers, among the more predatory in history. By refusing to risk its way of life, by rejecting the idea that the powerful might have to sacrifice for the common good, it clings to a set of social arrangements that allow it to monopolize progress and then give symbolic scraps to the forsaken—many of whom wouldn't need the scraps if the society were working right. This book is an attempt to understand the connection between these elites' social concern and predation, between the extraordinary helping and the extraordinary hoarding, between the milking—and perhaps abetting—of an unjust status quo and the attempts by the milkers to repair a small part of it. It is also an attempt to offer a view of how the elite see the world, so that we might better assess the merits and limitations of their world-changing campaigns.

There are many ways to make sense of all this elite concern and predation. One is that the elites are doing the best they can. The world is what it is; the system is what it is; the forces of the age are bigger than anyone can resist; the most fortunate are helping. This view may allow that this helpfulness is just a drop in the bucket, but it is something. The slightly more critical view is that this elite-led change is well-meaning but inadequate. It treats symptoms, not root causes; it does not change the fundamentals of what ails us. According to this view, elites are shirking the duty of more meaningful reform.

But there is still another, darker way of judging what goes on when elites put themselves in the vanguard of social change: that it not only fails to make things better, but also serves to keep things as they are. After all, it takes the edge off of some of the public's anger at being excluded from progress. It improves the image of the winners. With its private and voluntary half-measures, it crowds out public solutions that would solve problems for everyone, and do so with or without the elite's blessing. There is no question that the outpouring of elite-led social change in our era does great good and soothes pain and saves lives. But we should also recall Oscar Wilde's words about such elite helpfulness being "not a solution" but "an aggravation of the difficulty." More than a century ago, in an age of churn like our own, he wrote, "Just as the worst slave-owners were those who were kind to their slaves, and so prevented the horror of the system being realised by those who suffered from it, and understood by those who contemplated it, so, in the present state of things in England, the people who do most harm are the people who try to do most good."

Wilde's formulation may sound extreme to modern ears. How can there be anything wrong with trying to do good? The answer may be: when the good is an accomplice to even greater, if more invisible, harm. In our era that harm is the concentration of money and power among a small few, who reap from that concentration a near monopoly on the benefits of change. And do-gooding pursued by elites tends not only to leave this concentration untouched, but actually to shore it up. For when elites assume leadership of social change, they are able to reshape what social change is—above all, to present it as something that should never threaten winners. In an age defined by a chasm between those who have power and those who don't, elites have spread the idea that people must be helped, but only in market-friendly ways that do not upset fundamental power equations. The society should be changed in ways that do not change the underlying economic system that has allowed the winners to win and fostered many of the problems they seek to solve. The broad fidelity to this law helps make sense of what we observe all around: the powerful fighting to "change the world" in ways that essentially keep it the same, and "giving back" in ways that sustain an indefensible distribution of influence, resources, and tools. Is there a better way?

The secretary-general of the Organisation for Economic Co-operation and Development (OECD), a research and policy organization that works on behalf of the world's richest countries, recently compared the prevailing elite posture to that of the fictional Italian aristocrat Tancredi Falconeri, who declared, "If we want things to stay as they are, things will have to change." If this view is correct, then much of the charity and social innovation and give-one-get-one marketing around us may not be reform measures so much as forms of conservative self-defense—measures that protect elites from more menacing change. Among the kinds of issues being side-lined, the OECD leader, Ángel Gurría, wrote, are "rising inequalities of income, wealth and opportunities; the growing disconnect between finance and the real economy; mounting divergence in productivity levels between workers, firms and regions; winner-take-most dynamics in many markets; limited progressivity of our tax systems; corruption and capture of politics and institutions by vested interests; lack of transparency and participation by ordinary citizens in decision-making; the soundness of the education and of the values we transmit to future generations." Elites, Gurría writes, have found myriad ways to "change things on the surface so that in practice nothing changes at all." The people with the most to lose from genuine social change have placed themselves in charge of social change, often with the passive assent of those most in need of it.

It is fitting that an era marked by these tendencies should culminate in the election of Donald Trump. Trump is at once an exposer, an exploiter, and an embodiment of the cult of elite-led social change. He tapped, as few before him successfully had, into a widespread intuition that elites were phonily claiming to be doing what was best for most Americans. He exploited that intuition by whipping it into frenzied anger and then directing most of that anger not at elites but at the most marginalized and vulnerable Americans. And he came to incarnate the very fraud that had fueled his rise and that he had exploited. He became, like the elites he assailed, the establishment figure who falsely casts himself as a renegade. He became the rich, educated man who styles himself as the ablest protector of the poor and uneducated—and who insists, against all evidence, that his interests have nothing to do with the change he seeks. He became the chief salesman for the theory, rife among plutocratic change agents, that what is best for powerful him is best for the powerless, too. Trump is the reductio ad absurdum of a culture that tasks elites with reforming the very systems that have made them and left others in the dust.

One thing that unites those who voted for Trump and those who despaired at his being elected is a sense that the country requires transformational reform. The question we confront is whether moneyed elites, who already rule the roost in the economy and exert enormous influence in the corridors of political power, should be allowed to continue their conquest of social change and of the pursuit of greater equality. The only thing better than controlling money and power is to control the efforts to question the distribution of money and power. The only thing better than being a fox is being a fox asked to watch over hens.

What is at stake is whether the reform of our common life is led by governments elected by and accountable to the people, or rather by wealthy elites claiming to know our best interests. We must decide whether, in the name of ascendant values such as efficiency and scale, we are willing to allow democratic purpose to be usurped by private actors who often genuinely aspire to improve things but, first things first, seek to protect themselves. Yes, government is dysfunctional at present. But that is all the more reason to treat its repair as our foremost national priority. Pursuing workarounds of our troubled democracy makes democracy even more troubled. We must ask ourselves why we have so easily lost faith in the engines of progress that got us where we are today—in the democratic efforts to outlaw slavery, end child labor, limit the workday, keep drugs safe, protect collective bargaining, create public schools, battle the Great

Depression, electrify rural America, weave a nation together by road, pursue a Great Society free of poverty, extend civil and political rights to women and African Americans and other minorities, and give our fellow citizens health, security, and dignity in old age.

This book offers a series of portraits of this elite-led, market-friendly, winner-safe social change. In these pages, you will meet people who ardently believe in this form of change and people who are beginning to question it. You will meet a start-up employee who believes her for-profit company has the solution to the woes of the working poor, and a billionaire investor in her company who believes that only vigorous public action can stem the rising tide of public rage. You will meet a thinker who grapples with how much she can challenge the rich and powerful if she wants to keep getting their invitations and patronage. You will meet a campaigner for economic equality whose previous employers include Goldman Sachs and McKinsey, and who wonders about his complicity in what he calls "the Trying-to-Solve-the-Problem-with-the-Tools-That-Caused-It issue." You will meet one of the most powerful figures in the philanthropy world, who stuns his rich admirers by refusing to honor the taboo against speaking of how they make their money. You will meet a former American president who launched his career with a belief in changing the world through political action, and then, as he began to spend time with plutocrats in his post-presidential life, gravitated toward private methods of change that benefit rather than scare them. You will meet a widely lionized "social innovator" who quietly nurses doubts about whether his commercial approach to world-changing is what it is cracked up to be. You will meet an Italian philosopher who reminds us what gets sidelined when the moneyed take over change.

What these various figures have in common is that they are grappling with certain powerful myths—the myths that have fostered an age of extraordinary power concentration; that have allowed the elite's private, partial, and self-preservational deeds to pass for real change; that have let many decent winners convince themselves, and much of the world, that their plan to "do well by doing good" is an adequate answer to an age of exclusion; that put a gloss of selflessness on the protection of one's privileges; and that cast more meaningful change as wide-eyed, radical, and vague.

It is my hope in writing what follows to reveal these myths to be exactly that. Much of what appears to be reform in our time is in fact the defense of stasis. When we see through the myths that foster this misperception, the path to genuine change will come into view. It will once again be possible to improve the world without permission slips from the powerful.

CHAPTER 1

BUT HOW IS THE WORLD CHANGED?

Her college mind heavy with the teachings of Aristotle and Goldman Sachs, Hilary Cohen knew she wanted to change the world. Yet she wrestled with a question that haunted many around her: How should the world be changed?

It was 2014, the spring of her senior year at Georgetown University. She had to decide what was next. Should she be a management consultant? Should she be a rabbi? Should she go straight to helping people by working at a nonprofit? Or should she first train in the tools of business? She had absorbed the ascendant message, all but unavoidable for the elite American college student, that those tools were essential to serving others. The best way to bring about meaningful reform was to apprentice in the bowels of the status quo.

Her interest in world-changing, while commonplace in her generation, had not been inevitable given her background. She grew up in Houston, in a loving, tightly knit family of well-to-do *Wall Street Journal* subscribers, with a mother who actively volunteered in the mental health field and the Jewish community and a father who worked in finance (municipal bonds, real estate). In addition to more conventional father-daughter activities like coaching her sports teams, he trained her in investment analysis. He had her prowl the mall as a little girl, noting down which stores had the longest lines. Sometimes he bought stock based on her observations, and when they rose, sang her praises. His career paid for Cohen to attend, from pre-kindergarten through twelfth grade, the Kinkaid School in Houston, a preparatory academy founded on a philosophy of educating the "whole child" and of "balanced growth—intellectual, physical, social, and ethical." Her father dropped her there most mornings with a reminder to "learn something new." As with many students at such schools, there was a fair shot that she would bask in the inspiring ideals, fulfill the community service requirement, and land in a lucrative white-collar job like her father's.

But Cohen had also been interested in politics and public service for as long as she could remember. She had, she says, "served in every student government position you can imagine from third grade on." She had harbored childhood dreams of a "Hilary Cohen for 2032" presidential campaign—dreams bolstered virtually by a Facebook group and physically by actual T-shirts. In high school, she served on a youth council for the mayor of Houston, took a summer class at Harvard called "Congress: Policy, Parties, and Institutions," and interned on Capitol Hill. She ended up back in Washington to attend college at Georgetown, where she seemed to turn away from a trajectory like her father's and toward other suns.

She had arrived with an osmotic interest in business and her own passion for politics, and with a vague inclination to ground herself in math or one of the sciences or some other hard discipline. But she soon found herself changing. She was not the first college student to be overtaken by idealism amid old stone buildings and green quadrangles. She took a freshman seminar on education, and there read Aristotle's *Nicomachean Ethics*. She says that book "influenced me most, and probably redirected my course in college and then life."

The *Ethics*, as she read it, challenged many of the assumptions about life's purpose that one might absorb growing up in a prosperous neighborhood in Houston, learning at the knee of a financier, and being groomed by a prep school to enter the highly selective ranks of Georgetown. "The life of money-making is one undertaken under compulsion," Aristotle says, "and wealth is evidently not the good we are seeking; for it is merely useful and for the sake of something else." It stayed with her, this summons to search for a purpose greater than the material. "He goes through all the things you can mistake for the purpose of your life," she said. Glory. Money. Honor. Fame. "And he basically enumerates the reasons why, at the end of the day, those things are never going to fill you up." The only truly ultimate good is "human flourishing."

The class nudged Cohen toward a philosophy major. She also took classes in psychology, theology, and cognitive science because she wanted to understand how people grappled with these ancient dilemmas of how best to live. As she worked toward her degree, she decided that she wanted to pursue that idea of human flourishing for others. Like many of her classmates, she wanted to be an agent of positive change. If that desire was widespread in her cohort, it was perhaps because they were so often reminded of being among the lucky ones in a society with ever less grace toward the unlucky.

In Cohen's years at Georgetown, beginning in 2010, the anger about inequality and a seemingly elusive American dream had yet to peak. But it was already unavoidable. The country was still limping back to life after the Great Recession. The university's setting in Washington also made vivid the gentrification that since Cohen's birth had cut by half the black population as a fraction of the surrounding Ward Two—a fact impressed upon students by *The Hoya,* the campus newspaper. Two months after Cohen enrolled, and in a very different vein, the Tea Party won a significant victory in the 2010 midterm congressional elections. "They just didn't seem to care about the regular working person any more," the scholars Vanessa Williamson and Theda Skocpol quoted a Tea Partier named Beverly as saying in a dissection of the movement published in the spring of Cohen's freshman year and later taught at Georgetown.

The Occupy movement launched in the first weeks of Cohen's sophomore year. Thanks in part to its agitations, Google searches for "inequality" would more than double among Americans during Cohen's college career, and searches for "the 1 percent" would more than triple. In the spring of her junior year, a new pope was elected, a Jesuit like Georgetown's leaders. Pope Francis soon called for poverty to be "radically resolved by rejecting the absolute autonomy of markets and financial speculation and by attacking the structural causes of inequality," which he called "the root of social ills." *The Hoya* observed that these words ringing out of Rome were reverberating on campus. A Jesuit priest and political science professor named Matthew Carnes, with whom Cohen would soon work on a philanthropic project, told the newspaper that longtime critics of inequality on campus felt "vindicated" by the pope. And in the summer before Cohen's senior year, Black Lives Matter was born, drawing many of her classmates into one of the more trenchant critiques of inequality in modern American history. As Cohen's graduation neared, a little-known French economist named Thomas Piketty published the surprise bestseller *Capital in the Twenty-First Century*—a two-and-a-half-pound, 704-page assault on inequality.

Piketty and some colleagues would later publish a paper containing a startling fact about 2014, the year of Cohen's graduation and debut as a self-supporting earner. The study showed that a college graduate like Cohen, on the safe assumption that she ended up in the top 10 percent of earners, would be making more than twice as much before taxes as a similarly situated person in 1980. If Cohen entered the top 1 percent of earners, her income would be more than triple what a 1 percenter earned in her parents' day—an average of $1.3 million a year for that elite group versus $428,000 in 1980, adjusted for inflation. On the narrow chance that she entered the top 0.001 percent, her income would be more than seven times higher than in 1980, with a cohort average of $122 million. The study included the striking fact that the bottom half of Americans had over this same span seen their average pretax income rise from $16,000 to $16,200. One hundred seventeen million people had, in other words, been "completely shut off from economic growth since the 1970s," Piketty, Emmanuel Saez, and Gabriel Zucman wrote. A generation's worth of mind-bending innovation had delivered scant progress for half of Americans.

The realities of a bifurcating America were part of the atmosphere in which Cohen would make decisions about her future. The phrase that best captured her aspiration was, she said, a common one in the halls of Georgetown: "to change the lives of millions of people." It spoke of the widespread desire to work on social problems in an age not lacking in them. And it gave a hint of how that desire had been inflected by the institutions and mores of market capitalism.

Cohen explained that when she and her friends thought about improving the world for others, they did so with an ethos befitting the era in which they had come of age. It is an era in which capitalism has no ideological opponent of similar stature and influence, and in which it is hard to escape the market's vocabulary, values, and assumptions, even when pondering a topic such as social change. Socialism clubs have given way to social enterprise clubs on American campuses. Students have also been influenced by the business world's commandment, disseminated through advertisements and TED talks and books by so-called thought leaders, to do whatever you do "at scale," which is where the "millions of people" thing came from. It is an era, moreover, that has relentlessly told young people that they can "do well by doing good." Thus when Cohen and her friends sought to make a difference, their approaches were less about what they wanted to take down or challenge and more about the ventures they wanted to start up, she said. Many of them believed there was more power in building up what was good than in challenging what was bad.

A generation earlier, when their parents had spoken of "changing the world," many of them tended to follow that thought with language about taking on the "system," the "powers that be," the "Man." In the 1960s and '70s, Georgetown had been one of the more conservative campuses, thanks in part to its religious anchoring. Yet it was full of aspiring world-changers who protested the Vietnam War and raised questions about the system and joined groups like the Radical Union, which in 1970 put out a letter urging all who would listen to read the quotations of Chairman Mao. "Only about a fourth of the campus is hip—they wear rags," declared Susan Berman's 1971 book *The Underground Guide to the College of Your Choice*. "But then, things are progressing as three years ago some cats still wore sport coats and ties to classes."

One of those cats had been Bill Clinton, who enrolled at George-town in 1964 and returned sophomore year to discover, to his relief, that the shirt-and-tie requirement had been scrapped. The future president didn't think of himself as a radical, although at the time he told an interviewer, Maurice Moore, that he had many friends "whom I suppose would be classified as hippies or members of the off-beat generation." Clinton took care to distance himself from what he called the "rather unhealthy negativism" of the hippie move-ment. But his own alternative path illustrated how young people wanting to change things in those days thought about their options. He told Moore that he was thinking about a doctorate or law school and, after that, "domestic politics—electioneering, or some phase of it." He was enraptured by President Lyndon Johnson's sweeping initiatives on civil rights and poverty, and he believed what it wasn't strange to believe back then: that if you were sincere about chang-ing the world, you set out to work on the systems at the root of your society's troubles.

In the years since, though, Georgetown and the United States and the world at large have been taken over by an ascendant ideol-ogy of how best to change the world. That ideology is often called neoliberalism, and it is, in the framing of the anthropologist David Harvey, "a theory of political economic practices that proposes that human well-being can best be advanced by liberating individual entrepreneurial freedoms and skills within an institutional frame-work characterized by strong private property rights, free markets, and free trade." Where the theory goes, "deregulation, privatiza-tion, and withdrawal of the state from many areas of social provi-sion" tend to follow, Harvey writes. "While personal and individual freedom in the marketplace is guaranteed, each individual is held responsible and accountable for his or her own actions and well-being. This principle extends into the realms of welfare, education, health care, and even pensions." The political philosopher Yascha Mounk captures the cultural consequences of this ideology when he says it has ushered in a new "age of responsibility," in which "responsibility—which once meant the moral duty to help and support others—has come to suggest an obligation to be self-sufficient."

The founding parents of this revolution were political figures on the right such as Ronald Reagan and Margaret Thatcher, who rose to power by besmirching the role of government. Reagan declared that "government is not the solution to our problem; government is the problem." Two centuries earlier, the founding fathers of his country had created a constitutional government in order to "form a more perfect Union, establish Justice, insure domestic Tranquility, provide for the common defense, promote the general Welfare, and secure the Blessings of Liberty to ourselves and our Posterity." Now the instrument they had created, an instrument that had helped to make the United States one of the most successful societies in history, was declared the enemy of these things. Across the Atlantic, Thatcher echoed Reagan in saying, "There is no such thing as society. There are individual men and women, and there are families. And no government can do anything except through people, and people must look to themselves first." What their revolution amounted to in practice in America and elsewhere was lower taxes, weakened regulation, and vastly reduced public spending on schools, job retraining, parks, and the commons at large.

The political right couldn't pull off its revolution alone, however. That is where the need for a loyal opposition comes in. Thus neoliberals cultivated on the left half of the American political spectrum a tribe they could work with. This liberal subcaste would retain the left's traditional goals of bettering the world and attending to underdogs, but it would increasingly pursue those aims in market-friendly ways. Bill Clinton would become the paterfamilias of this tribe, with his so-called Third Way between left and right, and his famous declaration, regarded as historic from the moment it was uttered in 1996, that "the era of big government is over."

Clinton's evolution from embracing Johnson's big-government activism in the 1960s to declaring the end of big government in the 1990s spoke of a turning in the culture whose effects were palpable in the Georgetown that Cohen discovered in the early 2010s. When she and her peers were stirred by a desire to change things, their own ideas and the resources available to them tended to steer them toward the market rather than government as the place where problems are best solved. The age-old youthful impulse to reimagine the world was now often molded and guided by one of the reigning ideas of the age: that if you really want to change the world, you must rely on the techniques, resources, and personnel of capitalism. In 2011, for example, Georgetown found itself with a $1.5 million pot of money intended for student activities that the administration no longer wished to administer. It allowed students to vote on how to use the money. Out of several proposals, they chose one to create a "student-run endowment that invested in student and alumni innovative ideas that do good in the world." Cohen joined this Social Innovation and Public Service Fund as one of two students on its founding board of trustees. She served alongside a private equity executive and other businesspersons, as well as Georgetown professors. It was a perfectly laudable and well-meaning initiative, and it spoke to how many young people had been trained to think about change in an age dominated by a market consensus: as a thing that could be pursued by investment committee as much as by social and political action.

Boosters of business have done a remarkable job of reaching into campus life in recent decades and developing programs designed to coax students in their direction. In the early 1970s, for example, Georgetown received a gift from the family of the late George F. Baker, the founder of the bank that would grow to be called Citibank and the anchor donor of Harvard Business School. It was perhaps natural that the business school he had helped set up should have a Baker Scholars program, which recognized its most capable students. But it was even more deft to create a Baker Scholars program at Georgetown, focused on liberal arts students, offering them "a unique opportunity" to "learn about the world of business."

Cohen applied to the program, less because she wanted to be a businessperson and more because she was starting to be convinced by the idea that the business world offered useful general-purpose training in being effective. Her application earned her an interview, which turned out to be a four-on-one grilling by trustees, "most of whom are or have been in finance/consulting," she recalled. When she was asked to demonstrate her interest in business, she brought up the mall research she had done for her father. The interview questions, she said, reflected the tensions among older visions of changing the world, Georgetown's Jesuit traditions, and the ascendant values of the marketplace. "I remember being asked in the same day to assess the trade-offs should profit ever conflict with ethical standards, to describe how I'd lived the Jesuit ideal of 'women and men for others,' and to come up with a clear articulation of my 'personal brand' in two sentences or less," she said.

Her answers won her a berth as a Baker Scholar, and through the program she was treated to an inside tour of the business world of a kind seldom available to people interested in, say, legal aid. The program hosted regular meetings on campus and sent her on trips to other cities, where she visited companies such as Kiva, DoSomething, Kind, and NASCAR, as well as consulting firms, financial services firms, and companies in media and technology.

Even as the program sold liberal arts students on business, one of its trustees endeavored quietly to press a contrary message. He was a Jesuit named Kevin O'Brien, and he had been a Baker Scholar in the 1980s, which helped to prepare him for a career in corporate law. Then he had left that world for the priesthood. He hosted the nine Baker Scholars in Cohen's cohort for regular dinners. "Having tasted and departed the world most of us were about to enter, he would gently pose questions that ended up being far more provocative than those of the more buttoned-up trustees," she said. "He challenged us to think about our vocation more often and about being paid in the 'currency of our soul.'"

Father O'Brien's genre of advice was up against the tremendous force of corporate recruiters on campus—starting with the hawkers of internships. In the careerist culture that has overtaken many leading universities, productive summers that expose one to potential careers have become essential grooming for many ambitious students. Cohen pursued them. She began in 2010 with that internship on Capitol Hill, which many around her considered an old-fashioned way of learning how to make change. Starting companies and pursuing socially minded businesses like Toms Shoes or impact investment funds were more respected in her circles. While Cohen had trouble with this view, she didn't exactly resist it either. After the Hill, she interned at an educational technology company. Then, in the summer before senior year, as Black Lives Matter was getting under way, she followed many other aspiring do-gooders to a summer job as an analyst at Goldman Sachs.

It might seem an improbable choice for someone aspiring to help people. But it was not at all an unusual one in her circles. Cohen was hardly the first person to be impressed by an oft-heard view, espoused by firms like Goldman, that the skills they teach are vital preparation for change-making of any sort. Management consulting firms and Wall Street financial houses have persuaded many young people in recent years that they provide a superior version of what the liberal arts are said to offer: highly portable training for doing whatever you wish down the road. They also say, according to Cohen, "To be a leader in the world, you need this skill set."

She didn't capitulate to these notions all at once. She considered jobs in the nonprofit sector that had been advertised on campus or online. Somehow, though, they felt risky to her. Sure, she would be cutting to the chase of making a difference, but wouldn't she be forgoing the skill-building and self-cultivation offered by the big private-sector firms? Some of the NGOs she looked at seemed to have no career plan for a young person, no promise of a trajectory of growing responsibilities and impact. A lot of these places hired only one or two graduates per year and expected them to find their way with little structure, whereas the big firms recruited entire cohorts of them for entry-level analyst positions, referring to them as "classes," subtly playing into their nostalgia for dorm-room days.

She was still an Aristotelian; she believed that money is not the end in itself that so many think it to be. But it was a means, and she had absorbed the belief all around her that <u>one had to apprentice with money in order to make the world a better place.</u>

The big firms did all they could to portray themselves not only as springboards for future change agents but also as laboratories for present-day ones. For instance, Goldman had launched an initiative called 10,000 Women, through which it invested in female business owners and mentored them. Doing so, its promotional materials said, was "one of the most important means to reducing inequality and ensuring more shared economic growth"—goals for which Goldman was otherwise not well known. While Cohen was a summer analyst there, Goldman had also been involved in an experimental (and ultimately doomed) $10 million investment in a prison program in New York. Under the terms of a new financial instrument called a "social impact bond," it would profit if its investee, a prison education program, dramatically cut the recidivism rate.

Despite such efforts to win over people of Cohen's bent, a summer at Goldman revealed it to be not for her. It was a little far toward the "doing well" end of the "doing well by doing good" continuum. A more moderate choice, she felt, was McKinsey & Company. She liked the idea of going to a boot camp for solving problems at scale, which is how the campus recruiters framed it. The overwhelming share of McKinsey clients are corporate, but the recruiters, knowing the mentality of young people like her, played up the social- and public-sector projects. Cohen said, only half joking, that it was possible to come away from the information session thinking that if hired, you would spend most of your time helping Haiti with post-earthquake development and advising the Vatican.

Even as Cohen warmed to the idea, she feared she would be making "the least imaginative, most soul-sucking decision you can make," going to work at a consulting firm after talking big about changing people's lives. But McKinsey, like Goldman, had a persuasive story to tell her. It, too, was not just a springboard. It was a place where you could change the world now. A recruiting pamphlet from 2014, aimed at aspiring business analysts fresh out of college, seemed to cover all the right bases:

Change the world.
Improve lives.
Invent something new.
Solve a complex problem.
Extend your talents.
Build enduring relationships.

Lofty as the first three of these promises are, McKinsey tried to back them up. It had, for example, set up a Social Sector Practice, through which it published such insights as how "delivering financial services by mobile phone could benefit billions of people by spurring inclusive growth." Rival consulting firms had done the same. The Boston Consulting Group pledged "to change the world for both our social sector and our commercial clients." Bain & Company declared, "We're aiming to transform the whole social sector."

These firms were in fact channeling a widespread dogma: of the market as the place for world-changing and of market types as ideal world-changers. And so graduates like Cohen were bombarded not only by tales of economic woe and inequality, but also by an insistent message about how to defeat these scourges. They might have seen Morgan Stanley's advertising campaign "Capital Creates Change," in which it declares that "the value of capital is to create not just wealth but things that matter," and that working for Morgan Stanley is tantamount to "giving, literally, millions of people a shot at a better life." Like a reborn private-sector John F. Kennedy, it thunders, "Let's raise the capital that builds the things that change the world." They might have read influential books such as *How to Change the World: Social Entrepreneurs and the Power of New Ideas*, by David Bornstein, or come across articles such as "5 Companies Making a Splash for a Better World" in *Forbes* and "27 companies that changed the world" in *Fortune*. They perhaps agreed with Airbnb's conclusion in a research report that businesses like it were not about money but love: "Most people who share, do it because they want to make the world a better place," as *Fast Company* summarized the research. They might have seen a documentary like *The Double Bottom Line*, which told the story of two companies, D.light Design and LifeSpring Hospitals, that, like so many businesses now, merged two goals: to "change the world" and to "make a profit." They might have heard of companies becoming B Corporations and signing on to a new "Declaration of Interdependence," which committed them to using "business as a force for good" and fostering "the change we seek."

And they might have heard thinkers whom they respected say that these new, market-based ways of changing the world were not just additions to the existing ways, but in fact preferable to them. For example, Jonathan Haidt, a professor of psychology at New York University's business school and a popular TED speaker, was a left-wing student at Yale in the early 1980s, but he had since turned against the kind of power-busting world-changing he believed in then. He articulated the new belief well in an interview with the radio host Krista Tippett:

> People our age grew up expecting that the point of civic engagement is to be active, so we can make the government fix civil rights or something—we've got to make the government do something. And young people have grown up never seeing the government do anything except turn the lights off now and then. And so their activism is not going to be to get the government to do things. It's going to be to invent some app, some way of solving problems separately. And that's going to work.

That a scholar like Haidt could compare inventing an app to the civil rights movement gives a sense of the intellectual atmosphere around wavering graduates like Cohen. Maybe it wasn't a soul-sucking decision to go corporate, after all. Such a thought might be reinforced by the rampant talk among Cohen's peers about "social" everything—social innovation, social business, social enterprise, social investing. Indeed, during Cohen's final semester at Georgetown, the university launched on campus the new Beeck Center for Social Impact & Innovation, which was designed to promote the increasingly influential private-sector approach to world-changing that she was contemplating, and which highlighted its temptations and complications.

The center was founded thanks to a $10 million donation from Alberto and Olga Maria Beeck, who made much of their money in the mining business in South America. Wealthy donors such as they often had a financial interest in the world being changed in ways that left things like taxation, redistribution, labor laws, and mining regulations off the table. And Georgetown, like other universities, was happy to oblige. The new center's executive director was Sonal Shah, who had the perfect résumé for it as a veteran of Google, Goldman Sachs, and the White House, where she established the Office of Social Innovation and Civic Participation under President Obama. That office, according to its website, was "based on a simple idea: we cannot drive lasting change by creating new top-down programs from Washington." It was a striking statement from a liberal government—but not an uncommon one in an age dominated by market thinking—and it reflected a theory of progress that the rich and powerful could embrace.

Shah later built on the notion in an essay whose intellectual and pecuniary origins reflected the rising profile of private solutions to public problems. It was coauthored by Jitinder Kohli, who ran the public-sector practice at Monitor Deloitte, and it appeared as part of a think-piece series sponsored by Deloitte, the Skoll Foundation, and *Forbes*. The essay argued that the new private world-changing, led by people and entities like these, was preferable to the old-fashioned public, democratic way:

> In a bygone era government was solely responsible for addressing the Nation's biggest problems, from building the interstate highway system to the New Deal social programs.

However, today's challenges are more complicated and interconnected than ever before and cannot be solved by a single actor or solution. That is why government has an opportunity to engage with the actors in the Impact Economy from nonprofits to businesses.

It was curious to see the U.S. government, arguably the most powerful institution in human history, reduced to being a "single actor" among actors, one inadequate to modern problems. Building a continental highway network or waging a New Deal was easy, according to this view. But today's problems were too hard for the government. They had therefore to be solved through partnerships among rich donors, NGOs, and the public sector. There was no mention of the fact that this method, by putting the moneyed into a leadership position on public problem-solving, gave them the power to thwart solutions that threatened them. If your preferred way of solving big problems requires my money and gives me a board seat on the initiative, I may not encourage solutions involving inheritance taxes or the breakup of companies like the one from which I have made the money I am giving.

There are also subtler forms of influence to be reaped from the private push into world betterment. The promotional materials put out by the new Beeck Center illustrated, for example, how business language has conquered the sphere of social change and pushed out an older language of power, justice, and rights. The purpose of the center is to "foster innovation and provide a unique skill set." The center "engages global leaders to drive social change at scale." It provides tools to "leverage the power of capital, data, technology and policy to improve lives." The press release promised that "through the new center, students will learn how to design, organize and raise funds for careers in social impact, and be introduced to global leaders who will help with the incubation of their new ideas for small businesses or nonprofits." The solution of public problems through public action—changing the law, going to court, organizing citizens, petitioning the government with grievances—went all but unmentioned. Rather, the university promised a new focus on the "entrepreneurial spirit" as the solution to "some of the world's most pressing problems."

So when Cohen received her offer letter from McKinsey that year, it was possible to feel, as she did, that it was a dull and cynical choice; and it was possible to feel, as she also did, that it was an invitation into the new way of helping people. A meeting of another program she belonged to, known as Capstone, illustrated that she was far from alone. The program brought together small groups of college seniors to discuss the anxieties of the final year and future plans, with a professor's help. The host of the ninth meeting of Cohen's cohort, held in late March, circulated by email some readings to prime the discussion, one of which was a piece from *The George-town Voice,* a student-run newsmagazine founded in 1969 by former *Hoya* editors who objected to that newspaper's hesitancy to cover the Vietnam War. The article asked a question that Cohen was asking herself in those days: "Why Are So Many Georgetown Graduates Taking Jobs in Banking and Consulting?"

The article reported the striking fact that more than 40 percent of Georgetown graduates from the class of 2012 who found full-time work had gone into consulting or financial services. The writer observed that the trend "can seem contradictory for a University that prides itself on Jesuit values." It attributed the glut to the high salaries, the debt burden that many students take on, and a "culture that holds financial services and consulting jobs as prestigious." One student interviewed by the magazine added that "many fields that her friends are interested in do not realistically have entry-level positions available that do not require a few years of business experience." Other lines of work seemed to be internalizing the consulting and financial firms' tale of themselves as gateways. Cohen and her friends discussed the article that day, which mirrored her own agonizing over what to do about McKinsey. She says she sought an extension of the deadline for accepting the offer five times before deciding to join.

She says she was "simultaneously dazzled and horrified" by what she found. She was hugely impressed by the talent around her. "I remember sitting in orientation, and you have all of these well-groomed, super-articulate, high-performing people, and you have real questions about, 'Do I belong here? Am I really one of these people?'—that kind of thing. I was dazzled by the stature or seeming appearance of my peers and colleagues." She also soon came to be bothered by the overwork and by the reality that most of the projects were corporate humdrum, not world-saving. She had been pitched, as she saw it, on "the fact that you are going to have access to problems that typically people don't have access to for decades, the ways in which you're going to change the lives of your clients for the better." But most of the projects she came across were just your usual corporate advisory tasks, cutting costs here, devising a market-entry strategy there. "A lot of it is just executing on stuff that's a bit more mundane," she said.

And if the work was duller than the recruiters had promised, her fellow consultants' workaholism was out of step with that dullness. They worked as though they were solving the urgent problems they had been pitched on fixing but weren't. They built Excel models over dinner, which shocked Cohen, who grew up in a family "where you would be severely reprimanded and castigated" for answering the phone at mealtime. In a five-minute car ride from the hotel to a client's office, it was customary to get on the phone and seek to squeeze as much productivity as possible from that shard of an hour. "That's the reality," Cohen said. "It's just a crazy culture." Then, she added, "Slowly but surely, you too begin doing it."

Cohen began to doubt her decision, and she found herself wondering if she should instead be doing what those who knew her best often pressed her to do—training as a rabbi. So powerful, though, was the logic of business as a path to service that she told herself it was a useful prologue even for spiritual work—and if "the rabbi thing doesn't work out," she said, her time at McKinsey would give her a "backup plan." She added that it was probably better to be a rabbi known to have passed through McKinsey. "I think that we make sense of each other based on a very, very limited amount of information, and that certainly choices or brands or symbols signify certain things," she said.

In taking the McKinsey job, Cohen joined MarketWorld. MarketWorld is an ascendant power elite that is defined by the concurrent drives to do well and do good, to change the world while also profiting from the status quo. It consists of enlightened businesspeople and their collaborators in the worlds of charity, academia, media, government, and think tanks. It has its own thinkers, whom it calls thought leaders, its own language, and even its own territory—including a constantly shifting archipelago of conferences at which its values are reinforced and disseminated and translated into action. MarketWorld is a network and community, but it is also a culture and state of mind.

These elites believe and promote the idea that social change should be pursued principally through the free market and voluntary action, not public life and the law and the reform of the systems that people share in common; that it should be supervised by the winners of capitalism and their allies, and not be antagonistic to their needs; and that the biggest beneficiaries of the status quo should play a leading role in the status quo's reform.

In her first weeks at McKinsey, Cohen had yet to see MarketWorld for what it was, and despite her own discomfort with the work, she could tell herself what so many bright young people tell themselves these days and thereby get through the months and years: that they are entering the world of money in order to master the tools needed to help those it has forsaken. Cohen says she reassured herself: "Now that I've been trained to structure, break down, and solve business problems, I can apply those same skills to any issue or challenge I choose."

Then she began to see through that idea. From the outside, she had been awed by the claim that people trained in business would gain some elusive way of thinking that was vital to helping people.

Once inside, though, she realized that while this way of thinking was indeed useful for helping a tire company shave costs or a solar panel maker select a promising market for global expansion, it didn't deserve its status as a cure-all across domains. Accountancy, medicine, education, espionage, and seafaring all have their own tools and modes of analysis, but none of those approaches was widely promoted as the solution to virtually everything else.

Cohen began to worry that this idea of business training as a way station to world-changing was just a recruiter's ruse, and one made easier to sell by the glow of MarketWorld's seemingly noble intentions. What was the value in the problem-solving methods she had signed up to learn? Working on client projects, she began to run a parallel exercise in her own mind, ignoring the McKinsey toolkit and just asking herself what she thought the right answer was. "Very rarely, if ever, did the step-by-step, perfectly linear process of 'here's how we're going to conduct this exploration'—very rarely did that actually surface the right answer," she said. Often, that process—the thing for which McKinsey was famed—was "used primarily for communicating the answer, rather than generating it," she said. The answers were derived through intelligence and common sense, and then the team would make them look more like trademark McKinsey answers: "We would backfill them into the template," Cohen said.

Given what she felt to be the fallibility of the methods she was learning, she was amazed at the hunger for them outside the precincts of business. In our age, many domains lack confidence in their own methodologies and are often desperate to inject business thinking into their work. So successful is the belief in business as the universal access card for making progress, helping people, and changing the world that even the White House, with its pick of the nation's talent, under Republicans and Democrats alike, grew dependent on the special talents of consultants and financiers in making decisions about how to run the nation. In 2009, the *Economist* had declared it "McKinsey's turn to try to sort out Uncle Sam," suggesting that "Obama may favour McKinseyites in much the same way as his predecessor seemed addicted to hiring alumni of Goldman Sachs."

There was a case to be made that the very people being brought in to advise the government on the public good were implicated in many of the public's most urgent problems. Management consultants and financiers were critical protagonists in the story of how a small band of elites, including them, had captured most of the spoils of a generation's worth of innovation. The financial sector had extracted more and more value from the American economy, at the expense not only of consumers and workers but also of industry itself. More and more of the nation's financial resources were swilled around Wall Street without taking the form of new investment by companies or higher wages for workers. Meanwhile, the consultants had brought a productivity revolution to corporations. They had taught them how to optimize *everything*, which made their supply chains leaner and their income statements less volatile. This optimization, of course, made companies less hospitable to workers, who faced such things as layoffs, offshoring, dynamic scheduling, and automation as the downside of corporate progress. This was part of why their wages stagnated while companies' profits and productivity rose. Cohen said that her colleagues were often undeterred by these facts. "It's like, 'Okay, we caused these problems, but we also know how to solve problems,'" she said of the prevailing attitude. "So this is just the new problem that we're going to solve—the one that we have caused."

Cohen, though, was losing faith in the power of these solutions. And she had begun to flirt with the dangerous idea that she wasn't really being groomed to change the world. She pondered her next move.

Meanwhile, President Obama, who did his own post-collegiate teeth-cutting as a community organizer in Chicago, was approaching the end of his second term. In the modern custom, he would soon be creating a foundation and a library. He had resolved that the renewal of civic life would be among their priorities. He had often spoken of corporations and wealthy people having too much of a say in American life and of ordinary people having too little. Still, as this president turned his thoughts to making democracy more vital, he decided to seek advice from McKinsey, as so many change-makers now tended to do.

Cohen was asked to join the team, and she began to work on the question of what the president should do to reinvigorate citizenship. She said Obama's turning to McKinsey consultants to analyze the problem was both "a silencer of my doubts and the conjurer of many doubts." If a president whom she deeply admired thought McKinsey consultants should be thinking about these things, then maybe they should be. On the other hand, she suspected the president had been influenced by the same myths that had misled her. "Why wouldn't he go to a group of community organizers to do this work?" she wondered. The project gave her "more pause than hope," for it seemed to contribute to the business world's growing influence over social change. She felt conflicted: That McKinsey had been given the work made her uneasy; at the same time, it was the most exciting work she could imagine doing.

It was possible to interpret Cohen and her fellow consultants working to rethink democracy as capitalists stepping up, addressing a social challenge beyond their own self-interest. But it was also possible to ask, were the business elites chipping in, or were they taking over the work of changing the world? If the latter, perhaps putting the moneyed in charge of an effort to revive democracy would yield better results than putting others in charge. It is possible, but unlikely. For whoever treats a disease recasts it—with their own diagnosis, prescription, and prognosis. To take on a problem is to make it your own, and to gain the right to decide what it is not and how it doesn't need to be solved. The problem of human want, for example, had found very different solutions when it passed from the care of feudal lords to that of republics giving representation to property-holding men to that of democracies with universal adult suffrage.

The biggest risk of putting a corporate consulting firm in charge of designing fixes for societal problems is that it may sideline certain fundamental questions about power. The MarketWorld problem-solver does not tend to hunt for perpetrators and is not interested in blame. Cohen said she and her fellow consultants also risked ignoring or minimizing the concerns of people ill-served by democracy not out of malice or by design, but because of their mental model. If you think of the world as an engineering problem, a dashboard of dials you can turn and switches you can toggle and thereby make everything optimal, then you don't always register the voices of people who see a different world—one of people and systems that guard what is theirs and lock others out.

Eventually, Cohen would leave McKinsey and join the Obama Foundation full-time. But while she remained on the consulting firm's payroll, she and her colleagues were subject to the delicate balancing act of corporate social change. They were supposed to make democracy more vital and effective for ordinary people, but preferably without challenging their fellow winners too much. They were to grow the public's trust in institutions without digging too far into why the people leading those institutions were mistrusted.

Part of what still drew Cohen to the rabbinate was the chance it offered to flee the compromises that arose from seeking to do well by doing good. "I would a million percent say I'd prefer to live outside of that market logic and world," she said. But she would be lying if she said she didn't like the prestige and the lifestyle. And she clung to the dream of making change at scale. In her continuing attraction to religious training, she seemed to long for one faith to deliver her from another—from a market faith that she had not chosen so much as given in to.

This faith holds a great many decent, thinking people nowadays. Many of them are trapped in what they cannot fully see. Many of them believe that they are changing the world when they may instead—or also—be protecting a system that is at the root of the problems they wish to solve. Many of them quietly wonder whether there is another way, and what their place in it might be.

CHAPTER 2

WIN-WIN

Want to change the world? Start a business.

—JONATHAN CLARK, ENTREPRENEUR

I t is dinnertime, and Stacey Asher is sitting at a window-side six-top, talking about how she helps poor people using the power of fantasy sports. She lives in Highland Park, in Dallas, not far from former president George W. Bush. Asher runs a charity called Port-folios with Purpose. It calls itself "a powerful platform combining healthy competition with giving"—a short phrase that manages to hit the notes of techno-utopianism, capitalism, and charity. Though she appears to be in her thirties, she says she worked at "six or seven" hedge funds in New York before moving to Texas, where her new husband had a job, also in finance.

Like many from the business world who end up devoted to help-ing others, Asher has a story about an African epiphany. During a trip to climb Mount Kilimanjaro, she found herself at an orphan-age in Tanzania. There she met children who carried baby siblings on their backs for miles to secure a single daily meal. She learned that sometimes the orphanage kitchen shut down for lack of funds, though its operating cost was a mere $250 a month. "My life was forever changed in that moment," Asher later wrote.

She began to ponder how she could help. Like many Market-World do-gooders, she was more interested in starting something new than in examining how she and those around her—and the institutions they belonged to—might change their existing ways. She asked herself what she could do, but not what people in her universe might already have done. (It goes without saying, for example, that if hedge funders hadn't been enormously creative in dodging taxes, the income available for foreign aid would have been greater.)

At that very moment, one of the biggest banks in the world, Standard Chartered, was preparing to go to court in Tanzania to fight charges that it had knowingly bought "dirty debt," tainted by corruption, from an energy investment, and then petitioned the country's government to nationalize the project so as to pay the bank back with the money of ordinary Tanzanians. The practice was common—and was, at least theoretically, harmful to the government's ability to care for the orphans that Asher cared about. The African Development Bank Group has said that so-called vulture funds—of the very kind that Standard Chartered stood accused of creating—routinely buy bad debt at a steep discount and then sue African governments to repay them in full with taxpayer money, threatening their foreign assets if they contest. It has said that "these vulture funds undermine the development of the most vulnerable" countries, citing Angola, Burkina Faso, Cameroon, Congo, Côte d'Ivoire, Ethiopia, Liberia, Madagascar, Mozambique, Niger, São Tomé and Príncipe, Sierra Leone, and Uganda as victims of the practice, in addition to Tanzania.

A well-meaning person like Asher, knowledgeable about and well connected in high finance, was in a good position to take on an issue like this. Given that vulture funds had extracted nearly $1 billion from debtor countries, according to the development bank, there was great potential to help orphans by beating back this dubious practice and leaving more money for social spending. But this was precisely the kind of undertaking that tended to get overlooked when MarketWorld's winners took on the problems of others. Such an undertaking would be conflictual; it would name names of offending financial institutions; it would pick fights with people who might one day be useful to you. People like Asher were regularly told, and had come to believe, that there were less hostile ways of solving problems than systemic reform.

She knew millions of people like fantasy football, and everyone likes making a killing on the stock market, and who doesn't like helping people? Asher thought she would emulate the fantasy-football model, with stocks instead of players, and the proceeds directed to the winners' favorite charities. (Ninety percent of Portfolios with Purpose's players were said to work in finance—and at least one appeared to be an analyst at Standard Chartered.) As is often the case in MarketWorld, there is attendant irony: The same people who played the game could at the same time flash-trade commodities in ways that made prices unstable in the communities they were said to be helping, or continue to have their firms or clients buy up shady African debt, or pressure municipalities to repay their wealthy bondholders by raiding the pension funds of schoolteachers and firefighters. It captured MarketWorld values perfectly: You could change things without having to change a thing.

Asher was drawn to the tantalizing promise of the win-win approach to social change. That approach is much in vogue in an age of market supremacy, and its allure was captured by Stephen Covey in his 7 *Habits of Highly Effective People*, whose fourth habit had been "Think win-win":

> Win-win sees life as a cooperative arena, not a competitive one. Win-win is a frame of mind and heart that constantly seeks mutual benefit in all human interactions. Win-win means agreements or solutions are mutually beneficial and satisfying. We both get to eat the pie, and it tastes pretty darn good!

This idea fueled MarketWorld's approach to change and the rise of such things as social enterprises, social venture capital, impact investing, benefit corporations, double and triple bottom lines, "shared value" theories of business's enlightened self-interest, give-one-get-one products, and various other expressions of this presumed harmony between what is good for winners and good for everyone else. "Is Giving the Secret to Getting Ahead?" asked the headline atop a *New York Times Magazine* article on the research of an organizational psychologist and self-styled "thought leader" named Adam Grant. In an ideal version of these endeavors, the winner could enjoy an enticing combination of making money, doing good, feeling virtuous, working on hard and stimulating problems, feeling her impact, reducing suffering, spreading justice, exoticizing a résumé, traveling the world, and gaining a catchy cocktail-party spiel.

The widespread faith in win-wins is part of why Hilary Cohen had ended up at McKinsey. It was at work every time one bought a pair of cloth shoes and took comfort in knowing that another pair of shoes would soon be slipped onto a poor person's feet. It could be detected in a poster on a college campus: "Research shows that giving makes you happier. Be selfish & give." It could be seen in the buzzy idea of the "fortune at the bottom of the pyramid," promoted by the late management scholar C. K. Prahalad, who promised big business "a win-win situation: not only do corporations tap into a vibrant market, but by treating the poor as consumers they are no longer treated with indignity; they become empowered customers." It could be, for a World Bank adviser on refugee issues, a vital selling point for what once might have been advocated purely on compassionate grounds: "Getting Syrians back to work—a win-win for host countries and the refugees." To gain cachet in a world conquered by market thinking, one of the great humanitarian disasters since the Second World War needed to be marketed as an opportunity for the helpers, too.

What threads through these various ideas is a promise of painlessness. What is good for me will be good for you. And it is understandable that Asher had been drawn into this way of thinking. You could help people in ways that let you keep living your life as is, while shedding some of your guilt.

As Asher's example shows, there were many genuine win-wins awaiting discovery. But some amount of skepticism was warranted as well. When winners like Asher stepped in to solve a problem as they assessed it, using the tools they had and knew how to use, they often overlooked the roots of the problem and their involvement in it.

Justin Rosenstein seemed to agonize far more than Asher had about the best way to help people. Although he was largely unknown to the broader world, he was a star in Silicon Valley, instrumental in inventing several of its seminal technologies. A programming and product design phenom, he helped start Google Drive and was the coinventor of Gmail chat. Then he moved to Facebook, where he was the coinventor of Pages and the "like" button. More than a billion people were regularly using tools that Rosenstein crafted. He had been rewarded with stock said to be worth tens of millions of dollars. He wasn't yet thirty.

Rosenstein now faced a dilemma not uncommon among young entrepreneurs who have found early success: what to do with his money and his remaining decades on earth. He lived very modestly. He owned an iPhone that was several years out of date, drove a Honda Civic, and lived in a shared cooperative home in San Francisco with more than a dozen other people, many of whom worked in fields like art, activism, and counseling and couldn't fathom his level of resources. When he had the option to upgrade from coach to business class, he wondered how many lives could be saved by investing the extra cost in malaria nets. He wanted to give most of his money away to philanthropic causes.

Rosenstein considers himself to be deeply spiritual, which made him determined to serve others. "I think we're all in this together in a really deep sense," he said late one afternoon in San Francisco. "Somewhere deep down, we all actually share the same soul that we're basically just—I avoid the word God generally, but like consciousness—because we have basically one consciousness looking out through many different people." Rosenstein didn't believe in an abstract, external God so much as in other people: "It feels as though the deeper I go into the nature of my being, I come to a place where we all connect."

Guided by MarketWorld's win-win values, Rosenstein decided to improve the world by starting a company, Asana, which sold work collaboration software to companies like Uber, Airbnb, and Dropbox. Like Asher, he was eager to help, but it was hard to step outside of the realm of his assumptions and tools. He believed that Asana's software could be his most forceful way of improving the human condition. "When you think about the nature of human progress," he said, "when you think about the nature of, like, whether it's improving health care or improving government or making art or doing biotechnology or doing traditional philanthropy—whatever it is, all the things that can move the human condition forward, or maybe the world condition forward, all are about groups of people working together. And so we were, like, if we really could build a universal piece of software that could make everyone in the world who's trying to do positive things 5 percent faster, right?—I guess we'll also make terrorists 5 percent faster—but on the whole, we think that that's going to be really, really net-positive."

Rosenstein's desire to improve people's lives by making everyone a little more productive was noble. But one of the central economic challenges now facing his country is the remarkable stagnation in wages for half of Americans despite the remarkable growth in productivity. As the Economic Policy Institute, a think tank in Washington, puts it in a paper, "Since 1973, hourly compensation of the vast majority of American workers has not risen in line with economy-wide productivity. In fact, hourly compensation has almost stopped rising *at all*." The institute observes that the average American worker grew 72 percent more productive between 1973 and 2014, but the median worker's pay rose only about 9 percent in this time. In short, America doesn't have a problem of lagging productivity so much as a problem of the gains from productivity being captured by elites. The increasingly extractive financial sector is in part responsible. That sector could be arranged in other ways, including tighter regulations on trading, higher taxes on financiers, stronger

● ● ·

Summer is here! Pack your duffel bags & get out there for a much deserved fun and rest.

Thank you for the great start to the year & make sure to recharge for what should be memorable second half ahead of us :)

– Amir

labor protections to protect workers from layoffs and pension raid-ing by private equity owners, and incentives favoring job-creating investment over mere speculation. Such measures could help to solve the underlying problem by preventing the capture of the gains from growing productivity. Absent such measures, an initiative like Rosenstein's wouldn't bring the change it promised. It would serve to further increase an abundant thing likely to be hoarded by elites (productivity), instead of a scarce thing that millions need more of (wages).

The almost religious faith in the win-win helped to explain choices like Rosenstein's. "What's amazing about tech—and there's other industries like this, but I think it's something that is particularly common in tech—is that there are so many opportunities to have your cake and eat it, too, right?" he said. "There's a stereotype that you have to choose in life between doing good and making money. I think for a lot of people that's a real choice. They don't happen to have the skill set where there's a nice intersection. But for technol-ogy, there are a significant number of opportunities—Google search being the most massive example of all time—where we simultane-ously are doing something lucrative and really good for the world. And, in fact, I think that a lot of times you can get in situations where they're all aligned, where the bigger the reach of the good you're doing, the more money you'll make." It was a vision in which social justice and the concentration of power would somehow increase in tandem, ad infinitum.

"This is a great example where you've got to struggle, you've got to think really carefully, and it's complicated, it's messy, it's super easy to rationalize," he continued. "I'm sure I've done this at times, where I rationalize, like, 'Oh, well, this is going to be better for the world,' when really it's just going to make more money. But on the other hand, what's cool about for-profit endeavors—there's a lot of things for-profit endeavors are not suited to do, where you need the nonprofit sector, you need the government sector. But one of the things the for-profit sector is great at is self-sustaining, because you don't have to constantly be fund-raising."

This idea was important to many MarketWorlders: Business solutions could, despite appearances, be more compassionate than the alternatives because the profits they paid the winners assured their continued beneficence. The ideal business, Rosenstein said, has both revenue ("the value that it is capturing") and positive externalities ("the value that it creates in the world that it's not capturing"). Google's ad sales are revenue; the way it has made it effortless for anyone, anywhere, to look up anything is a positive externality. "In the case where you can create a system where you have both," he said, "where every dollar you make is also a positive externality, what's amazing about that is that now you can keep investing in that engine. You can do bigger things. You can reinvest. You can hire great people."

That business was a self-sustaining way to do good was especially convenient given Rosenstein's assessment of his peers. "The truth is, I've done a lot of research on this: Very few people are willing to make a big financial sacrifice to do good," he said. "Look at millennials. The majority of millennials want to have a job with meaning, but they're not willing to sacrifice having a good income for it. I do not blame them. I might feel the same way; it's very easy to feel that way. But I think there's more opportunities than people expect where we don't have to choose, where you can make good money and be doing good in the world."

Rosenstein's faith in such progress allowed him to overlook unintended consequences. When you build the kinds of tools that he believed in, you cannot know how people are going to use them. Rosenstein admitted as much. He sees teenagers obsessed with and anxious over the number of likes that their Facebook posts attract, and he wonders about his legacy. He could also be blind to the ways in which the companies he had served, Google and Facebook, could do well and do good, and at the same time accumulate a level of power—over information and news in a free society, over people's private details and whereabouts and the content of their every conversation—that is dangerous and quasi-monopolistic and needs to be watched over, if not broken apart.

When you ignore these kinds of concerns, it becomes easier for Asana to do well by doing good, the Silicon Valley way:

> By helping people work together more easily, we make it more effortless for groups to coordinate their collective action, so that they can achieve their goals and manifest the missions that drive them. In the next few years, we'll reach millions of people working in groups to improve the world we all share. Through them, we'll improve the lives of every person on the planet.

asana ...

It was an inspiring vision, notable for its appropriation of "collective action"—a term that traditionally connoted unions and movements and other forms of citizens making common cause in the public sphere. The vision reflected a bitter truth: Often, when people set out to do the thing they are already doing and love to do and know how to do, and they promise grand civilizational benefits as a spillover effect, the solution is oriented around the solver's needs more than the world's—the win-wins, purporting to be about others, are really about you.

Later that evening, Rosenstein drove from Asana to Agape, the communal home where he lives. It is an ornate and stately old mansion, the walls adorned with intricately carved wood. People were making their way to the dining room, where two tables had been pushed together, around which was a mix of chairs and an old church pew. As people met, they tended to hug. Many were young, waifish creative types for whom the modest rent was probably a stretch. It was a community that Rosenstein had cofounded and that he cherished. The group sat and held hands, and someone said a secular grace, and then everyone dove into the cartons of Cambodian takeout.

Behind Asher's Portfolios with Purpose, Rosenstein's Asana and countless other similarly minded initiatives, there stands a radical theory. It is a new twist on an old idea about the beneficial side effects of self-interest. The long-standing idea took root in the emerging commercial societies of urban Europe a few centuries ago. Its most famous statement is Adam Smith's declaration about the social benefits of human selfishness:

> It is not from the benevolence of the butcher, the brewer, or the baker that we expect our dinner, but from their regard to their own interest. We address ourselves, not to their humanity but to their self-love, and never talk to them of our own necessities but of their advantages.

This idea that self-love trickles down to others is an early ancestor of win-win-ism. In his *Theory of Moral Sentiments,* Smith elaborates on the idea with his famous metaphor of the "invisible hand." The rich, he writes,

> in spite of their natural selfishness and rapacity, though they mean only their own conveniency, though the sole end which they propose from the labours of all the thousands whom they employ, be the gratification of their own vain and insatiable desires, they divide with the poor the produce of all their improvements. They are led by an invisible hand to make nearly the same distribution of the necessaries of life, which would have been made, had the earth been divided into equal portions among all its inhabitants, and thus without intending it, without knowing it, advance the interest of the society.

The selfish pursuit of prosperity, Smith is arguing, takes care of everyone just as well as actually attempting to take care of everyone. From this general idea familiar theories derive. Trickle-down economics. A rising tide lifts all boats. Entrepreneurs expand the pie. Smith tells the rich man to focus on running his business on the assumption that positive social consequences will occur automatically, as a happy by-product of his selfishness. Through the magic of the "free market"—an oxymoron ever since the first regulation was imposed on it—he unwittingly arranges for the common good.

The kind of win-win represented by Portfolios with Purpose and Asana—as well as the new impact investment funds pledging to combine strong returns with poverty alleviation, and the new social enterprises, and the bottom-of-the-pyramid retail plays—innovated on this tradition by turning it upside down. The new win-win-ism was built on the same assumption of harmony in the interests of the winners and the losers, the rich and the poor, but it rejected the idea of social good as a by-product, a spillover. The winners of commerce were no longer told to ignore the social good and keep their contribution to it indirect and unintentional. They were to focus on social improvement directly and intentionally. Rosenstein shouldn't just start a software company, but one he thought most likely to improve the condition of humankind.

In the journey from Adam Smith's theory to that of the win-win, the entrepreneur is transformed from an incidental booster of the common good into a unique figure specially capable of tending to it. Business goes from being a sector with positive social benefits to being the principal vessel for human betterment. "Businesses acting as business, not as charitable donors, are *the most powerful force* [my italics] for addressing the pressing issues we face," the Harvard Business School professor Michael Porter declared in one formulation of the idea. "Business is the ultimate positive-sum game, in which it is possible to create a Win for all the stakeholders of the business," John Mackey, the chief executive of Whole Foods Market, and Raj Sisodia write in a book that has become a bible of the win-win faith, *Conscious Capitalism: Liberating the Heroic Spirit of Business.*

The new win-win-ism is arguably a far more radical theory than the "invisible hand." That old idea merely implied that capitalists should not be excessively regulated, lest the happy by-products of their greed not reach the poor. The new idea goes further, in suggesting that capitalists are more capable than any government could ever be of solving the underdogs' problems.

An influential statement of this new creed is found in the book *Philanthrocapitalism: How the Rich Can Save the World*. Published in the autumn of 2008, as millions of people watched the economies around them collapse and could have been excused for feeling that the rich were ruining the world, the book made the case for the wealthy as saviors. The authors, Matthew Bishop and Michael Green, stress that this salvation comes not in the old, happy-by-product way, but directly, when the winners assume leadership of social change:

Today's philanthrocapitalists see a world full of big problems that they, and perhaps only they, can and must put right. Surely, they say, we can save the lives of millions of children who die each year in poor countries from poverty or diseases that have been eradicated in the rich world. And back home in the United States or Europe, it is we who must find ways to make our education systems work for every child.

While Adam Smith's ideas were based on an analysis of how markets work, this new idea is based on a view of the moneyed themselves. Bishop and Green write that the "self-made" people who built their fortunes amid "the surge in entrepreneurial wealth in the last thirty years" are different from winners past, and not just because of their willingness to help others by parting with wealth they only just acquired. "Entrepreneurs are also, by nature, problem-solvers and relish the challenge of taking on tough issues," Bishop and Green write. They describe "philanthrocapitalists" as

"hyperagents" who have the capacity to do some essential things far better than anyone else. They do not face elections every few years, like politicians, or suffer the tyranny of shareholder demands for ever-increasing quarterly profits, like CEOs of most public companies. Nor do they have to devote vast amounts of time and resources to raising money, like most heads of NGOs. That frees them to think long-term, to go against conventional wisdom, to take up ideas too risky for government, to deploy substantial resources quickly when the situation demands it.

Under the new theory, entrepreneurship can become synonymous with humanitarianism—a humanitarianism that greases the wheels of entrepreneurship. "In the last decade, 'doing good' became a driving force for building successful, impactful businesses," writes Craig Shapiro, the founder of the Collaborative Fund, a venture capital firm in New York. "Once seen as sacrificial to growth and returns, pursuing a social mission now plays a big role when attracting both customers and employees." Shapiro used a Venn diagram to illustrate the investment thesis that his firm had created in view of this trend. One circle was labeled "Better for me (self-interest)"; the other was labeled "Better for the world (broader interest)." The overlap was labeled "exponential opportunity." A charitable interpretation of this idea is that the world deserves to benefit from flourishing business. A more sinister interpretation is that business deserves to benefit from any attempt to better the condition of the world.

Nowhere is this idea of entrepreneurship-as-humanitarianism more entrenched than in Silicon Valley, where company founders regularly speak of themselves as liberators of mankind and of their technologies as intrinsically utopian. After all, even a workplace software company like Rosenstein's Asana could claim that "we'll improve the lives of every person on the planet." A friend of Rosenstein, Greg Ferenstein, set out years ago to chronicle these grand claims and make sense of this new mentality radiating from the Valley. He was a reporter in the Bay Area who had written for various outlets, notably *TechCrunch*, the booster newsletter of Silicon Valley. He had become interested in the bigger ideas animating the people he covered—what win-win-ism imagines for the world and what, at times, it obscures.

Ferenstein interviewed many technology founders and distilled their ideas into a working philosophy. He calls this philosophy Optimism, though it seems to be just a slightly tech-inflected version of standard-issue neoliberalism. The ideology's central thrust, he said, is a belief in the possibility of the win-win and the harmony of human interests. "People typically think of government and market working in opposition to each other—and regulation being the tool by which government constrains the market," Ferenstein said. "This new ideology believes that government is an investor in capitalism. The government works not as a check on capitalism but for capitalism—to make capitalism successful, to ensure that the conditions for its success are in place": that there is a decent education system to produce the requisite number of workers, that trade agreements get written so as to allow companies to buy from and sell to far-off places, that the infrastructure allows trucks to get produce to the supermarket before it rots, that the air is clean enough that people live long and (more important) productive lives.

"The basis of old government is the notion of a zero-sum relationship between different classes—economic classes, between citizens and the government, between the United States and other countries," Ferenstein said. "If you assume that inherent conflict, you worry about disparities in wealth. You want labor unions to protect workers from corporations. You want a smaller government to get out of the way of business. If you don't make that assumption, and you believe that every institution needs to do well, and they all work with each other, you don't want unions or regulation or sovereignty or any of the other things that protect people from each other.

"Most politics and most institutions are built on a zero-sum relationship between some people in the group," Ferenstein went on. "This ideology is unique—and the reason I call it Optimism is because of the belief that everyone can get along. Or everyone has, to be more specific, overlapping preferences."

This idea seeks to push back against the modern democratic vision of society in which citizens are equal before the law, are understood to have divergent interests, and compete on the basis of those interests for resources and power, with different organs of the state designed to represent different kinds of needs. Optimism harkens back to a vision of harmony-as-progress that dominated the Middle Ages. It was distilled in "The Fable of a Man, His Belly, and His

Limbs," a twelfth-century poem by Marie de France about human body parts that resent each other until they realize their interdependence. At first, the hands and feet and head (representing the laborers) are enraged at the belly (representing the lords) for "their earnings that it ate." They cease to work, so as to deprive the belly of food—only to wither themselves when the belly has no material to digest and pass back to them as nutrients. The poem concludes:

> From this example one can see
> What every free person ought to know:
> No one can have honour
> Who brings shame to his lord.
> Nor can his lord have it either
> If he wishes to shame his people.
> If either one fails the other
> Evil befalls them both.

The fable allows that the hands and feet and head must thrive. But, it insists, they cannot thrive when the belly isn't thriving, too. To believe in this vision is not to cast the meek away. It is, rather, to say that their success can never be oppositional to that of the strong.

There is no discounting the audacity of this MarketWorld idea. It rejects the notion that there are different social classes with different interests who must fight for their needs and rights. Instead, we get what we deserve through marketplace arrangements—whether fantasy football to help African orphans or office software to make everyone more productive or the sale of toothpaste to the poor in ways that increase shareholder value. This win-win doctrine took on a great deal more than Adam Smith ever had, in claiming that the winners were specially qualified to look after the losers. But what do they have to show for their efforts, given that the age of the win-win is also, across much of the West, the age of historic, gaping inequality?

In a country that is losing its middle class, in a wider world racked by anxiety about globalization and technology and displacement, what is the win-win theory's response to the problem of suffering? "It's not an emphasis of this ideology," Ferenstein said. Suffering can be innovated away. Let the innovators do their start-ups and suffering will be reduced. Each entrepreneurial venture could take on a different social problem. "In the case of Airbnb, the way you alleviate housing suffering is by allowing people to share their homes," Ferenstein said. An Airbnb ad campaign along these lines featured older black women thriving now that the entrepreneurs had helped them to rent out rooms and make extra money. Of course, many poor people don't own homes or have a surplus of space to rent out. And many African Americans find it difficult to rent on the platform—hotels can no longer easily discriminate by race, but spare-room hoteliers often do. But what was even more striking than these blind spots was the notion, implied in Ferenstein's idea, that the winners should receive a kickback from social change.

Indeed, in the case of Airbnb and other so-called win-wins, the claim of a harmony of interests is hope masquerading as description. There are still winners and losers, the powerful and the powerless, and the claim that everyone is in it together is an eraser of the inconvenient realities of others. "This ideology radically overestimates who will benefit from change," Ferenstein admitted. Then what will happen as believers in win-win change amass ever more power—and not only economic power but also the power to guide the pursuit of societal betterment, one start-up at a time? "People will be left behind," Ferenstein said. "Unintelligent, poor, indigent, unmotivated—they will be left behind. The people who don't like change will be left behind. The people who like suburban small towns will be left behind. The people who don't want to work twenty-four hours a day will be left behind. The people who don't live to invent and create—and can—will be left behind." This list seemed to contradict the whole premise of Optimism—that we are all invested in each other's success and will prosper together. In fact, Ferenstein now seemed to be saying that the better the Optimists did, the more people would be beached. This claim jibed with what actually was going on in the world—the benefits of progress flowing primarily to the already fortunate; the widespread cutting loose of those on the wrong side of change.

It is fine for winners to see their own success as inextricable from that of others. But there will always be situations in which people's preferences and needs do not overlap, and in fact conflict. And what happens to the losers then? Who is to protect their interests? What if the elites simply need to part with more of their money in order for every American to have, say, a semi-decent public school?

Not long after moving to the Bay Area to run the Silicon Valley Community Foundation, Emmett Carson was told to drop his usage of the off-putting win-lose jargon of social justice. Given that social justice was his life's work, this might have posed a problem. But Carson understood one of the implicit rules governing the entrepreneurial class's contribution to change: It is more forthcoming when you frame problems in ways that make winners feel good.

Carson was raised on the South Side of Chicago, the son of municipal workers, a black boy in a neighborhood statistically unkind to black boys. When he was eight, though, a shooting outside of the Carsons' home prompted a move some thirty blocks south of the South Side to a better neighborhood called Chatham Village. Carson's life turned onto a different track. He made his way to Morehouse College, then to Princeton for graduate school, then to prestigious positions at the Ford and Minneapolis foundations. Then he went to Silicon Valley, where he became one of the leading advisers to technology entrepreneurs wishing to make a difference in the world.

That was when he was told to stop using the phrase "social justice." It had worked fine for him at Ford and Minneapolis. In Silicon Valley, it rubbed people the wrong way. "I spent twenty-five years working on social justice," he said to me one day, "and the first twenty years I thought it was important to use the term 'social justice.'" In Silicon Valley, "people interpret social justice different ways," often as win-lose thinking. "Some people say social justice is taking from the rich and giving to the poor," Carson said. "Some people say social justice is giving to people who didn't earn something." And so Carson started using the word "fairness."

The winners of the Valley preferred that. Fairness seemed to be more about how people were treated by abstract systems than about the possibility of the winners' own complicity. "I'm about getting to a solution," said Carson. "If using the word 'fairness' allows us to say something is wrong and needs to be changed, that's a better word for me. I'm about trying to minimize the distinctions and the splits, and creating frames that different people can say, 'I can buy into that.'"

Carson began to understand that if no one questioned the entrepreneurs' fortunes and their personal status quo, they were willing to help. They liked to feel charitable, useful. They liked the chance to sign off on the help that the poor received, not to have that help organized through democracy and collective action (in the pre-Asana meaning). "If the view is I took it from you, versus you gave it, it changes the entire dynamics of conversation," Carson said. Perhaps they had a feeling "that I'm being targeted because I've been successful, I've worked hard, I made it; and because I made it, I am now the target, that you think you deserve some of my success that you haven't earned." Carson made clear that he did not believe they were right in their sense of victimhood. But in order to get his job done, he decided to honor the feeling.

Carson had spent his life working on poverty, opportunity, and inequality. But now, living and working among the rising philanthrocapitalist class, he had decided to play by their rules. And what these winners wanted was for the world to be changed in ways that had their buy-in—think charter schools over more equal public school funding, or poverty-reducing tech companies over antitrust regulation of tech companies. The entrepreneurs were willing to participate in making the world better if you pursued that goal in a way that exonerated and celebrated and depended on them. Win-win.

· · ·

Think back to the Venn diagram of Craig Shapiro, the venture capitalist. There is, he tells us, a vast sphere of things that would make the world better for oneself and another vast sphere of things that would make the world better for others. Where they meet offers tremendous possibility. Moreover, "pursuing a social mission now plays a big role when attracting both customers and employees." But what about the people with little and the world at large?

The obvious gain is access to the resources, brains, and tools of the moneyed world. Suddenly its capabilities can be harnessed to address your problem. But in Shapiro's Venn diagram, it is worth noting that the lion's share of each circle remains outside the overlap of the win-win—what mathematicians call the relative complement. What becomes of those interests of others that do not jibe with the winners' interests?

That question hovered over Jane Leibrock as she sat behind the wheel of the rattling yellow Ford Bronco that was serving as the official vehicle of the start-up she had recently joined, cruising the Nimitz Freeway in the Bay Area.

Leibrock had left Facebook, where she investigated such things as how people grapple with privacy settings, for a new company called Even. She was drawn to Even's attempt to address a massive social problem: the growing volatility of millions of working-class Americans' income, thanks to the spreading practice of employing people erratically, the rise in part-time jobs and gigs, and the new on-demand economy that left many eternally chasing work instead of building livelihoods.

When your paychecks surge and dive willy-nilly, it is hard to pay bills, make plans, and create a future. Even came along offering a Silicon Valley–style solution to this problem, in the form of, naturally, a phone app. It would smooth the spiky incomes of working-class people, for a fee. The initial plan was to sell them a service, costing $260 a year, that squirreled away some of their money when they made more than the usual, and then in weeks when their pay fell short supplemented it with some of what was squirreled away. Say you made $500 a week on average, but with considerable swings.

In a week when you earned $650, $500 would go to your regular bank account and $150 would be deposited into your virtual Even account. In a week when you earned $410, $500 would be placed in your bank account, courtesy of your former surpluses. Even would endeavor, with characteristic Silicon Valley ambition, to counteract the effects of a generation's worth of changes in the lives of working-class Americans, rooted in policy choices and shifts in technology and the world situation—including outsourcing, stagnant wages, erratic hours, defanged unions, deindustrialization, ballooning debt, nonexistent sick leave, dismal schools, predatory lending, and dynamic scheduling—while doing nothing about those underlying problems. Like Rosenstein and other believers in win-wins, the founders of Even wanted very much to help, but thought it best to help in a way that would create some opportunity for them, too.

Leibrock was among the Even founders' first hires, and she was on the Nimitz that day driving from interview to interview, learning about the lives and needs of the working poor so that Even could most effectively serve them as customers. She is a graduate of Yale and the private schools of Austin, Texas, with no trace of an accent. She was part of the great brain rush to California that was turning the Bay Area into one of the most unaffordable, unequal, and tense parts of the country, with resentful locals famously throwing rocks at the Google buses that ferried employees to and from the South Bay. Leibrock and her colleagues at Even were awash in noble intentions, but it was still reasonable to ask if Even's for-profit safety net was the most appropriate response to the problem its founders had identified. Could it be read as a lucrative bet that the new economy would inevitably entrap a permanent underclass, whose incomes could only be smoothed, not lifted—and smoothed not by restricting certain business practices by law (win-lose) but by charging workers a fee for security (win-win)? "If you want to feel like you have a safety net for the first time in your life, Even is the answer," the company's website said. But this was a new kind of MarketWorld "safety net" that did not ask the public and government to help in any way.

Here was Leibrock in a Starbucks, talking to a single mother about trying to balance her job and her education and her embarrassment at relying on free diapers from her parents. Here was Leibrock with an employee of a Nike store, who was explaining how her bosses kept her hours low to avoid paying her benefits, while requiring her to remain available most of the week, which prevented her from taking a second job. Here was Leibrock at a strip mall, asking a grocery stocker named Ursula about the mental gymnastics of managing too little money, working hours that fluctuated week to week, complicating the making of plans. Despite working thirty-six hours a week on average at the supermarket, she couldn't afford the gas necessary for picking up her grandkids from school in San Francisco. Ursula talked of the depression that gripped her, her father's Parkinson's, and her mother's dementia.

Leibrock's job brought her into contact with a section of America that the Valley mostly ignored. Interview by interview, Leibrock was cultivating a sense of this other country. One day she was interviewing via Skype a woman named Heather Jacobs about her life and finances. The conversation began awkwardly, because Jacobs had misunderstood what was on offer. Her husband had told her that Even provided free credit, which it didn't.

When Leibrock asked about Jacobs's work, she knew to choose her words carefully: "Tell me about your—you're being paid for something. What's your job, or jobs?"

Jacobs said she worked at a corporate massage chain and freelanced for extra money. "So I'm pretty much working every day for the rest of my life," she said. She explained how she usually got twenty-six to thirty-two hours a week at her job. Besides that, she went to people's houses for private sessions or went to gyms; they didn't pay her, but she was allowed to keep the tips.

Every month she went slightly crazy when money was running out, bills were due, and she hadn't made enough. She felt like "I'm about to go a little insane and pull out my hair. That's when I'm like desperate, going everywhere I can, just to find people to rub." She added, "It's usually around the twenty-seventh, because that's when my credit card bill is due. The minimum payment is about $90 at the moment. So that's when I freak out."

Jacobs explained the details of how she got paid. She explained how, like so many American workers, she bore much of what was once properly considered a company's risk. If the company was able to secure many massages for her, she could make $18 an hour or so, excluding tips. If the company didn't get a lot of bookings, her pay dropped to minimum wage and her hours might be cut back—the way so many Americans were now employed. In some two-week pay periods, she had made $700; in others, she had made $90.

It was all adding up lately—the forty-four-mile commute; the old debt she was paying down for her husband, Greg, a part-time delivery driver for a Red's BBQ who was studying at California State University, Channel Islands; her own bruised credit score, thanks to the $3,700 of massage school tuition that she still owed on her credit card; the dog who needed to be fed. She described this confluence of things as "suffocatingly stressful." She said, "It's coming apart a little," before wandering into her own thoughts.

"I don't deal very well with a lot of stress," she said a moment later, "because I'm anxiety bipolar, so I go immediately to straight full stress, and then I have a panic attack."

Jacobs got the attacks when she thought of money—what was due, what was coming in. When an attack came on, she got a jolt to her gut—"like you're about to get into a car accident." It felt, she said, like a bear hug from someone you don't want hugging you. (It happens that one of the founders of Even had been put on the path of starting the company by reading an article in the journal *Science*, "Poverty Impedes Cognitive Function," about how the thought of money can be psychologically damaging when you are poor. The study found that going up to poor people in a mall and asking them a hypothetical question about money, such as whether to make an expensive repair to an imaginary car, could drop their IQ on a subsequent test by 13 points relative to people of similar means not reminded of money, a plunge comparable to the effect of being an alcoholic or losing a night's sleep.)

Jacobs went on, "So I have to try to get medication, but the medication, it is $60 a month."

Leibrock asked how Jacobs imagined a healthier, more satisfying life might be.

"I would think it's more inspiring to have a stable income. Just to go outside and go see a movie without having to debate for an hour whether it's worth it," she said. "Should we just go get a thing of ice cream and watch something on Netflix instead? Or should we actually have a date night? I mean, we haven't had a date night in probably a year and a half, to be honest with you. We're always inside, and we're never going out with friends, because we can't afford it."

Jacobs and her husband used to shop at Walmart, but in leaner times they had downshifted to the Dollar Store. They were both putting on weight with the new food. The high salt and sugar content in the cheap, processed items they were buying was getting to her. She was convinced that the food was responsible for the ache she now felt in the mornings getting out of bed.

Jacobs came from that other America whose residents' lives had grown more and more insecure in the years of Silicon Valley's ascendancy—117 million people for whom a generation's worth of dazzling innovation had brought barely any extra income on average. America had been churning out some of the most ambitious and impressive companies in history, connecting a billion people here and a billion people there on their networks, and in the shade of their growth was a country ever more unkind to ordinary people. "Society tells me I have to go to school, get a good job, and then I'll get a salary, because I'm in America," Jacobs said on another occasion. "And that's what I did, and now I'm in debt. And now I'm suffocating."

Jacobs's story exposed multiple malfunctions in the machinery of American progress. It implicated the country's health care system and the problem of unaffordable drugs; its public transport system; its wage and labor laws; its food system and food deserts; its student debt crisis; its so-called great risk shift, through which corporate America has stabilized its own income statements over a generation by off-loading uncertainty onto workers; and the ways in which shareholders were running companies more and more for themselves, to the detriment of every other stakeholder.

[Vinod Khosla,]the billionaire venture capitalist whose firm led an early investment round in Even, had taken to sounding alarms about lives like Jacobs's being the looming reality for most Americans, unless the government intervened. He saw through the triumphalism of his Valley circle. Sitting in his second-floor conference room one morning, nursing a cold, Khosla said he expected the disruptions that had already wreaked so much havoc in working-class lives to continue and intensify as automation spread through the economy. He expected the world to continue to overflow with innovation but remain short on progress, if progress implies the flourishing of human beings. He believed that seven or eight out of ten people in the not-too-distant future might not have steady work available to them. To him, this coming future was both an entertainment problem (how would we occupy the minds of all those people?) and a political one (how would we keep them from revolting?).

Khosla, interestingly, did not seem to think that apps like the one he had bet on in Even were the right response to the problem. The thing that could stave off social unrest, he said, is "if—big if—we do enough redistribution, if we handle minimum standards of living for everybody where they work when they want to work, not because they need to work." He knew that such redistribution could cost people like him dearly, in the form of higher taxes. But it was a good investment, he felt. "To put it crudely, it's bribing the population to be well enough off," he said. "Otherwise, they'll work for changing the system, okay?"

The rather different approach proposed by Even had winners charging people like Jacobs money to facilitate her insuring of herself, helping her stabilize her life while turning a profit for themselves. It was understandable, and revealing, that a winner who had already made more money than he would ever need felt free to call out the limitations of such an approach—in a way that his young investees, with their fortunes yet to be made, did not. The billionaire investor was describing a massive collective social obligation, which the founders he had invested in were trying to turn into a win-win of a personal-finance app.

This reframing was a source of worry to Jacob Hacker, a Yale political scientist who coined the "great risk shift" with an eponymous book and whose work helped to inspire Even's founders. "Even is a personal solution to a public problem," he told me. Hacker, who was among the first to make rising income volatility a national issue, said he was "fascinated" by Even. He thought the idea "deeply attractive and intriguing," with "many questions to be worked out, but also much to admire" in the business model. Yet he was concerned. "Does its introduction lessen the pressure for collective action, either private collective action like unions or public collective action like social movements?" he asked. "It would be a sad irony if a great new Band-Aid headed off the major surgery—expanded unemployment insurance, paid family leave, unions and new union alternatives, and so on—that an insecure citizenry so desperately needs." Hacker was referring back to groups of individually powerless citizens potentially banding together to gain strength in numbers and stand up to powerful interests—the idea, in short, of political action. That idea was now up against a far more seductive approach: the winners of the world deciding what and how much largesse to give, or concentrating on the Venn diagram overlap of solutions to underdogs' problems that also served them—and doing just enough of these things to keep at bay that very explosive impulse of banding together.

If you asked the question, "What is the best way to help Heather Jacobs?," the honest answer probably wouldn't be to charge her $260 a year to smooth her income. If you were a person of education, privilege, and access to resources, as everyone at Even was, you might conclude that you should do something to repair the systems that are working to keep Jacobs poor. But if those problems were solved, you wouldn't have much of a win-win business to grow. If it became illegal to employ the Heather Jacobses of the world in the way that she was, or if Khosla's idea of massive redistribution were to be realized, Even might become unnecessary.

CHAPTER 3

REBEL-KINGS IN WORRISOME BERETS

One recent November, Stacey Asher and Greg Ferenstein and a few thousand other citizens of MarketWorld found themselves aboard a 145,655-register-ton Norwegian cruise ship bound for the Bahamas. The idea of doing well for yourself by doing good for others is a gospel, one that is celebrated and reevangelized at an unending chain of tent revivals around the world. The citizens of MarketWorld can reinforce the mission at conference after conference: Davos, TED, Sun Valley, Aspen, Bilderberg, Dialog, South by Southwest, Burning Man, TechCrunch Disrupt, the Consumer Electronics Show, and now, at Summit at Sea, on a cruise ship full of entrepreneurs wishing to change the world.

Summit at Sea was a four-day-long maritime bacchanal honoring the credo of using business to change the world—and perhaps of using "changing the world" to prosper in business. It brought together a great many entrepreneurs and financiers who invest in entrepreneurs, some artists and yoga teachers to keep things interesting and healthy, and various others who tend to run in those circles and whose bios refer to them using terms like "influencer," "thought leader," "curator," "convener," "connector," and "community manager." Summit, being one of the hotter MarketWorld tickets, had drawn to this cruise ship the founders or representatives of such venerable institutions as AOL, Apple, the Bitcoin Foundation, Change.org, Dropbox, Google, Modernist Cuisine, MTV, Paypal, SoulCycle, Toms Shoes, Uber, Vine, Virgin Galactic, Warby Parker, and Zappos. There were some billionaires and many millionaires on board, and lots of others who had paid a typical American's monthly salary to attend.

Selena Soo, a New York publicist who was on board and represented many of these entrepreneur types, perfectly captured the prevailing view. "I work with clients whose personal mission is to improve the lives of others," she writes on her website. "When their business grows, the world becomes a better place." Blair Miller, who was also on the ship and has long worked at what she sees as the nexus of business and social good, once put it this way in an interview published by a clothing boutique:

> The question for me was never if I should devote my career to social impact, it was always HOW can I make the most impact? Business is a dominant force in the world today and I believe that if I can influence how business is done, I can change the lives of millions around the world.

Once you believe that business is how you change things these days, a conference of entrepreneurs offers unlimited possibilities. Indeed, many boarding the ship had recently received an inspirational message from one of the conference's organizers that framed Summit's mission in world-historical terms:

> The winds are picking up in the east and in six short days something transformational is going to be born from the sky and the moon and it might just change history. We may not see the full effect now . . . but that's the case with any great shift in culture. Any great seismic shift amongst the plates of planet earth.

A motivational speaker and thought leader named Sean Stephenson would offer a slightly more candid, if no less ambitious account of Summit's purpose in a welcome speech to the attendees. It came in the form of three pointers for making the most of this chance. First: "In this room you can make contacts that will help you have cascading effects on humanity." Second: "You're going to make friends who are going to impact your pocketbook." Third: "The Boat's not about getting drunk and getting naked. Well, it's sort of about that. But it's also about social justice."

And yet the stubborn facts of an age of stark inequality clouded this vision of the pocketbook-impacting approach to social justice and the use of business to unlock potential and birth transformational things. The more these entrepreneurs waxed about changing the world, the more those facts got in their way, mocking their grandiose and self-serving claims. And this was most acutely true for a subtribe of the attendees of Summit at Sea: those hailing from Silicon Valley and the world of technology, with its audacious claims, even by MarketWorld standards, that what was good for business was great for mankind.

The new barons of technology were the Rockefellers and Carnegies of our time, amassing giant fortunes, building the infrastructure of a new age, and often claiming to operate in the service of civilization itself. "What's amazing about tech," Justin Rosenstein had said in light of his experiences at Google, Facebook, and his own start-up to change the world, "is that there are so many opportunities to have your cake and eat it too, right?" Yet there was no denying that as they chewed away, these technologists were also partly responsible for prying inequality as unsustainably wide as it had gotten. (It was no accident that the city they had adopted, San Francisco, had become perhaps the most cruelly unequal of American cities, with less and less space and chance for ordinary people to make a life.) Many of them had clamored for the dismantling of systems designed, among other things, to protect equality, such as labor unions, zoning regulations, or the laws that assured job security and benefits for workers.

How was the faith in the win-win maintained in the face of widespread evidence that one was in fact contributing to inequality? How did these new barons relieve the cognitive dissonance they might have felt from claiming to improve others' lives while noticing that their own were perhaps the only ones getting better? One day at

Summit at Sea, in the well of the Bliss Ultra Lounge, on the seventh floor of the ship, a high priest of this technology world, a venture capitalist named Shervin Pishevar, was demonstrating one form of relief.

Pishevar was among the leading venture capitalists in the Valley, a status he had cemented by placing early bets on Airbnb and Uber. Those investments earned the kind of returns that could allow one's grandchildren to be full-time philanthropists. Pishevar was an Iranian-born immigrant whose adopted country, through its Department of Homeland Security, had named him an Outstanding American by Choice. He was a kingmaker in the Valley, whom the founder of Uber, Travis Kalanick, had reportedly leaned on as a tutor in the art of going clubbing in Los Angeles, with Pishevar providing "club clothes," according to the *New York Times*. And the entrepreneurs at Summit at Sea knew that a VC like Pishevar, whose firm was called Sherpa Ventures, was in a position, should he so choose, to guide any of them to the mountaintop.

This knowledge helped explain the crush of bodies that had come to see Pishevar's talk, titled "All Aboard the Hyperloop: Supersonic Storytelling with VC Shervin Pishevar." People were curled up on armchairs and sofas; some sat and others lay down on the ground; still others hovered above, ringed a few deep around a balcony on the eighth floor, peering down. The crowd was listening in rapt, reverent silence.

What they heard was a powerful man who seemed at pains to explain his power away and to cast himself as a man in pursuit of things nobler than money. "Sharing is caring," Pishevar said at one point. He admitted it was corny, but he said he truly believed it. "At the end of the day, it's not about the money," he continued. "It's about the love and those moments of character." The Summit people clapped hard and whooped in recognition. They believed it wasn't about the money for them either, one would guess.

Pishevar turned to the topic of life-extending technology, which was a major focus of his work now. He was hardly the only Valley man pursuing the elongation of the lives of people who presumably could pay. "The next twenty, thirty years, my best piece of advice is stay alive," Pishevar said. "Don't take really stupid risks"—this clashed with his business mantra of taking as many risks as possible—"physically, I'm saying. And get ready, because the things that are coming down the pipe in terms of genetic research, our life spans and the health of our lives are going to be longer, and it's going to challenge the very basis of our current civilization: The way things are structured today are not going to be relevant to what the reality is going to be of people who are going to have so much knowledge and living so long and healthier lives. The idea of retiring at seventy is gonna seem like people telling you at thirty to retire."

Here Pishevar was engaging in advocacy that disguised itself as prophecy, which was common among technology barons and one of the ways in which they masked the fact of their power in an age rattled by the growing anxieties of the powerless. VCs and entrepreneurs are considered by many to be thinkers these days, their commercial utterances treated like ideas, and these ideas are often in the future tense: claims about the next world, forged by adding up the theses of their portfolio companies or extrapolating from their own start-up's mission statement. That people listened to their ideas gave them a chance to launder their self-interested hopes into more selfless-sounding predictions about the world. For example, a baron wishing to withhold benefits from workers might reframe that desire as a prediction about a future in which every human being is a solo entrepreneur. A social media billionaire keen to profit from the higher advertising revenue that video posts draw, compared to text ones, might recast that interest—and his rewriting of the powerful algorithms he owns to get what he wants—as a prediction that "I just think that we're going to be in a world a few years from now where the vast majority of the content that people consume online will be video." (*New York* magazine had skewered Mark Zuckerberg after he issued that prediction at the Mobile World Congress in Barcelona: "The Vast Majority of Web Content Will Be Video, Says Man Who Can Unilaterally Make Such a Decision.")

In the Valley, prediction has become a popular way of fighting for a particular future while claiming merely to be describing what has yet to occur. Prediction has a useful air of selflessness to it. Predictors aren't caught in the here and now of their own appetites and interests. It seems like they aren't choosing how things will be in the future any more than they chose the color of their eyes. Yet selecting one scenario among many possible scenarios and persuading everybody of its inevitability—and of the futility of a society's exercising its collective choice among these futures—is a deft way to shape the future.

As he predicted the elongation of life and other such "things that are coming down the pipe," Pishevar was in fact pushing those things down the pipe. He was part of a group of elites who had been very smart and very lucky with start-up investments, and who now got to make decisions of enormous social consequence about what to do about the human life span. This power gave them great responsibility and exposed them to the possibility of resentment—unless they convinced people that the future they were fighting for would unfold automatically, would be the fruit of forces rather than their choices, of providence rather than power. Hence the cleverness of Pishevar's passive framing of his own goals: "The way things are structured today are not going to be relevant to what the reality is going to be." Longer lives for rich people were just something that happened to be coming down the pipe. Not so much a better health care system for all.

"What are the characteristics of people who are able to do world-changing ideas?" someone in the crowd asked during the Q-and-A portion.

This question set Pishevar up well to present himself—and his fellow elites—as rebels up against the powerful, and not as power itself. The characteristic that world-changers have in common, Pishevar said, is a willingness to fight for the truth. It had nothing to do with their being more luckily born than you, unburdened by racial and gender discrimination and with greater access to seed capital from family and friends. It was that they were braver, bolder than you—some might say ruthless—willing to take on power, no matter the cost. Citing Travis Kalanick of Uber and Elon Musk of Tesla, he said, "They are most comfortable in the uncomfortable places. What that means is, they're very comfortable having uncomfortable conversations. And most of us want to just be kumbaya, everything's great, I'm happy, you're happy, we're good, besties, BFFs—and it's like, 'No. Fuck that. Let's challenge each other. What's going on here? What is the truth?' When things get uncomfortable, the reason it's getting uncomfortable is because there's a conflict between something that's true and something that's not true. And the only way to suss that out, figure it out, is to poke at it. And people like that who make big ideas happen don't run away from those conflicts. They actually embrace it."

This idea of the start-up pursuing its singular truth in this fashion was part of Pishevar's rebellious self-conception. A king presides over a multitude of truths. But a rebel, who takes no responsibility for the whole, is free to pursue his singular truth. That is the whole point of being a rebel. It is not in the rebel's job description to worry about others who might have needs that are different from his. By Pishevar's lights, when a company like Uber challenged regulators and unions, there were not rival interests at play so much as a singular truth vying with opposition, and insurgent rebels going up against a corrupt establishment. This became even clearer with his answer to the following question:

"How do you find the balance between morality and ambition and having to compete?"

Because Pishevar did not think himself powerful, because he refused to see the companies he invested in as powerful, he seemed not to understand the question. It takes a certain acceptance of one's own power to see oneself as facing moral choices. If instead what you see in the mirror is a rebel outgunned by the Man, besieged, fighting for your life, you might be tempted to misinterpret the question in the way that Pishevar now did. He interpreted it as being about how he, a moral man, representing a moral company—again, he chose the example of Uber—stood up against immoral forces.

"My biggest thing is existing structures and monopolies—one

example is the taxi cartels—that is a very real thing," he said. "I've been in meetings where I've been threatened by those types of characters from that world. I've seen them beating drivers in Italy. You see the riots in France, and flipping over cars and throwing stones. I took my daughter to Disney. We were in the middle of that. We had to drive our Uber away from basically the war zone that was happening.

"So from a moral perspective, anything that's fighting against morally corrupt, ingrained systems that are based on decades and decades of graft within cities, within city councils, with mayors, etcetera—all those things, they are real, actual things that are threatened by new technologies and innovations like Uber and other companies in that space. So from that perspective, bring it on. That is something we should be fighting. And from a moral perspective, we have a responsibility to fight those types of pockets of control. And they exist at all levels—in the city level to the state, and even at the national and global."

[Pishevar] was not only casting venture capitalists and billionaire company founders as rebels against the establishment, fighting the powers that be on behalf of ordinary people. He was also maligning the very institutions that are meant to care for ordinary people and promote equality. He referred to unions as "cartels." He cast protests, which were a fairly standard feature of labor movements, as a "war zone." He spoke of taxi drivers and their representatives in the language of the corrupt, mafioso Other: "those types of characters from that world." Here was a leading investor in a company, Uber, that had sought to shatter democratically enacted regulations and evade the unions that have a record of actually, and not just rhetorically, fighting for the little guy, and he was proudly portraying himself as the one who was truly fighting for the people against the corrupt power structure. "In the era when political power corrupts, social and crowdsourced power cleanses," Pishevar once wrote. "We must stir the hornet's nest to build immunity to the sting of corruption."

Speaking of the regulations he didn't like and unions he didn't like, Pishevar said, "Finding companies that can disrupt those is one way of having some kind of ethical philosophy of saying, 'We are going to use our capacity and our knowledge to improve our world by getting rid of some of those points of control.'" In short, technological disruption was the venture capitalist's way of making the world a better place for everyone's benefit.

Applause and whoops.

Pishevar spoke as an insurgent, with none of the grace and sense of obligation of the man who accepts his own arrival. Nor did his bearing suggest any awareness that Uber and Airbnb, of which he loved to speak, now faced serious charges of exploitative and illegal behavior toward people who genuinely lacked power. In Pishevar's mind, he and those companies were the weak ones. There he was driving in Paris, with protesting drivers creating a "war zone" and threatening him and his child. There he was trying to cleanse corruption by defying local city regulations. There he was clinging to his unpopular truth like Martin Luther reincarnated as a VC, nailing theses to the doors of the New York City Taxi and Limousine Commission. VCs are among the most powerful people in the world today, but in his mind he was the little guy. When your leader still wears the beret from his days in the rebel army, you should be afraid.

As the Q-and-A ended, Pishevar praised the Summit conference as "a movement of value creation," seamlessly merging the language of Selma and Harvard Business School.

To take the edge off of "value creation," a phrase that risked reminding people that he was a powerful gazillionaire, he once again invoked mushy language. Value creation, he said, was brought into one's life by value creators—people who put you "in an environment of love, faith, support." Here he was appropriating a language of movements and love, solidarity and selflessness, and even the therapeutic language of sharing being caring, and using it to dress up the naked truth of his oligarchic visions. He had the audacity to board an expensive, exclusive, invitation-only cruise-ship conference full of entrepreneurs, and yet claim it was taxi drivers who constituted the unjust cartel. He could profit from and defend a company doing everything in its power to smash the idea of a labor movement, while unabashedly speaking of this conference in the language of movements. He could, as a Silicon Valley venture capitalist, be the very picture of what was making the country less equal, while claiming to be fighting on behalf of the common man.

Shervin Pishevar's refusal to own up to his power was not an isolated occurrence. Such modesty is a defining feature of Silicon Valley, an epicenter of new power. "They fight as though they are insurgents while they operate as though they are kings," writes Danah Boyd, a technology scholar. She came of age among hackers and renegades and then grew frustrated with their failure to accept victory. They now owned the tools of modern power. But the group's self-image as "outsiders," a hangover from the sector's countercultural origins, left it "ill-equipped to understand its own actions and practices as part of the elite, the powerful," Boyd argues. And powerful people who "see themselves as underdogs in a world where instability and inequality are rampant fail to realize that they have a moral responsibility." As it happens, the two companies that had made Pishevar a legend got into legal trouble for engaging in that very sort of denialism.

Airbnb's troubles began some months before Summit at Sea, when an African American woman named Quirtina Crittenden took to Twitter to complain of being racially profiled when trying to book accommodations. Posting screenshots of rejections by hosts whose rentals had been listed as available for a given date range, Crittenden added the tag #AirbnbWhileBlack. Over time, others began to add their testimonies to Crittenden's, especially after she was profiled by National Public Radio the following year. The stories began to fly: "One bachelor's degree, one master's degree, and one doctorate's degree later, and I still can't rent your apartment. SMH #AirbnbWhileBlack." Then a black user named Gregory Seldon shared a story of how he had "made a fake profile as a white guy and was accepted immediately." Seldon's tweet went viral, and a social media firestorm was born.

Because of how Airbnb and other Silicon Valley platforms work, the company faced a choice of how to respond. Airbnb could claim that the platform itself has little power, that it cannot be held responsible for what occurs between two autonomous people on its site. But it surprised many by putting out a report some months later in which it committed to make "powerful systemic changes to greatly reduce the opportunity for hosts and guests to engage in conscious or unconscious discriminatory conduct." These steps were admirable—and also voluntary.

Two months after the viral explosion of #AirbnbWhileBlack, however, when the company received complaints from California's Department of Fair Employment and Housing alleging that it "may have failed to prevent discrimination against African American guests" and "may have engaged in acts of discrimination" itself, Airbnb retreated. "While Airbnb simply operates a platform and is not well positioned to make determinations regarding the booking decisions Hosts make in each case," the company said in a legal response, "Airbnb has recognized on its own based on available data that some third-party hosts on its site are likely violating Airbnb's policy against racial discrimination, and that its policies and processes have, to date, been insufficient fully to address the problem." Yet despite a Harvard Business School study that backed up users' claims of discrimination, the company said it was merely engaged in the "publication of rental listings," a humble role that it said "immunizes" it against liability. Airbnb, it argued, "cannot be held legally liable for the conduct of its third-party users." The law, the company said, "does not impose a duty to prevent discrimination by others."

At the time #AirbnbWhileBlack launched, Shervin Pishevar's other star investment, Uber, was embroiled in its own case about whether it was as humble and powerless as it claimed. A group of drivers had sued Uber, as well as its rival Lyft, in federal court, seeking to be treated as employees under California's labor laws. Their case was weakened by the fact that they had signed agreements to be contractors not subject to those laws. They had accepted the terms and conditions that cast each driver as an entrepreneur—

a free agent choosing her hours, needing none of the regulatory infrastructure that others depended on. They had bought into one of the reigning fantasies of MarketWorld: that people were their own miniature corporations. Then some of the drivers realized that in fact they were simply working people who wanted the same protections that so many others did from power, exploitation, and the vicissitudes of circumstance.

Because the drivers had signed that agreement, they had blocked the easy path to being employees. But under the law, if they could prove that a company had pervasive, ongoing power over them as they did their work, they could still qualify as employees. To be a contractor is to give up certain protections and benefits in exchange for independence, and thus that independence must be genuine. The case inspired the judges in the two cases, Edward Chen and Vince Chhabria, to grapple thoughtfully with the question of where power lurks in a new networked age.

It was no surprise that Uber and Lyft took the rebel position. Like Airbnb, Uber and Lyft claimed not to be powerful. Uber argued that it was just a technology firm facilitating links between passengers and drivers, not a car service. The drivers who had signed contracts were robust agents of their own destiny. Judge Chen derided this argument. "Uber is no more a 'technology company,'" he wrote, "than Yellow Cab is a 'technology company' because it uses CB radios to dispatch taxi cabs, John Deere is a 'technology company' because it uses computers and robots to manufacture lawn mowers, or Domino Sugar is a 'technology company' because it uses modern irrigation techniques to grow its sugar cane." Judge Chhabria similarly cited and tore down Lyft's claim to be "an uninterested bystander of sorts, merely furnishing a platform that allows drivers and riders to connect." He wrote:

Lyft concerns itself with far more than simply connecting random users of its platform. It markets itself to customers as an on-demand ride service, and it actively seeks out those customers. It gives drivers detailed instructions about how to conduct themselves. Notably, Lyft's own drivers' guide and FAQs state that drivers are "driving for Lyft." Therefore, the argument that Lyft is merely a platform, and that drivers perform no service for Lyft, is not a serious one.

The judges believed Uber and Lyft to be more powerful than they were willing to admit, but they also conceded that the companies did not have the same power over employees as an old-economy employer like Walmart. "The jury in this case will be handed a square peg and asked to choose between two round holes," Judge Chhabria wrote. Judge Chen, meanwhile, wondered whether Uber, despite a claim of impotence at the center of the network, exerted a kind of invisible power over drivers that might give them a case. In order to define this new power, he decided to turn where few judges do: the late French philosopher Michel Foucault.

In a remarkable passage, Judge Chen compared Uber's power to that of the guards at the center of the Panopticon, which Foucault famously analyzed in *Discipline and Punish*. The Panopticon was a design for a circular prison building dreamed up in the eighteenth century by the philosopher Jeremy Bentham. The idea was to empower a solitary guard in the center of the building to watch over a large number of inmates, not because he was actually able to see them all at once, but because the design kept any prisoner from knowing who was being observed at any given moment. Foucault analyzed the nature and working of power in the Panopticon, and the judge found it analogous to Uber's. He quoted a line about the "state of conscious and permanent visibility that assures the automatic functioning of power."

The judge was suggesting that the various ways in which Uber monitored, tracked, controlled, and gave feedback on the service of its drivers amounted to the "functioning of power," even if the familiar trappings of power—ownership of assets, control over an employee's time—were missing. The drivers weren't like factory workers employed and regimented by a plant, yet they weren't independent contractors who could do whatever they pleased. They could be fired for small infractions. That is power.

It can be disturbing that the most influential emerging power center of our age is in the habit of denying its power, and therefore of promoting a vision of change that changes nothing meaningful while enriching itself. Its posture is not entirely cynical, though. The technology world has long maintained that the tools it creates are inherently leveling and will serve to collapse power divides rather than widen them. In the mid-1990s, as the Internet began reaching into people's lives, Bill Gates predicted that technology would help to equalize a stubbornly unequal world:

> We are all created equal in the virtual world, and we can use this equality to help address some of the sociological problems that society has yet to solve in the physical world. The network will not eliminate barriers of prejudice or inequality, but it will be a powerful force in that direction.

It is hard to overstate how influential this belief has become in MarketWorld, especially in Silicon Valley: The world may be cruel and unfair, but if you sprinkle seeds of technology on it, shoots of equality will sprout. If every girl in Afghanistan had a smartphone . . . If every classroom were linked to the Web . . . If every police officer wore a body camera . . . Mark Zuckerberg and Priscilla Chan have vowed to connect the unconnected as part of their philanthropic work, because the Internet "provides education if you don't live near a good school. It provides health information on how to avoid diseases or raise healthy children if you don't live near a doctor. It provides financial services if you don't live near a bank. It provides access to jobs and opportunities if you don't live in a good economy." Some in the Valley have become downright glib about the leveling bias of technology. "Thanks to Airbnb," the venture capitalist Marc Andreessen says, "now anyone with a house or apartment can offer a room for rent. Hence, income inequality reduced." Investors like

Andreessen, according to this view, are just like the Occupy movement, but with bigger houses and clearer results.

Networks are the basis for much of this new power—networks
that simultaneously push power out to the edges and suck it into
the core. This idea comes from an authority on networks, Joshua
Cooper Ramo, a journalist turned protégé of Henry Kissinger, who
some years ago became interested in how new varieties of power
were upending the old laws of strategy and geopolitics. His study
of networks and interviews with their owners became a book, *The
Seventh Sense,* in which he says that this new

> power is defined by both profound concentration and by mas-
> sive distribution. It can't be understood in simple either/or
> terms. Power and influence may yet become even more cen-
> tralized than it was in feudal times and more distributed than
> it was in the most vibrant democracies.

Ramo is arguing that the Ubers and Airbnbs and Facebooks and
Googles of the world are at once radically democratic and dangerously oligarchic. Facebook emancipates people in Algerian base-
ments to write whatever they want, for all the world to see. Airbnb
allows anyone to rent out their home. Uber allows anyone going
through financial hardship to download the app and, without much
hassle, get started making money. These platforms *are* pushing
power out to the edges—power once controlled by media companies, hotel chains, and taxi unions. But networks tend toward
extreme concentration as well. It is no fun if half of your high school
friends are on the other social network, so Facebook becomes a de
facto monopoly. A core tenet of network theory is that the bigger the
network, the more juice it will be able to squeeze from every new
connection. Networks, then, are those rare beasts that get healthier,
tougher, and faster the fatter they become.

This simultaneous concentrating and diffusing of power has real
consequences for the distribution of societal power. "Tech people
like to picture their industry as a roiling sea of disruption, in which

every winner is vulnerable to surprise attack from some novel, as-yet-unimagined foe," writes Farhad Manjoo, who covers the sector for the *New York Times*. In fact, he notes, the industry is more concentrated than most, with Amazon, Apple, Facebook, Google, and Microsoft controlling much of everything. By almost any measure, the Frightful Five, as Manjoo calls them, are "getting larger, more entrenched in their own sectors, more powerful in new sectors and better insulated against surprising competition from upstarts." If technology keeps spawning Goliaths, it is because of the concentrating pressure of networks that Ramo described: Those players have built certain foundational networks, often called "platforms," that upstarts have ever less of a choice but to build on the bigger those networks get. "These platforms," Manjoo writes, "are inescapable; you may opt out of one or two of them, but together, they form a gilded mesh blanketing the entire economy."

Facebook, despite calling itself a "community," single-handedly redefined the word "friend" for much of humanity, based on what was best for its own business model. Another company, Google, can know everything you search for and buy, every off-color joke you have ever typed, every utterance you have spoken in your home in the presence of its kitchen helper, every move you've made in front of its home security camera. Airbnb boasted of 1.3 million people staying in one of its properties on a single New Year's Eve. As technologies like these have eaten the world, a relatively small number of people have come to own much of the infrastructure on which ever more human discourse, motion, buying, selling, reading, writing, teaching, learning, healing, and trading are done or arranged—even as many of them make public pronouncements about fighting against the establishment.

David Heinemeier Hansson is the cofounder of a Colorado-based software company called Basecamp, a successful but modest business that stayed relatively small and avoided the lure of Silicon Valley and of trying to swallow the world. "Part of the problem seems to be that nobody these days is content to merely put their dent in the universe," he has written. "No, they have to fucking own the universe. It's not enough to be in the market, they have to dominate it. It's not enough to serve customers, they have to capture them."

Maciej Ceglowski, the founder of a start-up called Pinboard, made waves in the Valley and beyond when he gave a talk comparing VCs first to the landed lords of feudal England, then to the central planners who once ran his native Poland:

> There's something very fishy about California capitalism.
>
> Investing has become the genteel occupation of our gentry, like having a country estate used to be in England. It's a class marker and a socially acceptable way for rich techies to pass their time. Gentlemen investors decide what ideas are worth pursuing, and the people pitching to them tailor their proposals accordingly.
>
> The companies that come out of this are no longer pursuing profit, or even revenue. Instead, the measure of their success is valuation—how much money they've convinced people to tell them they're worth.
>
> There's an element of fantasy to the whole enterprise that even the tech elite is starting to find unsettling.
>
> We had people like this back in Poland, except instead of venture capitalists we called them central planners. They, too, were in charge of allocating vast amounts of money that didn't belong to them.
>
> They, too, honestly believed they were changing the world, and offered the same kinds of excuses about why our day-to-day life bore no relation to the shiny, beautiful world that was supposed to lie just around the corner.

Over a generation, America has grappled with one problem after another that could be said to have contributed to the decay of its politics and many people's livelihoods. The American social contract has frayed, and workers' lives have grown more precarious, and mobility has slowed. These are hard and important problems. The new winners of the age might well have participated in the writing of a new social contract for a new age, a new vision of economic security for ordinary people in a globalized and digitized world. But as we've seen, they actually made the situation worse by seeking to bust unions and whatever other worker protections still lingered and to remake more and more of the society as an always-on labor market in which workers were downbidding one another for millions of little fleeting gigs. "Any industry that still has unions has potential energy that could be released by start-ups," the Silicon Valley venture capitalist Paul Graham once tweeted.

As America's level of inequality spread to ever more unmanageable levels, these MarketWorld winners might have helped out. Looking within their own communities would have told them what they needed to know. Doing everything to reduce their tax burdens, even when legal, stands in contradiction with their claims to do well by doing good. Diverting the public's attention from an issue like offshore banking worsens the big problems, even as these Market-Worlders shower attention on niche causes.

As life expectancy declined among large subpopulations of Americans, winners possessed of a sense of having arrived might have chipped in. They might have taken an interest in the details of a health care system that was allowing the unusual phenomenon of a developed country regressing in this way, or in the persistence of easily preventable deaths in the developing world. They might not have thought of themselves at all, given how long they were likely to live because of their tremendous advantages. "It seems pretty egocentric while we still have malaria and TB for rich people to fund things so they can live longer," Bill Gates has said.

Perhaps the most unlikely featured speaker at Summit at Sea was Edward Snowden, American whistleblower, scourge of the National Security Agency. He was in Russia, coming to the ship via video. His interviewer was Chris Sacca, a wildly successful VC (Instagram, Kickstarter, Twitter, Uber). One of the founders of Summit walked onstage and said, "We need truth-tellers and thought leaders like Chris Sacca." Two truth-tellers for the price of one.

Sacca, taking the stage, praised Summit for becoming what he called "a platform for entrepreneurship, for justice." He said it as if the two were the same. Then he interviewed Snowden for a time, eliciting what had become his whistleblower stump speech. At one point, the man in Moscow began to say what would quicken the heart of any chaser of Valley glory. The world's most famous leaker spoke of the need to build new communication tools that went beyond encryption to be entirely untraceable so that even the fact of a conversation having occurred between two people would remain unknown. He talked about "tokenizing identity," giving people ways of participating in the online communities of the age without becoming vulnerable to being followed from platform to platform and having people know every book they had read, every movement they had participated in, every friend they had made.

"When we think about the civil rights movement," Snowden said, "when we think about every social progress that's happened throughout history, going all the way back to the Renaissance, going back to people thinking about heretical ideas—'Hey, maybe the world is not flat'—even making these arguments, challenging conventions, challenging the structures of law on any given day itself is a violation of law. And if the minute somebody starts engaging in heretical thinking, the minute somebody breaks a law, even if it's a simple minor regulation, if that can be instantly detected, interdicted, and then remediated through some kind of penalty or sanction, not only would we never see start-ups like Uber get off the ground, but it will freeze human social progress in place. Because you'll no longer have the chance to challenge orthodoxies without being immediately singled out, thrown off in the pen, having no possibility or capability to build a critical mass that could lead to change."

Perhaps in an effort to be courteous to his entrepreneurial audience, Snowden had tucked a mention of a start-up into his much grander vision of heresy, thereby destroying whatever chance he had for his ideas to be heard as they were intended. He had ensured that Sacca, and presumably many others, would now hear his revolutionary words and think only of investment.

"So I invest in founders for a living," Sacca said, staring up at the giant screen. "And I gotta tell you, as I listen to you, I smell a founder here. You're talking about these things that need to be built. Are you going to build any of them? Because there's probably investors waiting for you here."

Snowden seemed taken aback. Here he was talking about heresy and truth and freedom, and now he was being asked about a start-up. Flummoxed, he tried to let Sacca down politely: "I do have a number of projects that are actively in motion. But I take a little bit of a different view from a lot of people who need venture capital, who are trying to get investors. I don't like to promote things. I don't like to say I'm working on this particular system to solve this particular problem. I would rather simply do it, at the minimum expenditure of resources, and then be judged on the basis of results. If it works, if it expands, that's wonderful. But ultimately, for me, I don't tend to think that I'm going to be working in a commercial space. So I would rather say, 'Let's wait and see.'"

It was a kindly delivered rebuke to MarketWorld's way of life. Here was a man who didn't like to promote himself, who didn't crave money, who was actually fighting the system, and willing to lose for the greater good to win.

At Summit, Snowden called for "one spot, anywhere in the world, where we can experiment, where we can be safe." For him, this was a serious vision perhaps involving life and death. Entrepreneurs, as if to mimic genuine renegades, tended to invoke the same idea, but in their case it was less about challenging power than about amassing and protecting it. The entrepreneur and investor Peter Thiel called for floating "seasteading" communities far from the reach of law. Larry Page, the cofounder of Google, reportedly said, "As technologists, we should have some safe places where we can try out new things and figure out the effect on society." The technology investor

Balaji Srinivasan called for the winners of the digital revolution to secede from the ungrateful world of Luddites and complainers—"Silicon Valley's ultimate exit," as he put it—using tools, like those Snowden had imagined, to "build an opt-in society, ultimately outside the United States, run by technology."

What connects these various notions is a fantasy of living free of government. These rich and powerful men engage in what the writer Kevin Roose has called "anarchist cheerleading," in keeping with their carefully crafted image as rebels against the authorities. To call for a terrain without rules in the way they do, to dabble in this anarchist cheerleading, may be to sound like you wished for a new world of freedom on behalf of humankind. But a long line of thinkers has told us that the powerful tend to be the big winners from the creation of blank-slate, rules-free worlds. A famous statement of that finding came from the feminist writer Jo Freeman, who in her 1972 essay "The Tyranny of Structurelessness" observed that when groups operate on vague or anarchic terms, structurelessness "becomes a smokescreen for the strong or the lucky to establish unquestioned hegemony over others."

Freeman's idea could be traced back to the Enlightenment and Thomas Hobbes. Hobbes also believed that structurelessness wasn't all it was cracked up to be, especially for the weak. The powerful Leviathan for which he advocated is often treated as shorthand for monarchy or authoritarianism. But in fact what Hobbes suggested was that the choice is not between authority and liberty, but between authority of one sort and authority of another. Someone always rules; the question is who. In a world without a Leviathan, which is to say a strong state capable of making and enforcing universal rules, people will be ruled by thousands of miniature Leviathans closer to home—by the feudal lords on whose soil they work and against whom they have few defenses; by powerful, whimsical, unaccountable princes.

Hobbes articulated a vision of an authority in which everyone had a formal legal investment, an authority that belonged to us in common and that trumped local authorities. He believed that there could be greater liberty under such an authority than in its absence: "Men have no pleasure, but on the contrary a great deal of grief, in keeping company where there is no power able to overawe them all." In a world without rules, he wrote, "nothing can be unjust. The notions of right and wrong, justice and injustice, have there no place. Where there is no common power, there is no law; where no law, no injustice." The cardinal virtues in a such a world are "force and fraud."

The self-styled entrepreneur-rebels were actually seeking to overturn a major project of the Enlightenment—the development of universal rules that applied evenly to all, freeing people from the particularisms of their villages, churches, and domains. The world that these elites seemed to envision, in which rules receded and entrepreneurs reigned through the market, augured a return to private manors—allowing the Earl of Facebook and the Lord of Google to make major decisions about our shared fate outside of democracy. It would be a world that let them deny their power over the serfs around them by appropriating a language of community and love, movements and win-wins. They would keep on speaking of changing the world. But many, down in the world, would feel, not without reason, that what was bleak in the world somehow wasn't changing.

It is not inevitable that what passes for progress in our age involves the concentration of power into a small number of hands and the issuance of stories about the powerful being fighters for the little guy. There are people thinking about other, more honest ways of making the world a better place, and thinking freely, without the burdensome MarketWorld requirement that progress must tend to the winners and obey their rules. But it is not easy to compete with MarketWorld for the resources and branding power it is able to throw at its works.

A few months after Summit, an event at the Goethe Institute in New York offered a very different vision for the digital age. It was a meeting of a budding movement called "platform cooperativism." Here was a conversation about making the world better that eschewed the win-win commandment that the powerful should benefit from any change for that change to be worth doing. Platform cooperativism is a movement that seeks to make true what Silicon Valley claims is already occurring, proposing "a new kind of online economy," as one of its digital pamphlets put it:

> For all the wonders the Internet brings us, it is dominated by an economics of monopoly, extraction, and surveillance. Ordinary users retain little control over their personal data, and the digital workplace is creeping into every corner of workers' lives. Online platforms often exploit and exacerbate existing inequalities in society, even while promising to be the great equalizers. Could the Internet be owned and governed differently?

To talk like this was to flirt with the actual, and not rhetorical, changing of the world. One did not regularly encounter ideas like this in MarketWorld, even though the suppositions behind them were obvious: that sometimes the builders of technology serve only themselves; that sometimes humanitarianism and entrepreneurship are actually distinct things. The subversive premise of platform co-op, as the cause was casually known, ought not to have been as subversive as it was: that ordinary people, and not just the winners of MarketWorld, should have some say in how technology develops; that it could develop in more than one direction; that some of those directions would be better than others at turning innovation into progress for most people.

One heard from speakers ways of thinking that were all but barred from MarketWorld: the idea that there were such things as power and privilege; that some people had them in every era and some people didn't; that this power and privilege demanded wariness; that progress was not inevitable, and that history was not a line but a wheel; that sometimes astonishing new tools were used in ways that worsened the world; that places of darkness often persisted even under new light; that people had a long habit of exploiting one another, no matter how selfless they and their ideas seem; that the powerful are your equals as citizens, not your representatives.

The attendees didn't confine their speech to win-wins. They spoke of exploitation and abuse and solidarity. They spoke of problems. They were not bound by the genteel MarketWorld consensus. The audience was cynical rather than utopian, critical rather than boosting. They knew what wasn't new. The speakers, for their part, had none of MarketWorld's customary slickness. Presentations weren't smooth. No lavalier microphones were on offer. No one roamed the stage like a lion on the savanna. There were few, if any, jokes in the talks. People just spoke to the problems they wished to solve. The event was a thrillingly democratic contrast with Summit at Sea and other MarketWorld forums.

Trebor Scholz stepped up to the podium and explained why, a few years earlier, he had written a short essay on an idea that he coined as platform cooperativism. As he surveyed the world being remade by Silicon Valley, and especially what was once called the sharing economy, he began to see through the fantasy-speak. Here were a handful of companies thriving by serving as middlemen between people who wanted rides and people who offered them, people who wanted their Ikea furniture assembled and people who came over to install it, people who defrayed their costs by renting out a room and people who stayed there. It was no accident, Scholz believed, that these services had taken off at the historical moment that they had. An epic meltdown of the world financial system had cost millions of people their homes, jobs, and health insurance. And as the fallout from the crash spread, many of those cut loose had been drafted into joining a new American servant class. The precariousness at the bottom, which had shown few signs of improving several years after the meltdown, had become the fodder for a bounty of services for the affluent—and, Scholz noted, for the "channeling of wealth in fewer and fewer hands." Somehow, the technologies celebrated by the Valley as leveling playing fields and emancipating people had fostered a slick new digitally enabled upstairs-downstairs line in American social life.

It didn't have to be this way, said Scholz. Technology was neither inherently feudal nor inherently democratic. It had, as Ramo wrote, both tendencies. Which tendency would win out depended on the values of the age and what people chose to fight for. We live in an era in which it is remarkably easy, by historical standards, to build a platform like Uber or Airbnb. Yet for all this ease, the big platforms tend to be owned by small cliques of investors like Shervin Pishevar and Chris Sacca, run for their benefit, and given to extracting as much value from workers as they can, at very low prices. If it is so easy to build platforms these days, Scholz wondered, why couldn't workers and customers create their own platforms?

Scholz had embarked on a global adventure to locate and study various attempts to do just this. The idea lived already, in many little embryos. There was Fairmondo and Loconomics and Members Media and various others. But it wasn't just about these companies, Scholz said: "I'm not really talking about an app. I'm not really talking about technology per se, but it is really about the change of a mind-set, a mind-set that is now based on this kind of extractive economy but is working towards one that is really based on mutualism and cooperativism." Here was a rarity: a no-strings-attached idea for actually changing the world.

When Scholz spoke at events, he was asked over and over how democratically owned tools could ever compete with powerful corporate platforms. "How can we achieve scale?" people would ask. "How can we reach out to the masses?"

"We are the masses," Scholz reminded them.

He ceded the floor to people working on various aspects of platform co-op. Brendan Martin was the founder of the Working World, a cooperative financial institution active in Argentina, Nicaragua, and the United States. He was seeking to build what he called "non-extractive finance." He told the audience that the challenge represented by platform co-op was part of a very old human story:

The fight over platforms, whether they are cooperative or owned by just a few—you can look and you can distill history down to essentially being that fight. Class warfare can really be about who gets to own it, a couple of us or all of us. It is things that have public benefit that are owned by a couple of people, and they get to extract what they will from those who have to use it—or they are shared for the collective benefit. What is new about technology here, it's just a new space to have that battle in.

Who owns what no one has any choice but to use? It is an ancient question that has become central to a new age. Martin looked at the new platforms and saw links to earlier platforms—the platforms of granaries, of gold, of land. Revolution after revolution over the ages had called for the cancellation of debts and the redistribution of land. "We might change that now to cancel the debts and redistribute the platform," Martin said.

Then there was Emma Yorra, who codirected the Cooperative Development Program at the Center for Family Life in Brooklyn. She was running a social service program that had little apparent connection to technology. The center had some years earlier begun to organize worker cooperatives to help poor immigrants locate work in housecleaning, child care, pet care, and the like, and to keep as much of the pay as possible, rather than forking it over to a middleman.

One day Yorra was taking the subway, and she saw an ad that angered her. It was for one of the slick new digital platforms offering super-easy housecleaning. As she recalled it:

It's an ad that's really promoting itself for its technological ease of use. I think it's like, "Get a clean apartment with one click." And it's just got this hand that is a yellow-gloved hand. It's kind of disembodied, and it's got a sponge and you're going to get this clean apartment cleaned by someone you

don't see, some magical elf who has a yellow hand. And it's
not really a person, right? It's all about the technology.

This was what had bothered Yorra. The technology, which had
made the service easier to procure, had also changed the nature of
the interaction. The one-click app obscured the messy human reality of the working people behind it, who now had less bargaining
power.

Yorra had begun to build what she imagined as a cooperative
answer to the one-click cleaning service. Because MarketWorld is so
hard to escape even when you are rejecting it, she had taken funding from the Robin Hood Foundation, financed by the titans of Wall
Street, to build her service. The effort was still in progress that night
at the Goethe Institute. (Eventually, her organization would release
a new app called Up & Go, which allowed consumers to book housecleaning services, and which channeled 95 percent of the money
directly to the workers, who also owned the businesses.) That evening, with the app more than a year away from release, Yorra had a
long way to go to make progress against a statistic that appalled her:
the news, put out by the charity Oxfam, that just sixty-two billionaires possessed as much wealth as the bottom half of humanity
(3.6 billion people), down from three hundred billionaires a few
years ago. In fact, it was nine billionaires, not sixty-two, as Oxfam
would later say when better data came in. And the following year,
the number of billionaires it took to account for half the world's
resources dropped from nine to eight.

Six of those eight made their money in the supposedly equal-
izing field of technology: Gates, Zuckerberg, Jeff Bezos of Amazon,
Larry Ellison of Oracle, Carlos Slim of Telmex and other Mexican
businesses, and Michael Bloomberg, the purveyor of computer ter-
minals. Another, Amancio Ortega, who built the retailer Zara, was
famous for applying advanced technology to manufacturing and for
automating his factories. The final member of the gang of eight,
Warren Buffett, was a major shareholder in Apple and IBM.

CHAPTER 4

THE CRITIC AND THE THOUGHT LEADER

It is difficult to get a man to understand something when his salary depends on not understanding it.

—UPTON SINCLAIR

In October 2011, in the sleepy village of Camden, Maine, Amy Cuddy prepared to give her first proper talk outside academia. Cuddy was a social psychologist at Harvard Business School who had spent more than a decade publishing papers on the workings of prejudice, discrimination, and systems of power. She had written of how the sexism that women face is a strange amalgam of the envy men feel toward career women and the pity they feel for women who don't work. She had written of how "socialized obedience" and "conformity" played into the decisions of both the 9/11 hijackers and the American guards at Abu Ghraib who tortured their prisoners. She had written of how white people taking computerized implicit-bias tests became more prejudiced when informed that the tests' purpose was to measure racism. She had written of how, in the aftermath of Hurricane Katrina, people more easily perceived "anguish, mourning, remorse," and other "uniquely human" emotions in people of the same race as them than in people of other hues. She had written of the "model minority" stereotype that shadows so many Asian Americans.

That autumn, she was continuing to work with a team on a long-term project to study how men's hegemony, that most global of phenomena, adapts to local conditions so as to enroot itself. In America, where being independent and self-oriented are the leading "cultural ideals," she and her colleagues wrote, the society tends to cast men as independent and self-oriented. In South Korea, where being interdependent and others-oriented are more prized, the society tends to cast men as interdependent and others-oriented. As a working paper put it, "Men in general are seen as possessing more of whatever characteristic is most culturally valued." Like much of her work, the paper didn't offer solutions. It was part of a noble intellectual tradition of plumbing the depths of a problem. Which was perhaps why none of Cuddy's work had led to giving a talk beyond the walls of academia—until now.

She had been invited to speak at a conference called PopTech. It was, like Summit at Sea, an important stop on the MarketWorld circuit. It had been founded by a group of people who wanted to bring big ideas to Maine—including the inventor of Ethernet and a former chief executive of Pepsi and Apple. At PopTech, the ideas went down easy amid the lobster rolls and twilight deck parties overlooking West Penobscot Bay and nightcaps at Natalie's at the Camden Harbour Inn. Like many MarketWorld conferences, PopTech charged a sizable attendance fee, and it relied on corporate sponsors. When MarketWorld organized such events, it could be difficult to keep its tastes and ways of seeing from shaping what ideas were offered and how. It was not clear what these MarketWorld types would make of Cuddy, since she tended to speak of problems rather than easy solutions, and of challenging power and systems, and appeared little interested in the milquetoast change of win-wins.

Fortunately, Cuddy had a guide to this new world in the form of Andrew Zolli, who, as PopTech's curator, was her host at the conference. Zolli was a kind of MarketWorld producer, standing at the profitable intersection of companies wanting to associate themselves with big ideas, networkers looking for their next conference, and writers and thinkers who wanted to reach a broader audience and perhaps court the influential elites of the circuit. Zolli, who called his conference "a machine to change the world," was a consultant and strategic adviser to companies like General Electric, PricewaterhouseCoopers, Nike, and Facebook, as well as NGOs, start-ups, and civil society groups; he was on the boards of various MarketWorld organizations; and he was a fixture on the paid lecture circuit, where he spoke on topics like resilience. His book on the subject would praise such things as smart electrical grids and marine conservation as win-wins.

Zolli was, in other words, an expert in and perpetuator of MarketWorld culture and its way of seeing. He understood what ideas would be useful to MarketWorlders, helping them to anticipate the future and make their killings, and he understood what ideas made winners feel socially conscious and globally aware but not guilty or blamed.

An essay he wrote to promote his book on resilience argued that the world should focus less on rooting out its biggest problems, including poverty and climate change, and more on living with them. The message had reassuring implications for those who were perfectly content with the status quo and preferred the kinds of changes that essentially preserved it. Zolli believed that the desire to solve underlying problems is "an alluring and moral vision," but ultimately wrong. The problems were perhaps here to stay, and it was more important, he argued, to teach people to cope.

Zolli promoted various projects that devote resources to helping people weather bad situations rather than to improving those situations. For example, he praised research at Emory University that illustrates how "contemplative practice" can "bolster the psychological and physiological resilience of children in foster care," which was a lot easier than fixing foster care. He spoke of inflatable bridges and electrical micro-grids that could help communities survive exploding transformers as sea levels continue to rise. He was quick to admit that none of these kinds of fixes "is a permanent solution, and none roots out the underlying problems they address." He knew he had critics: "If we adapt to unwanted change, the reasoning goes, we give a pass to those responsible for putting us in this mess in the first place, and we lose the moral authority to pressure them to stop." But this was the kind of thinking mostly heard from people who didn't make a living as corporate consultants and MarketWorld idea generators, and Zolli didn't buy it. He made clear that he wasn't saying "there aren't genuine bad guys and bad ideas at work, or that there aren't things we should do to mitigate our risks. But we also have to acknowledge that the holy war against boogeymen hasn't worked and isn't likely to anytime soon. In its place, we need approaches that are both more pragmatic and more politically inclusive—rolling with the waves, instead of trying to stop the ocean." You can talk about our common problems, but don't be political, don't focus on root causes, don't go after bogeymen, don't try to change fundamental things. Give hope. Roll with the waves. That is the MarketWorld way.

Cuddy was nervous about speaking, for the first time, to hundreds of strangers who weren't in her field, who weren't enthusiastic students who had signed up for her class, who didn't know any of the basic concepts of social psychology. Although her work on images of men in individualist and collectivist societies was on her mind, it may not have exhilarated PopTech. Another paper she had published, in *Psychological Science,* "Brief Nonverbal Displays Affect Neuroendocrine Levels and Risk Tolerance," would become the basis for her talk.

The stage lights came up from darkness. Cuddy stood center stage with her hands on her hips, her feet planted shoulder-width apart, tucked into a pair of brown cowboy boots that only added to what would come to be called her signature "power pose." On the giant screen behind her was an image of Wonder Woman, whose hands and feet were in the same powerful posture, engaged in the same willful taking of space. What she and her colleagues had found was that standing in a forceful position like this could stir confidence in people—and perhaps blunt some effects of the sexism that she had long studied. For twenty seconds that felt like eternity, Cuddy stood there, looking powerful and remaining silent, as the Wonder Woman theme song played. She pivoted from side to side, holding her position. Then she broke character and smiled.

"I'm going to talk to you today about body language," she began. The title of her talk, revealed on the second slide, was "Power Posing: Gain Power Through Body Language." She began to explain her and her colleagues' research showing that without changing any of the larger dynamics of power and sexism and prejudice, there were poses people could strike in private that would help them gain confidence. Without necessarily intending to, she was giving MarketWorld what it craved in a thinker: a way of framing a problem that made it about giving bits of power to those who lack it without taking power away from those who hold it. She was, to use a metaphor she would later employ, giving people a ladder up across a forbidding wall—without proposing to tear down the wall. Or as Zolli might have put it, she was giving people a way of "rolling with the waves, instead of trying to stop the ocean."

I t is the best of times for thought leaders. It is the worst of times for public intellectuals," declares Daniel Drezner, a foreign policy scholar, in his recent treatise *The Ideas Industry*, a part-academic, part-first-person account of how an age of inequality, among other things, has distorted the work of thinking.

Drezner starts out by defining two distinct kinds of thinkers, who share in common a desire to develop important ideas and at the same time reach a broad audience. One of these types, the dying one, is the public intellectual, whom Drezner describes as a wide-ranging "critic" and a foe of power; she perhaps stays "aloof from the market, society, or the state," and she proudly bears a duty "to point out when an emperor has no clothes." The ascendant type is the thought leader, who is more congenial to the plutocrats who sponsor so much intellectual production today. Thought leaders tend, Drezner says, to "know one big thing and believe that their important idea will change the world"; they are not skeptics but "true believers"; they are optimists, telling uplifting stories; they reason inductively from their own experiences more than deductively from authority. They go easy on the powerful. Susan Sontag, William F.

Buckley Jr., and Gore Vidal were public intellectuals; Thomas L. Friedman, Niall Ferguson, and Parag Khanna are thought leaders. Public intellectuals argue with each other in the pages of books and magazines; thought leaders give TED talks that leave little space for criticism or rebuttal, and emphasize hopeful solutions over systemic change. Public intellectuals pose a genuine threat to winners; thought leaders promote the winners' values, talking up "disruption, self-empowerment, and entrepreneurial ability."

Three factors explain the decline of the public intellectual and the rise of the thought leader, according to Drezner. One is political polarization: As American politics has grown more tribal, people have become more interested in hearing confirmation of their views, by whoever will offer it, than in being challenged by interesting, intellectually meandering thinkers. Another factor is a generalized loss of trust in authority. In recent decades, Americans have lost faith in virtually every institution in the country, except for the military, thanks in part to years of hard economic realities and a dysfunctional public sphere. Journalists have come to be trusted less than chiropractors. This loss of faith has pulled public intellectuals down a few notches, and created new space for the less-credentialed idea generators to vie for attention. Yet in Drezner's view it is rising inequality that has most altered the sphere of ideas. It has had a paradoxical effect. On one hand, extreme inequality has created "a thirst for ideas to diagnose and treat the problems that seem to plague the United States." On the other, it has spawned "a new class of benefactors to fund the generation and promotion of new ideas." So America is more interested than ever in the problem of inequality and social fracture—and more dependent than ever on explainers who happen to be in good odor with billionaires.

Drawing on his own surveys and scholarship by others, Drezner shows how these explainers get pulled into MarketWorld's orbit—how thinkers like him and Cuddy and others are coaxed to abandon their roles as potential critics and instead to become fellow travelers of the winners. "As America's elite has gotten richer and richer, they can afford to do anything they want," he writes. "It turns out a surprising number of them want to go back to school—or, rather, make school go to them." Thinkers are invited to become the elite's teachers on the circuit of "Big Idea get-togethers"—"TED, South by Southwest, the Aspen Ideas Festival, the Milken Institute's Global Conference, anything sponsored by *The Atlantic*." These thinkers often find themselves having become thought leaders without realizing it, after "a slow accretion of opportunities that are hard to refuse."

It could be added to Drezner's analysis that even as plutocrats were providing these alluring incentives, less corrupting sources of intellectual patronage were dwindling. On America's campuses in recent decades, the fraction of academics on tenure track has collapsed by half. Newsrooms, another source of support for those in the ideas game, have shrunk by more than 40 percent since 1990. The publishing industry has suffered as bookstores vanish and print runs dwindle. We live in a golden age for digitally beaming out ideas, but for many it has been a dark age for actually making a living on them. Many thinkers have no expectation but that a life making ideas will be grueling, unremunerated, and publicly unsung. But for those drawn to money or stardom or solo influence, publicly oriented sources of support have been eclipsed by privately oriented ones, and the new patrons have their tastes and taboos.

It can be said that MarketWorld's circuit, and the world of the thought leader more generally, has had many virtuous effects. It has made ideas more accessible and available to many people. It has created, with the new form of videotaped talks, an alternative to the heavy tomes that many people, frankly, didn't read a generation ago and aren't about to start reading now. It has extended the opportunity to reach a wide audience to people from backgrounds long shut out by the old gatekeepers at publishing houses and newspapers.

But the world of thought leadership is easily conquered by charlatans. It is long on "affirmation without any constructive criticism," as Drezner argues, emphasizing beautiful storytelling and sidelining the hurly-burly of disputation that helps ideas to get better and keeps bad ones from attracting too many adherents. And it puts thinkers in a compromised relationship to the very thing they are supposed to keep honest and in check: power.

The phenomenon Drezner details matters far beyond the world of thinkers, because on issue after issue, the ascendant thought leaders, if they are positive, unthreatening, mute about larger systems and structures, congenial to the rich, big into private problem-solving, devoted to win-wins—these thought leaders will edge out other voices, and not just at conferences. They get asked to write op-eds, sign book deals, opine on TV, advise presidents and premiers. And their success could be said to come at the expense of the critics'. For every thought leader who offered advice on how to build a career in a merciless new economy, there were many less-heard critics aspiring to make the economy less merciless.

The Hilary Cohens and Stacey Ashers and Justin Rosensteins and Greg Ferensteins and Emmett Carsons and Jane Leibrocks and Shervin Pishevars and Chris Saccas and Travis Kalanicks of the world needed thinkers to formulate the visions of change by which they would live—and to convince the wider public that they, the elite, were change agents, were the solutions to the problem, and therefore not the problem. In an age of inequality, these winners longed to feel, on one hand, that they had "some kind of ethical philosophy," as Pishevar put it. They needed language to justify themselves to themselves and others. They needed the idea of change itself to be redefined to emphasize "rolling with the waves, instead of trying to stop the ocean." The thought leaders gave these winners what they needed.

Cuddy's choice of topic at PopTech paid off. She hadn't talked about the structural power of men. She had talked about poses that individuals can do to feel more powerful, and the crowd had loved it. Word of her compelling, digestible research and her Wonder Woman shtick got out, and soon afterward she was asked to give a main-stage TED talk.

She said she had no desire to sugarcoat reality in the talk. But she decided to speak of the feeling of powerlessness that many women experience without getting into the causes of that sentiment. In an interview years later, she was straightforward about the motivation behind her "power pose" research. It came, she said, from watching her female students not speak in class: "Seeing their body language, watching them shut down and curl themselves up, that truly was it for me. It was watching that and then seeing myself behaving the same way when I got into an interaction with a man who I found intimidating." In the interview, Cuddy minced no words about the cause of the behavior. It flowed from "sexism." But in the talk she sanded the rough edges of these ideas. She described the class-rooms in which she had taught, where some students come in "like caricatures of alphas," physically and conversationally expansive, and others are "virtually collapsing when they come in." Then she casually mentioned the gender factor, even though it was the founding observation of the research. The collapsing behavior, she said, "seems to be related to gender. So women are much more likely to do this kind of thing than men. Women feel chronically less power-ful than men, so this is not surprising."

Cuddy was a leading authority on why women chronically feel less powerful than men, who does that to them, and how. But that story was not for this stage. Instead, Cuddy led the audience toward the findings of her and her colleagues' study of "power poses."

It was already known that being and feeling powerful made peo-ple stand more grandly and spaciously. But what if you did not have to redress those larger power imbalances to get more women speak-ing up in the classroom? What if you could teach them to stand grandly and spaciously in the hope of making them feel, and even be, more powerful? What Cuddy and her colleagues wondered, she said that day at TED, was: "Can you fake it till you make it? Like, can you do this just for a little while and actually experience a behav-ioral outcome that makes you seem more powerful?" Their big con-clusion was that you can. "When you pretend to be powerful, you are more likely to actually feel powerful," she said. "Tiny tweaks," she added a moment later, "can lead to big changes." In closing, she asked the audience to share the poses far and wide, because, she said, "the people who can use it the most are the ones with no resources and no technology and no status and no power." Now at least they had new tools for pretending.

More than forty million people would eventually watch Cuddy's TED talk, making it the second most popular talk of all time—even as some began to question her research. Members of the "replication movement" in social psychology, who have been pushing for more rigorous standards of double-checking, re-tested her findings and reported the effects of posing on hormones to be nonexistent, while acknowledging some effect on people's self-reported feelings. The ensuing battle turned bitter at times, with one of Cuddy's own coauthors publicly disavowing the power-pose work. Cuddy acknowledged on the TED website that "the relationship between posture and hormones isn't as simple as we believed it to be," even as she has continued to defend—and further research—the effects of power posing on people's emotional states. And the controversy in academia did nothing to deter people from stopping her in the street to thank her tearfully for giving them confidence. Her email inbox began to overflow. She would soon land a book deal. And she would become one of those people known for a phrase that you can never escape—the "power pose" woman forevermore.

Cuddy was still Cuddy, was still a strong feminist, was still a scholar and dangerously equipped foe of sexism. She remained better qualified than most people on earth to explain why women weren't born feeling powerless but had that feeling implanted in them. But she had pulled a punch in her talk, leaving out the critic-style utterances and making a pleasant, constructive, actionable, thought-leaderly case, and the world had rewarded her by listening.

As Cuddy figured out how to address these new forums and audiences, she had the benefit of many surrounding examples. The culture was full of instruction, if you were open to it, about how to become more hearable as a thinker—how to move toward the thought-leader end of the critic/thought-leader continuum. This becomes apparent when you consider some of Cuddy's contemporaries who have also gone the thought-leader way. You start to see a few basic dance steps in common—what we may call the thought-leader three-step.

"Focus on the victim, not the perpetrator" is the first of these steps. The phrase itself comes from Adam Grant, an organizational psychologist who has surged to the highest altitudes of thought leadership in recent years—"one of his generation's most compelling and provocative thought leaders," as his own book jacket declares. When faced with a problem, the human instinct is often to hunt for a culprit. But that is a win-losey approach to solving a problem. Grant proposed a more congenial way to deal with problems such as sexism. "In the face of injustice, thinking about the perpetrator fuels anger and aggression," he wrote. "Shifting your attention to the victim makes you more empathetic, increasing the chances that you'll channel your anger in a constructive direction. Instead of trying to punish the people who caused harm, you'll be more likely to help the people who were harmed."

The second step is to personalize the political. If you want to be a thought leader and not dismissed as a critic, your job is to help the public see problems as personal and individual dramas rather than collective and systemic ones. It is a question of focus. It is possible to look at a street corner in Baltimore and zoom in on low-hanging pants as the problem. It is possible to zoom out and see the problem as overpolicing and a lack of opportunity in the inner city. It is possible to zoom out further and see the problem as the latest chapter in a centuries-long story of the social control of African Americans. Many thinkers tend to be zoomers-out by nature and training, seeing things in terms of systems and structures. But if they wish to be thought leaders who are heard and invited back, it is vital to learn how to zoom in.

Brené Brown, who has become a friend of Cuddy's, offers a case study in how to zoom in successfully. She was a scholar of social work, a field that has produced few, if any, major thought leaders

besides her. That may be because social work is almost constitution-
ally a zoom-out discipline. A psychologist's analysis of a troubled
child may not go much further than the parents and home environment. But a social work scholar is educated to consider and write
journal articles in venues like *Families in Society* about the systems
beyond the home that implicate us collectively—crime-ridden neighborhoods, failing foster care programs, chronic poverty, threadbare
health care offerings, lack of nutrition options. This makes social
workers poor candidates for thought leadership, because at any
moment they might say something critical and win-losey.

As a researcher at the University of Houston, Brown started by
studying human connection, which led to studying shame, which
led to studying vulnerability—"this idea of, in order for connection
to happen, we have to allow ourselves to be seen, really seen." She
studied this for six years, after which time she came to one inescapable conclusion: "There was only one variable that separated
the people who have a strong sense of love and belonging and the
people who really struggle for it. And that was, the people who have
a strong sense of love and belonging believe they're worthy of love
and belonging. That's it." Now, scholars of social work tend not to
speak like this. They are experts in the thicket of circumstances that
keep so many of us from being our fullest selves—some of them
escapable through individual effort, but many of them not, being
structural in nature, or depending on the choices of many other
actors we do not control.

Brown did not emphasize all of the other reasons and circumstances and forces—poverty, family abuse, police treatment,
addiction—that made some people feel worthy and others unworthy.
She became a thriving, Oprah-backed thought leader. She, too, gave
one of the most popular TED talks of all time. "We live in a vulnerable world," she said, in which people got sick, struggled in marriage,
got laid off, had to lay others off. The country was deep into an economic crisis when she said this. Millions had lost jobs and homes
and even loved ones as a complication. Brown warned people that

numbing the pain wasn't the answer, though that is what Americans were doing as "the most in-debt, obese, addicted, and medicated adult cohort in U.S. history." (Following the first step, about focusing on the victim rather than the perpetrator, she did not mention the powerful interests pushing debt and fat and opioids and mood medications on people.) The answer to these woes was, for Brown, in acceptance—in saying, "I'm just so grateful, because to feel this vulnerable means I'm alive." In an age awash in vulnerability, an age in which the winners were reluctant to change anything too fundamental, this mantra of feeling grateful for vulnerability caught on. "There are 1,800 Facebookers today whose lives will never be the same," a Facebook executive said after Brown spoke there. The winners loved her, Oprah loved her, and then everyone loved her. And everyone was now able to have their piece of Brown as she became that rarest of social work scholars—the productized one. She offered an array of electronic courses that promised to train people to be daring leaders, to "fully show up" in life, to engage in "self-compassion," to live bravely and vulnerably.

This second step was, in a sense, to do the opposite of what a generation of feminists had taught us to do. That movement had given the culture the phrase "the personal is political," credited to this passage from Carol Hanisch: "Personal problems are political problems. There are no personal solutions at this time. There is only collective action for a collective solution." It was an important and fruitful idea in February 1969. It helped people to see that things that happened in the quiet of personal life, and yet happened over and over again at the scale of the system, and happened because of forces that no individual was powerful enough to counteract alone— that these things had to be seen as and acted on politically, grandly, holistically, and, above all, in the places where the power was. A man beating a woman wasn't just one man beating one woman; he was part of a system of male supremacy and laws and a culture of looking away that put the problem beyond solution by the woman in question. The shame one felt in getting an abortion wasn't a feeling cooked up by the feeler; it was engineered and constructed through public policy and the artful use of religious authority. The feminists helped us to see problems in this way.

In our own time, the thought leaders have often been deployed to help us see problems in precisely the opposite way. They are taking on issues that can easily be regarded as political and systematic—injustice, layoffs, unaccountable leadership, inequality, the abdication of community, the engineered precariousness of ever more human lives—but using the power of their thoughts to cause us to zoom in and think smaller. The feminists wanted us to look at a vagina and zoom out to see Congress. The thought leaders want us to look at a laid-off employee and zoom in to see the beauty of his feeling his vulnerability because at least he is alive. They want us to focus on his vulnerability, not his wage.

The third move is to be constructively actionable. It is fine and good to write and say critical things without giving solutions—but not if you want to be a thought leader. A compelling example of this comes from Charles Duhigg, a *New York Times* reporter and editor who has managed, better than most, to straddle the lives of the critic and the thought leader. A journalist with a Harvard MBA, Duhigg once spent a summer making financial models about the turnaround of distressed companies, before concluding that he would rather be a newspaper reporter. He won a Pulitzer Prize for an investigation revealing Apple's business tricks in managing foreign plants, paying and dodging taxes, and claiming patents. He also exposed corporations for violating pollution laws more than half a million times, and probed Fannie Mae's near-fatal decision, in the run-up to the Great Recession, to enter the "more treacherous corners of the mortgage market." Despite his business degree, he had become what MarketWorld did not appreciate: a critic who pointed out what was wrong without offering digestible lists of tips on how to fix things.

Several years later, Duhigg began to write books. He could have done so in the same vein, and one assumes that the books would have been important. But would they have sold? "An investigative series in the *New York Times* never makes a good book, because if an investigative series in the *Times* works, basically it tells you everything that's wrong with the world or with a particular company or with a situation," he told me. "But when you read a book—nobody really wants to read a book to just learn about how much things suck, right? I mean, those books do exist, and they're very, very valuable. But they tend to have, you know, limited audiences." People, especially the winners who shape tastes and patronize thought leaders, want things to be constructive, uplifting, and given to hope. "In addition to learning what's wrong, they want to learn what's right," Duhigg said. And they like easy steps: "They want to learn what they can do and how they can make themselves or the world a better place."

Duhigg didn't believe in this kind of solutions peddling when wearing his investigative reporting hat, but he found it useful in his emerging life as a thought leader. "Investigative reporting is trying to avoid speculation," he said. "Whereas in a book, at least half of your effort should be speculating at solutions." Yet if Duhigg was right about the preference for solutions, it left less and less space for the kinds of thinkers and critics who have been important to our society in the past. And it made ever more room for the kinds of books that Duhigg began to write.

He produced books that MarketWorlders instantly loved, because they either helped them or taught others to be like them. The first was about how habits are made and broken, and it easily cleared the hurdle of being constructively actionable. It included a story about how Duhigg learned to stop eating a cookie every afternoon. And it was his race to finish this first book that inspired the second. He was busy, doing a little bit of everything and doing nothing well, he felt. He longed to be more productive. Thus began a book on productivity, which would teach readers "to become smarter, faster, and better at everything we do." To MarketWorld, Duhigg became less threatening. He now wanted to learn from the kinds of people he used to bust. A centerpiece of the book was about what we could learn from the most productive teams at Google, which at the time of the book's release was close to dethroning Duhigg's former target Apple as the most valuable company on earth.

Duhigg became a heavily sought-after thought leader—a fixture of the bestseller lists, a denizen of the paid lecture circuit. "I'm blessed," he said. "I'm very lucky in that businesspeople want to hear what I'm talking about and thinking about." This gave him special pleasure because of what some of his HBS classmates seemed to think when he first went into journalism: that, as he put it, "someone handed you the winning lottery ticket and you decided to use it as toilet paper." He said, "I think they thought, economically, I was making a foolish choice because I was going into an industry where I was not going to make money—which, generally, that's been wrong, actually, but for a long time was true."

One of the things that turned that dire assessment of his economic prospects from true to false was speaking engagements. Duhigg was adamant that his reliance on the income from those speeches, as on making money from selling constructively actionable books, in no way altered his ideas or corrupted him or caused him to self-censor. Invoking the debate over his lecture circuit fellow traveler Hillary Clinton's speeches to Goldman Sachs, he said that his experience "has been exactly the opposite" of what Clinton's critics had said about her corruption from such speeches—and rather parallel to her own defense of them. "They literally just want me to give the speech," he said. "I'm kind of like the entertainment, right? Not someone that they're trying to buy access to."

He thought for a moment about whether living off of speaking gigs might cause thought leaders to self-censor. "Do you think people begin not going down path lines of intellectual inquiry because they're worried that it will be alienating to a potential audience?" he asked out loud. "Or do they skew their thinking in a way that would make it more palatable to a business audience?" Sure, he conceded, there must be some people who do, but it wasn't a big problem. Yet a moment later he added, "The question is, do you want to be wealthy as a writer or do you want to be an intellectually honest, responsible writer?"

Some years ago, another heavyweight of thought leadership, Malcolm Gladwell, who, like Duhigg (and unlike many thought leaders), had managed to retain social respectability, wrote a long "disclosure" note on his website grappling with the complications of wearing his "two hats" as a writer and a speaker. He argued:

> Giving a speech does not buy my allegiance to the interests of my audience. Why? Because giving a paid speech to a group for an hour is simply not enough to create a bias in that group's favor. . . . Financial ties are in danger of being corrupting when they are ties, when they are, in some way, permanent and when resources and influence and information move equally in both directions.

Gladwell may be right that each speech is its own thing, not enough to corrupt an honest person on its own. But can a speaking career as a whole never form something like "ties" that have some degree of permanence and a two-way flow of influence and information? Many gigs insist on a phone call with the speaker, during which the organizers inform the speaker about the context of the event and what is "top of mind" for attendees, and perhaps offer suggestions to make the talk more relevant. Each gig is certainly its own, but many of them grow out of a commercial world that does harbor a consistent set of values and preferences for the depoliticized, the actionable, the perpetrator-free. It is not easy to build a career catering to these institutions while being as sure as Gladwell is that the cumulative effect of this catering, and of wanting to succeed rather than fail, does not affect you.

"It's got to be about what I write. Don't criticize me for who I talk to," the *New York Times* columnist Thomas L. Friedman once said, similarly insisting on his incorruptibility. Yet even if one were to take Friedman and Gladwell at their word about the effect of money on them as individuals, it is hard to accept the conclusion that the plutocratic funding of ideas has no effect on the marketplace of ideas as a whole.

The money can liberate the top thought leaders from the institutions and colleagues that might otherwise provide some kind of intellectual check on them, while sometimes turning their ideas into advertisements rather than self-contained work. As Stephen Marche has written of the historian turned thought leader Niall Ferguson, who reportedly earns between $50,000 and $75,000 per speech:

> Nonfiction writers can and do make vastly more, and more easily, than they could ever make any other way, including by writing bestselling books or being a Harvard professor. . . .
>
> That number means that Ferguson doesn't have to please his publishers; he doesn't have to please his editors; he sure as hell doesn't have to please scholars. He has to please corporations and high-net-worth individuals.

While individual thought leaders like Gladwell might resist the temptations of changing their ideas for, say, a banking convention, the plutocrats' money amounts to a kind of subsidy for ideas they are willing to hear. And subsidies have consequences, as the Harvard Business School professor Gautam Mukunda observes in a piece about how Wall Street clings to power, including by cultivating ideas that make us believe "that those with power are good and just and doing the right thing":

> The ability of a powerful group to reward those who agree with it and punish those who don't also distorts the marketplace of ideas. This isn't about corruption—beliefs naturally shift in accord with interests. As Upton Sinclair said, "It is difficult to get a man to understand something when his salary depends on not understanding it." The result can be an entire society twisted to serve the interests of its most powerful group.

The idea that thought leaders are unaffected by their patrons is also contradicted by their very own speakers bureau websites, which illustrate how the peddlers of potentially menacing ideas are rendered less scary to gatherings of the rich and powerful.

Anat Admati is a Stanford economist and prominent critic of the financial industry. "Bankers are nearly unanimous" about this "persistent industry gadfly," the *New York Times* reports: "Her ideas are wildly impractical, bad for the American economy and not to be taken seriously." Admati's writing has been praised for her ability "to question the status quo"; she is someone who "shreds bankers' scare tactics" and "exposes as false the self-serving arguments against meaningful financial reform advanced by Wall Street executives and the captured politicians who serve their interests." Admati is also a thought leader, represented by the Leigh Bureau, a speaking agency, which takes the hard, critical edge off in advertising a speaking topic from her: "We can have a safer, healthier banking system without sacrificing any of its benefits."

Anne Applebaum, a *Washington Post* columnist who writes about rising nationalism, Russian aggression, and other dark geopolitical currents, is presented on her speaker page as a lecturer on "The Politics of Transition—Risks and Opportunities."

Jacob Hacker is a political scientist at Yale. He was the one concerned about the Even app, and a trenchant critic of America's economic direction over the last generation. He has written such books as *American Amnesia: How the War on Government Led Us to Forget What Made America Prosper* and *The Great Risk Shift: The New Economic Insecurity and the Decline of the American Dream*. He is a very win-losey thinker, and one of the most insightful critics of corporate America. This presents a challenge to his agents, who nonetheless find a way out: Hacker, somewhat denuded, becomes a "policy thought leader on restoring security to the American dream."

One may protest that these are just superficial tweaks in language that do not alter the underlying message. Yet even were that true in some cases, it is not self-evident that giving in to such tweaks is without its costs. There is tremendous pressure to turn thoughts into commodities—into tiny, usable takeaways, into Monday morning insights for the CEO, into ideas that are profitable rather than compelling for their own sake. To give in to this pressure, to make your thoughts more actionable, to enter the business world's domain of language and assumptions is in effect to surrender. In the poem "Conversation with a Tax Collector About Poetry," by Vladimir Maya-kovsky, the poet realizes that he has no chance of getting his way because the language in which he is forced to speak belongs to another domain. The businessperson's amortization is factored into his tax bill, but what about the poet's "amortization of the heart and soul"? The businessperson gets a break for his debts, but can the poet claim the same advantage for his indebtedness "to everything/ about which/I have not yet written"?

Thought leaders can find themselves becoming like poets speaking a tax collector's language, saying what they might not say or believe on their own. And the danger isn't only in what they say in this new language, but also in the possibility that they might somewhere down the line stop thinking in their native one.

Five years after giving her TED talk, Cuddy continued to live in the beautiful new world it had built for her. She was now famous, among the top thought leaders of her time.

Still, success, and the particular way in which it had come, had caused a dilemma for her. She had been studying prejudice and sexism for nearly twenty years, and even after her breakout continued to work on those topics with academic colleagues. She had often taken on such themes in harsh, perpetrator-blaming ways. But a viral TED talk all but drowned out every other thing she had ever said, and now she was fielding lucrative invitation after invitation to offer her ideas in that same safe way.

She found herself repeatedly being asked to speak or do workshops that came with a corporate expectation of usability. "Here's what's frustrating me," Cuddy told me. "Everyone wants me to come in, and, basically, they want me to address prejudice and diversity and fixing it. First of all, without saying those words, because that might alarm people. And in one hour people want this to be done.

They have the sense that you can come in and reduce prejudice in an hourlong talk, which is absurd. I'm tired of people asking me questions like, 'I really don't know how to get the women to speak up more in a boardroom.'" She had, as she saw it, tried to make things a little easier for them with her talks. Now they wanted her to morph into a quick-acting drug.

Cuddy saw herself as a person who had fought in the trenches against sexism for most of her career, but now she was being played back to herself as the dispenser of easy fixes. Even if she thought of it as merely adding an aria to her repertoire, the world more and more saw her as capable of singing just one song. When Market-World likes you, it wants you as a product.

She worked to defy that perception. She was asked to teach one of Harvard's executive education seminars, at which midcareer business executives from around the world fly into Boston for some intellectual refreshment. The organizers wanted her to talk to the group about prejudice and diversity. They gave her roughly an hour and hoped she could cover sexism, racism, and other topics. She asked for three hours; they agreed on an hour and a half. She insisted on focusing on one topic alone—sexism—and on flying out a male collaborator, Peter Glick, at her own expense, to help her deal with a crowd that she expected to be tough. It was a highly global group, largely male, and she had the bad luck of teaching them during a World Cup match that some of them soon made clear they would rather be watching.

Cuddy, a body language expert, walked into a room that was a textbook case of people closed off from the beginning. Nonetheless, she tried to wear the hat of the critic, not the thought leader. In fact, she and Glick started by flouting the first rule of thought leadership. Instead of focusing on the victim, they spoke of the perpetration of sexism. "We tried to start really soft by explaining how we're all bigots," she said. So they were refusing to talk about the feeling of powerlessness that women get without naming who gives them that feeling. But they were trying to be gentle about it. Glick, a leading authority on the psychology of sexism, tried a classic tactic with men wary of being called sexist: He spoke of his own sexism. He told a story of how he once stepped in it by buying his wife a princess mug.

This approach did not help. "I actually stopped in the middle of the class and I said, 'I feel how frustrated people in this room are, so can we stop for a moment and talk about what's going on?'" But talking didn't help. "We had two slides at the end," Cuddy said. "One was individual things you can do to reduce sexism in your organization, and the second one was organizational things or structural things. And we didn't even get to them because there was so much pushback on just the idea that there was a problem with sexism."

Knowing even more now about the tastes and boundaries of MarketWorld, Cuddy looks back and sees how she could have handled the situation another way, although she isn't sure that doing so would have been honorable. "If I had gone in and said, 'Hey, let's talk about empowerment and how to get the best out of our employees,' that would've been totally different," she said. People "would've accepted that something is going on that makes it harder for women to speak up. They would've accepted that because it would've been about the bottom line. It would've been about making your organization the best. But when you go in and say, 'Hey, here's the truth. The system is set up in a biased way. It favors white guys. Sorry, but it does'—I mean, you cannot get past that statement. That's it. You're stuck there."

Cuddy felt it harder and harder to speak truths like this the better known she became. She became a target of the sexism she had long drily studied: the almost inevitable fate of the online superstar. "The misogyny that I experience as a female scientist who's had success—it's repulsive, it's awful, it's disgusting," she said. The attacks had a paradoxical effect on her. On one hand, they made even more vivid and personal to her the sexism she had studied through an academic lens. Deemphasizing talk of the system had made her ideas more accessible, which caused her to become even more aware of how dismal the system was. Yet at the same time, the constant vitriol made her less interested in devoting her work to fighting sexism as a system. "I think there was a point where I said, 'I'm tired of fighting this fight. I feel alone,'" Cuddy said in the interview. "As a woman, I find it harder to do. It's unpleasant, either dealing with people who don't believe me"—by this she meant men—"or who I'm really disappointing"—now she spoke of women—"by telling, 'Yeah, you're right. You think there's prejudice? There is, and it's hurting you.'" She hated to say it, but she didn't "see the -isms going away"—by which she meant sexism, racism, and other prejudices. "That is largely because I do not see the people at the top really willing to wrestle with them, really willing to take them on." She stopped believing that "people are going to make the big sweeping changes that are actually going to change these things."

If she was right, she felt that her best strategy was to help women see the kinds of small-scale changes they could make without changing anything. "Basically, I can give them armor so that they can buffer themselves and push through it even when it's happening." She would teach them to roll with the waves. She would focus on the victims, not the perpetrators.

The irony of all this is dark: Scaling back her critique of the system had allowed her to be wildly popular with MarketWorld elites and more easily digested by the world at large; and so she became famous, which drew the system of sexism into her life as never before and heightened her awareness of it; and its ferocity convinced her not to take on that system but to conclude that it might never change; and this acquiescence made her turn from uprooting sexism to helping women survive it. She had been drafted into a growing brigade: the theorists of the kind of change that leaves the underlying issues untouched.

"I might have a view that's a little bit unorthodox," said Cuddy, "which is that, actually, we have done a really good job of documenting the problems and the mechanisms underlying them," she said. "We really fully understand all of the structural and psychological and neurological mechanisms that lead to prejudice. We get it." This view of scholars' work perhaps made it easier to justify the punch-pulling for MarketWorld, but it was also problematic. After all, her academic colleagues in other fields like race, gender, and sexuality—

to cite just a few examples—worked, in a slow, winding, often un-heralded way, producing tangible change in an entire culture's way of talking. Sometimes even the most risk-averse politicians now casually voiced concepts coined at universities: "micro-aggressions" (Chester Pierce, psychiatry, Harvard, 1970); "white privilege" (Peggy McIntosh, women's studies, Wellesley, 1988); "gender identity" (Johns Hopkins School of Medicine); "intersectionality" (Kimberlé Williams Crenshaw, critical race theory, University of California at Los Angeles, 1989).

Nonetheless, Cuddy believed that in her field, the real need was for serious scholars, equipped with serious money, to work on solutions and the implementation of what had already been learned. "I actually think we need to start now doing really deep science on interventions that work, and they are not going to be easy," she said. The interventions she had in mind involved something deeper and more sustained than one-off diversity trainings and the like: "It's going to be lifelong."

But what about the charge from some of her critics that power poses, and perhaps other similarly oriented interventions, were just feminism lite? Cuddy insisted not. She saw such interventions as "tiny incremental change that over time can lead to downstream measurable changes in your life." She added, "This is not light-weight shit. This is real stuff that happens, and it works a lot better than trying to make a big change like a New Year's resolution." But was this truly a workable plan to change the system, or just acceptance of the system adorned with feedback loops?

Strangely, one of the things that makes it easier to accept the system is that when you do, you will find yourself being told more often that you are changing things. Many genuine agents of change must make peace with never being seen as such, at least within their own lifetimes. One presumes that the scholars mentioned above, having coined the new verbiage of a nation awakening to the realities of identity and power, were rarely stopped on the street and told about the difference they had made in so-and-so's life. And Cuddy, during her years of throwing scholarly rocks at sexism and other prejudices, had to trust that she was changing things, but wasn't told so by the public. Yet when she scaled back her claims, when she depoliticized, when she focused on the actionable, when she accepted that she didn't "see the -isms going away," when she focused on how individual women could navigate a bad system, ironically, at that very moment of relinquishing hope of changing systems in a serious way, she began to be stopped everywhere she went by women who thanked her for changing their lives. Even if she had narrowed her ambitions, she was attracted to the personal gratification that came with the more doable kind of change.

Cuddy was raised in a working-class town in Pennsylvania, and she has come to feel, thanks to the fame that power posing brought her, that she is helping the kinds of people she grew up with. "Most of the people that I hear from who say, 'You really changed my life,' are not the powerful people," she said. "They're the people who really do deal with incredible adversity and figure out these ways to get through it."

Cuddy says she remains committed to fighting sexism as a system of power, and she still conducts research along those lines. But it is, she says, "and I'm just being honest, less personally gratifying." Still, she seemed to wonder about her choices: "It's not the way I thought I would go when I started in this field."

If Cuddy was caught between the polarities of criticism and thought leadership, Simon Sinek was confidently and comfortably ensconced at the thought-leader end of things. Sinek is now famous for the idea that companies and people should "start with why"— should discover and organize their lives around a single animating purpose. His own "why," he said, is "to inspire people to do what inspires them."

He was put onto the path of thought leadership, he said, by the fact that as a young man he was largely unable to read. His mind hopped and twirled too much to stay on the page; he had an attention deficit issue. But Sinek likes to see problems as opportunities in disguise: "I believe that the solutions we find to our challenges as children become our strengths as adults." He realized he couldn't learn through reading. He could learn only through talking. When he became a thought leader, and a highly successful one, and the time came for him to write a book, he did his research in a curious way. "If books need to be read, I'll ask somebody to read it for me and then explain it to me, and let me ask him questions," he said. This was his own, very particular way into a quality that defined many thought leaders: a certain freedom from any kind of intellectual tradition, a comfort with pronouncing on a subject without being burdened by what others had said about it before. This advantage, as Sinek saw it, was soon compounded by another: several years of training in advertising, which was useful because the thought leader's work was often to make ideas as catchy and sticky and digestible as ads, and to use ideas as advertisements for workshops, paid speeches, and consulting.

Sinek had initially set out to study law in Britain, but he realized not long after the course began that "it didn't fit me and I didn't fit it." He quit in the middle of his first year, to his parents' horror, and went into the world of advertising. There he "learned the importance of the role of emotions," he said; "that it's not just an argument but rather that you can make somebody feel a certain way or connect to them in a certain way." He learned that "rather than just facts and figures, if you can get someone to associate their lives and themselves to whatever it is you're doing, and assert whatever it is you're doing into their lives, you're more likely to create not only a saleable product but love."

He remained in advertising for several years, working for such clients as Enron and Northwest Airlines. Then he started his own marketing agency, taking on clients such as Oppenheimer Funds, ABC Sports, GE, and AOL. But his passion for the work waned, and he grew stressed with the duty to perform for clients and employees. "I spent most of my days lying, hiding, and faking," he said. "And it became darker and darker, and more and more stressful. I would go to business conferences to learn how to do things right, and they would actually make me feel worse. Because this guy would stand on the stage and tell me everything I wasn't doing."

One day, a friend asked whether he was alright. Sinek told her he felt depressed. Getting that off his chest "gave me the courage to start seeking a solution." At the heart of the solution that would emerge was an idea that Sinek branded as "the Golden Circle." Imagine a circle. The core of the circle is the "why," the purpose or cause, of a business. The ring outside the core is the "how," the actions the company takes to live out the purpose. The ring outside that is the "what"—the results of those actions, measured in products and services.

Sinek had come up with the rudiments of the framework while trying to figure out "why some advertising works and some doesn't." One day he was at a "black-tie affair," he said, and he sat beside a guest whose father was a neuroscientist. Sinek says the neuroscientist's daughter began telling him about her father's work with "the limbic brain and the neocortex." This led Sinek to follow up with his own research on the brain. "I started realizing that the way the human brain made decisions was the same as this little idea that I had on a shelf," he said. As he would later put it, "None of what I'm telling you is my opinion. It's all grounded in the tenets of biology. Not psychology, biology. If you look at a cross section of the human brain, from the top down, the human brain is actually broken into three major components that correlate perfectly with the Golden Circle." The why and how of what people do is, according to Sinek's (incredibly controversial and highly oversimplified) brain theory, controlled by the limbic brain, while the what of what people do is controlled by the evolutionarily newer neocortex. The science may have been dubious, but it did sound fancy.

He started his new career as a thought leader by helping people find their whys for $100 each. He would sit with them and interview them for four hours about their "natural highs," their moments of peak inspiration, and then inform them of their purpose in life. The service caught on, and it would eventually lead him to giving a wildly successful TED talk, publishing widely read business books, and racking up gig after gig speaking to and advising corporate types. This rocket-ship success as a thought leader has a (slightly apocryphal-sounding) founding story. In Canada on a business trip, Sinek went out for breakfast with a former client. His friend asked:

> "What are you up to these days?" As I did everywhere, I pull out a napkin and started drawing circles. And he says to me, "This is amazing. Can you come and share those with my CEO?" And I looked at my watch, and I go, "Sure." So we walked over to his company. I sit down with the CEO. It's a small business. I take her through the Golden Circle and the concept of the "why," and she says, "This is amazing. Can you help our company discover their 'why'?" I said, "Sure." She said, "Could you do it this afternoon?" I was like, "Sure." She says, "How much is it?"
>
> And, of course, what goes through my head is $100. So I said, "It's $5,000," and she said, "Okay." And I made five grand for two and a half hours' worth of work and literally walked out of there giggling. I literally was walking the street, laughing out loud at the ridiculousness of this whole day. But more importantly, I realized that I could actually make a living doing this thing. I was literally doing math in my head: how many days I could work at five grand a pop to make the same living that I was making, which wasn't very much.

Sinek was not burdened by a multiplicity of ideas. This was his one big idea, and he now set out to spread it. "I'm a preacher of a gospel, and I'm looking for people to join me in the gospel and help me preach the good word," he said. For the aspiring thought leader, it is less important to have an undergirding of scholarly research than it is to *be* your idea—to perform and hawk it relentlessly. Sinek was good at this: He embodied his own dogma about living one's life in service of a single, pulsing "why." He had confidence and zeal and persistence. He knew how to "productize" his thoughts, as they say in the business world. He gradually built up a vast business with two divisions: One was for all the things he did himself, such as speaking and writing; the other was for all the things others did without him, such as speeches given by more junior thought leaders he had recruited to his network and the sales of his books and other wares.

That there is someone out there willing to promote some questionable gospel is nothing strange. What is more striking is how elites embrace an idea such as this. Sinek lectures to and consults for a variety of influential institutions and people, including (according to his literary agency) Microsoft, American Express, the U.S. Department of Defense, members of Congress, the United Nations, and foreign ambassadors. Thought-leaders-in-the-making might have to compromise themselves, but that compromise can be lavishly rewarded. And in the embrace they receive, it is not their values that are revealed so much as the values of those MarketWorld elites who are their patrons and impassioned base: their love of the easy idea that goes down like gelato, an idea that gives hope while challenging nothing. Their susceptibility to scientific authority, no matter how thin or disputed. Their need for ideas to be useful, results-oriented, profitable in order to receive their support. Their wariness of collective political purpose, and their preference for purpose to be privatized into something small and micro, trapped inside companies and executives. Their interest in a man like Sinek giving their workaday businesses the glow of heroism, change-making, mission—of a cause. That ideas like these guide the rich and powerful in their business lives is what it is. But is this the kind of thinking we want to guide the solution of our biggest shared problems?

Sinek himself seemed to have doubts about the thought leaders' ascendancy. While he obviously believed in his own ideas, he made a point of criticizing thought-leader charlatans whom he fretted were being birthed by a new age of plutocratically backed ideas and the commodification of thought. "I have contempt for people in the speaking circuit," he said, even though he was one of the leading figures on the speaking circuit. "Even though I'm getting lumped in with people who do have speaking goals and call themselves motivational speakers or whatever they call themselves, I have contempt for these guys who I love, who I think are brilliant, and I see them stand on stages presenting to companies that I know they disagree with, saying shit that I know is not true," he said. "I go up to them after, and I'm like, 'Dude, why would you do that?' And they'll say, 'Simon, I've got to make a living,' and I think 'got to make a living' is a rationalization we tell ourselves to do things without integrity." Although some describe Sinek himself in precisely the same terms, he viewed such pandering as something that he had managed to stay above.

"Sometimes it's very difficult, and I'm empathetic with the struggle," he went on. "Somebody offers you a massive amount of money to do something, and you say no in integrity. And then they offer you more money because they thought it was a matter of money, and it wasn't. And then you sit there and go, 'Oh man. I could just do one. I could just do one.'"

Not long ago, he was invited to an advice circle. It was ten or so people, and many in the group were big-name thought leaders like Sinek. "We're supposed to be talking about how we can combine our efforts to advance the greater good," he said. "That's why I showed up. And every single one of them talked about how they can increase their mailing lists, how they can get an extra dollar for X, Y, Z, how they can sell more products. And I literally sat there, and I was disgusted." Even if he perfectly embodied how ideas were being turned into products, he had found a way to see himself as a purist among sellouts. "It becomes a business," he said. "And, look, there's a lot of guys whose first book, their breakout, is absolutely all integrity—took them their whole lives to get there. And then the money gets involved, and the business gets involved, the TV gets involved, the TED gets involved, and it becomes seductive. And some give in to the seduction, and some are able to sort of manage the seduction, and it's not easy. Like I said, I turned down things, but it doesn't mean it's not stressful to turn them down, because it's a lot of money, and I can rationalize fast."

The world of ideas "is just another industry," he said after a moment. "There's good product, and there's bad product." The question is whether a republic can thrive when ideas are thought of as an industry, and the prevailing incentives so heavily favor bad product. Is this how we want ideas to be generated? And are the elites who embrace and sponsor such ideas the people we trust to arrange our future?

Amy Cuddy wants to believe the thought leader can use the tricks of her trade to transcend the pitfalls of thought leadership. She wants to believe there is a micro way into the macro—that we can Sheryl Sandberg our way to a Simone de Beauvoir–worthy society. She wants to believe that a thought leader can also be a critic, that she can use her embrace by MarketWorlders to effect change from within. She thinks the secret to cajoling them toward systemic reform may lie in blending two disparate concepts from her field. One is about how to get people to care about a problem by zooming in on a vivid person. The other is about how to get them to care by zooming out from one person to see a system.

The first of these concepts is known as the "identifiable-victim effect." As Deborah Small and George Loewenstein, scholars at Carnegie Mellon University, write in a major paper:

> People react differently toward identifiable victims than to statistical victims who have not yet been identified. Specific victims of misfortune often draw extraordinary attention and resources. But, it is often difficult to draw attention to, or raise money for, interventions that would prevent people from becoming victims in the first place.

Small and Loewenstein's research confirms what many budding thought leaders intuit by reading the faces in the crowd: that people feel and care more when you help people to see a problem in terms of individuals. In Cuddy's case, she experienced this whenever she spoke about young girls, rather than adult women, shrinking physically. A light would go off in the heads of men with daughters. "A sixty-year-old man would come up to me and go, 'Oh my God, thank you so much. This is so important for my daughter and for her kids.' They were open to it. Suddenly, the audience that I could never capture when I talk about, 'You need to change as a leader; you need to say that this is not okay; you need to do this and that'—those people who completely turned off to me were suddenly open when I was talking about their daughters and the opportunities their daughters would have."

Cuddy wondered if a thought leader could use feedback like this to her advantage. If you want to talk about the structural power of sexism, first make people think of their daughters. "People want their daughters to have every opportunity, but they don't feel like that about their female coworker," Cuddy said. For a thought leader, the advantage of zooming in, of telling the story of sexism and power and systems as a story about *your* daughter is that you hook people. The risk, which the thought leader may or may not acknowledge, is that you change the nature of the problem by that act of zooming. By framing it as a problem for their daughter, you shrink the issue. "There's this problem where people don't generalize beyond their daughter, because their daughter is different from other girls," Cuddy said. "They call it subtyping." It is the age-old phenomenon of the racist who says, "My black friend is different."

Many thought leaders, facing this pressure, give in. And Cuddy insists that it is not because they don't wish to press for bigger changes but because they are human. "It's not that you, as a thinker, are forgetting that it's about the group. You're not," she says. "When you're talking to other humans, you want a response, you want to see them move, you want something other than a neutral facial expression. You want an interaction. You crave that. And so when you find over time, talking about these ideas, that when you start talking about individuals, suddenly people start becoming animated, I see how you're led down that path or how you follow that path. It's not just more gratifying; it gives you hope. You actually feel like people are going to change. I think that's where you start to think, *Now I have to reach all of them as individuals.*"

Listening to Cuddy, it was possible to understand the symbiosis that developed between MarketWorld elites and their thought leaders. The thought leaders put out a variety of ideas and, being human beings, noticed what moved people at places like the Aspen Ideas Festival and TED. What especially moved such audiences was the rendering of social problems as unintimidating, bite-sized, digestible. The thought leader picked up on this and spoke more and more in these terms. The audience responded more and more rapturously. The actual nature of the problem receded.

This is why Cuddy was interested in the possibilities of the second social psychology concept, the one involving zooming out. She felt it might break up this limiting symbiosis. The formal term for the concept is the "assimilation effect," and it occurs when people link the personal and specific to the surrounding social context. You tell the story of that one girl, and those men think of their daughters, but then they also "assimilate the concept of their daughter to other girls. It's the girls who don't look like their daughter. It's the girls who have brown skin and who are from poor families," she said. The challenge, as Cuddy sees it, is to humanize a vast political and social problem without triggering the opposite reaction, which is called the "contrast effect." "Oh my God, but my daughter is so special," Cuddy said, mimicking the contrast reaction. "She's so different from all of the other girls. I need to protect her from that. I need to protect only her."

The thought leader, when he or she strips politics from the issue, makes it about actionable tweaks rather than structural change, removing the perpetrators from the story. It is no accident that thought leaders, whose speaking engagements are often paid for by MarketWorld, whose careers are made by MarketWorld, are encouraged to put things in that way. To name a problem involving a rich man's daughter is to stir his ardor. To name a problem involving everyone's daughter, a problem whose solution might involve the sacrifice of privilege and the expenditure of significant resources, may inspire a rich man to turn away.

For her own sense of integrity, Cuddy wants to find an escape from this trap: to focus on helping victims, to draw people into problems by zooming in, but to avoid giving power a pass. "How do you bring these things together?" she asked. "Messages about what the in-group is doing wrong, unless it's with the lining of hope that here's an easy thing you can do to be a better person—I think that those messages are the ones that get shut down."

What happens to a society when there is not one Amy Cuddy but thousands of thought leaders, each making their private bargains, pulling punches in order to be asked back, abiding certain silences? What is the cumulative effect of all of these omissions?

In part, they have given rise to watered-down theories of change that are personal, individual, depoliticized, respectful of the status quo and the system, and not in the least bit disruptive. The more genuine criticism is left out and the more sunny, actionable, take-away-prone ideas are elevated, the shallower the very idea of change becomes. When a thought leader strips politics and perpetrators from a problem, she often gains access to a bigger platform to influence change-makers—but she also adds to the vast pile of stories promoted by MarketWorld that tell us that change is easy, is a win-win, and doesn't require sacrifice.

What the thought leaders offer MarketWorld's winners, wittingly or unwittingly, is the semblance of being on the right side of change. The kinds of changes favored by the public in an age of inequality, as reflected from time to time in some electoral platforms, are usually unacceptable to elites. Simple rejection of those types of changes can only invite greater hostility toward the elites. It is more useful for the elites to be seen as favoring change—*their* kind of change, of course. Take, for example, the question of educating poor children in a time of declining social mobility. A true critic might call for an end to funding schools by local property taxes and the creation, as in many advanced countries, of a common national pool that funds schools more or less equally. What a thought leader might offer MarketWorld and its winners is a kind of intellectual counteroffer—the idea, say, of using Big Data to better compensate star teachers and weed out bad ones. On the question of extreme wealth inequality, a critic might call for economic redistribution or even racial reparations. A thought leader, by contrast, could opine on how foundation bosses should be paid higher salaries so that the poor can benefit from the most capable leadership.

When this denuding of criticism happens on not one or two issues but every issue of import, the thought leaders are not merely suppressing their own ideas and intuitions. They are also participating in MarketWorld's preservation of a troubled status quo by gesturing to change-making. Not long ago, Bruno Giussani, the man who had hosted Amy Cuddy's TED talk, was grappling with his own role in this phenomenon. Giussani is one of a small handful of curators of the TED organization, and the host of some of its events. It was from his stage in Edinburgh that Cuddy catapulted to global stardom several years earlier. A former journalist from Switzerland, Giussani is one of the small team of senior executives who decide on presenters for the conference's main stages, who coach the speakers and edit the talks, and who help disseminate their ideas. He is known to be something of a dissenter from the technology-loving, market-admiring ethos that dominates TED events, but obviously not to the extent that he doesn't still work for TED. He is a behind-the-scenes operator who doesn't have a household name but has helped to make many of them.

Giussani was meant to be on a long-awaited sabbatical. But he had quit his respite a few months early, because the rise of populism around the world and the spreading politics of anger had him worried and wondering about what had happened to societies gone mad.

At first the anger at elites could seem puzzling, for in Giussani's own social circles he saw a plethora of organizations and people socially concerned and socially active. "You go to any dinner, and not only at TED or at Skoll or at Aspen or anywhere else, but you go to any dinner with people in this circle," he said, "and to your right is somebody who just sent $1 million to an NGO in Africa, and to your left there is somebody whose son just came back from spending six weeks operating on somebody in a field hospital." Giussani joked that there were so many elite do-gooders trying to change the world that "if everybody would jump at the same time, it would probably tilt the axis of the earth." And yet look what was happening to the world—seething populism, anger, division, hatred, exclusion, and fear.

In recent years, Giussani noticed how elites seemed increasingly guided by lite facsimiles of change. These ideas largely exempted markets and their winners from scrutiny, despite their immense power in deciding how people's lives were lived and their support for a system that produced extraordinary fortunes and extraordinary exclusion. These notions of change were shaped and hemmed in by the complex of "intellectual assumptions that have dominated the last two decades," Giussani said. Among them: "Businesses are the engines of progress. The state should do as little as possible. Market forces are the best way at the same time to allocate scarce resources and to solve problems. People are essentially rational, self-interest-driven actors." Speaking as a man who had controlled access to one of the most powerful stages in the world, Giussani said that over this period, "certain ideas have got more airtime because they fit into those intellectual assumptions." Others fit less well.

MarketWorld finds certain ideas more acceptable and less threatening than others, he said, and it does its part to help them through its patronage of thought leaders. For example, Giussani observed, ideas framed as being about "poverty" are more acceptable than ideas framed as being about "inequality." The two ideas are related. But poverty is a material fact of deprivation that does not point fingers, and inequality is something more worrying: It speaks of what some have and others lack; it flirts with the idea of injustice and wrongdoing; it is relational. "Poverty is essentially a question that you can address via charity," he said. A person of means, seeing poverty, can write a check and reduce that poverty. "But inequality," Giussani said, "you can't, because inequality is not about giving back. Inequality is about how you make the money that you're giving back in the first place." Inequality, he said, is about the nature of the system. To fight inequality means to change the system. For a privileged person, it means to look into one's own privilege. And, he said, "you cannot change it by yourself. You can change the system only together. With charity, essentially, if you have money, you can do a lot of things alone."

This distinction ran parallel to Cuddy's reframing of her antisexism message in her TED talk. What motivated her to study the topic was inequality—specifically, a lack of power in one set of students because of the power held by another set (and people like them). This was a crime with a victim and a perpetrator. By the time this idea made it to TED, the inequality, as we've seen, had been resculpted into poverty. "Women," Cuddy said, "feel chronically less powerful than men." The crime was still a crime, but now it wanted for suspects.

Giussani had a clearer view than most of how thinkers were tempted into this kind of thought leadership. It wasn't as though you had no choice but to compromise. You could easily develop your ideas and promote them through what he labeled "marginal magazines" and "militant conferences." But your reach would be limited. If you had acquired from the age something like what Hilary Cohen had acquired, the sense of wanting to help others at Coca-Cola-like scale, and you knew your ideas could help, you could feel that your purity would limit your reach, which would hurt rather than help all the people who needed you. Your alternative, Giussani said, was to do what Cuddy had done: Bite your tongue to open their ears. "You can go out and make this stuff known by packaging it in a way that it becomes appealing to big stages, high-level audiences or large audiences, hoping that in that context you can still put in enough of those ideas that are supposed to drag them along, rather than just those ideas that are supposed to please them or satisfy them or just keep them there listening to you."

There is a tendency in MarketWorld to deny what Cuddy and

Giussani candidly admit: that one does, often but not always, have to keep certain ideas at bay in order to gain a hearing. "You need to cut some of your moral corners or some of your convictions in order to package your ideas to make them palatable to this kind of environment," Giussani says. For many thought leaders, he said, it was still a terrific deal. "If that's your belief," he said, "you want to be able to repeat that next week and the following week—and by repeating it and by reinforcing it and by keeping researching on it and by touching more and more people, you're trying to have an impact to create change."

Many thinkers cut these moral corners and contort themselves in these ways because they are so reliant on the assent of Market-World for building their careers. Some manage to forge robust careers without a single paid speaking gig, without summer panels at the Monsanto- and Pepsi-sponsored Aspen Ideas Festival, without the usage of platforms like TED or Facebook, where sunnier ideas have more of a shot. There remains, Daniel Drezner observes in *The Ideas Industry,* "a middle class of intellectuals housed in the academy, think tanks, and private firms." But they have few of the opportunities of the thought leaders shooting past them into the stratosphere of fame and public recognition. "To stay in the superstar rank, intellectuals need to be able to speak fluently to the plutocratic class," Drezner writes, adding, "If they want to make potential benefactors happy, they cannot necessarily afford to speak truth to money."

It isn't that any of those elites had ever telephoned Giussani and told him to keep this or that person offstage. It does not happen like that, he said. These invisible mantras are enforced subtly. One means of enforcement is the preference these days for thinkers who remind winners of their victorious selves, Giussani said. A critic in the traditional mold is often a loser figure—a thorn, an outside agitator, a rumpled cynic. The rising thought leaders, even though their product is ideas, are less like that and more like sidekicks of the powerful—buying parkas in the same Aspen stores, traveling the same conference circuit, reading the same Yuval Noah Harari books, getting paid from the same corporate coffers, accepting the same basic consensus, observing the same intellectual taboos.

"People like winners, and we don't like losers, and this is the reality," he said. And, yes, he knew one could argue that people like him should defy that preference rather than pander to it. "If conferences don't put losers onstage, then they will forever remain losers," Giussani said, anticipating his critics. But he told himself that it was unfair "asking a conference organizer or the *New York Times* to solve a social problem at the end of the chain that exists because people like winners and don't like losers. If I put only losers onstage, I become one of them because nobody comes to my conference." (He said he was using "losers" in thick quotation marks, to capture how they are perceived, not his own view. And, to be fair, Giussani has smuggled a number of critics onto the TED stage, most notably Pope Francis.)

It wasn't necessarily malice or cynicism that sustained these patterns, but, in Giussani's telling, something far more banal. The people who served as tastemakers for the global elite—people like Giussani—were, like many, in an intellectual bubble. "The French have an expression for that, which is *une pensée unique*. The sole way of thinking? Everybody thinks the same way." In his world, he said, that meant an unspoken consensus (widespread but not total) on certain ideas: Progressive views are preferable to conservative ones; globalization, though choppy, is ultimately a win-win-win-win; most long-term trends are positive for humanity, making many supposed short-term problems ultimately inconsequential; diversity and cosmopolitanism and the free flow of human beings are always better than the alternatives; markets are the most realistic way to get things done.

What this *pensée unique* did was cause his tribe to "ignore a lot of issues that were relevant to other people and not to us," Giussani said. "And so the more this went on, the more we kind of left behind a lot of these issues and sensitivities and culture eventually—culture in a broad sense that then came back and is haunting us." By this he meant the rising populist anger, for which he blamed himself in a modest way.

Of course, it wasn't only curators and arbiters like him who protected their own worldview and shut out others. It was also the elite audiences who heard only what they wanted to hear. He gave the example of Steven Pinker's popular TED talk on the decline of violence over the course of history, based on his book *The Better Angels of Our Nature*. Pinker is a respected professor of psychology at Harvard, and few would accuse him of pulling his punches or yielding to thought leadership's temptations. Yet his talk became a cult favorite among hedge funders, Silicon Valley types, and other winners. It did so not only because it was interesting and fresh and well argued, but also because it contained a justification for keeping the social order largely as is.

Pinker's actual point was narrow, focused, and valid: Interpersonal violence as a mode of human problem-solving was in a long free fall. But for many who heard the talk, it offered a socially acceptable way to tell people seething over the inequities of the age to drop their complaining. "It has become an ideology of: The world today may be complex and complicated and confusing in many ways, but the reality is that if you take the long-term perspective you will realize how good we have it," Giussani said. The ideology, he said, told people, "You're being unrealistic, and you're not looking at things in the right way. And if you think that you have problems, then, you know, your problems don't really matter compared to the past's, and your problems are really not problems, because things are getting better."

Giussani had heard rich men do this kind of thing so often that he had invented a verb for the act: They were "Pinkering"—using the long-run direction of human history to minimize, to delegitimize the concerns of those without power. There was also economic Pinkering, which "is to tell people the global economy has been great because five hundred million Chinese have gone from poverty to the middle class. And, of course, that's true," Giussani said. "But if you tell that to the guy who has been fired from a factory in Manchester because his job was taken to China, he may have a different reaction. But we don't care about the guy in Manchester. So there are many facets to this kind of ideology that have been used to justify the current situation."

Here is an expert example of Pinkering, from the social psychologist Jonathan Haidt. Notice how accurate observations about human progress between the time of hunter-gatherers and the present creep into criticism-shaming:

> We're this little, tribal species that was basically just sort of beating each other up, and competing with each other in all these ways, and somehow or other, we've risen so vastly far above our design specifications. I look around at us and I say, go humanity. We are fantastic. Yeah, there's ISIS, there's a lot of bad stuff, but you people who think that things are bad, you are expecting way too much.

As a TED curator, Giussani was one of many people who had helped to build a new intellectual sphere in recent decades. It turned thought leaders into our most heard philosophers. It put many on the payroll of companies and plutocrats as their means of making a living. It promoted a body of ideas friendly to the winners of the age. It beamed out so many thoughts about why the world was getting better in recent years that its antennae failed to detect all the incoming transmissions about all the people whose lives were not improving, who didn't care to be Pinkered because they knew what they were seeing, and what they were seeing was a society in which a small number of conference-going people and their friends were hoarding much of the progress they claimed to be inevitable, abundant, and beneficial to all.

Now in America, in Europe, and beyond, revolts were under way. People were rejecting the winners' consensus that Giussani had described. Had MarketWorld's commandeering and distortion of the realm of ideas contributed to the anger that so disturbed him? "Of course that distortion contributed," he said. "I believe even that it is one of the biggest engines of it." MarketWorld elites spun an intellectual cocoon for themselves, and kept repeating the stories that insured against deep change. Meanwhile, Giussani said, millions around the world were "feeling that a big chunk of their reality was being ignored at best, censored, or ridiculed even."

Eventually, they would do something about it.

CHAPTER 5

ARSONISTS MAKE THE BEST FIREFIGHTERS

*No one knows the system better than me, which is why
I alone can fix it.*

—DONALD J. TRUMP

The master's tools will never dismantle the master's house.

—AUDRE LORDE

As the win-win approach to social change spread around the world, George Soros had been something of a holdout. With a net worth in the double-digit billions, Soros was one of the richest men on earth. He was also one of the most generous and influential, having set up a philanthropic empire that planned to give away $931 million in 2016. Until lately, his giving had been guided by assumptions that somewhat clashed with those of MarketWorld. Soros, who in his youth in Hungary had lived as a Jew under Nazism and a would-be capitalist under communism, was more interested than many rich people in justice and movements, rights and good government. His Open Society Foundations described their mission as being "to build vibrant and tolerant societies whose governments are accountable and open to criticism, whose laws and policies are open to debate and correction, and whose political institutions are open to the participation of all people." In 2016 the foundations were planning to give $142 million for human rights and democratic practice, $21 million for journalism, and $42 million for justice reform and the rule of law. Soros was giving much of his money to the kinds of non-market-oriented causes that don't necessarily benefit winners.

But as the win-win gospel conquered ever more territory, it had come to be believed in many quarters that the best way to help people was through the marketplace; there were new demands for new kinds of change. In the course of their work, Soros's team reported encountering a young Roma woman in Europe whose attitude was emblematic of a shift in the culture. She told them that the older generation of Roma in Europe wanted rights, but the rising generation wanted to be social entrepreneurs. The woman's either/or schema was dubious, for social enterprises might well be said to depend on underlying rights, but it bespoke the era. In a time of market supremacy, an organization that fought for people's rights and equality under the law was in danger of disappointing them by failing to invest in their for-profit social justice businesses.

The foundations' Economic Advancement Program was born in 2016 as an answer to this hunger of the age. Embracing win-win language, the foundations said the program would "work at the nexus of economic development and social justice," and "encourage economic transformation that increases material opportunity in ways that promote open and prosperous societies." Soros's foundations had largely avoided this kind of work in the past, out of concern that it might be viewed as a conflict of interest—a man still active in the markets advocating to countries how their markets should be arranged and regulated. But avoidance was no longer an option. The new program could make traditional philanthropic grants, fund research into what fosters more just and inclusive economies, lend money to other organizations, and advise governments on policy; moreover, in the ultimate win-win, the program would administer an impact investment fund whose task was to make investments in for-profit companies that promote more open societies and "advance the interests of underserved populations."

A new approach to changing the world required a new leader,

and so the foundations had hired Sean Hinton, late of McKinsey, Goldman Sachs, and the mining conglomerate Rio Tinto, as the program's chief executive. Hinton and his team had spent months coming up with a working theory of what makes for more inclusive and just economies, a theory that would guide their work. Now they needed feedback on it. They wanted people from outside the foundations to help them debate important underlying questions such as: How could they foster fast-growing economies that also promoted justice, governance, empowerment, social cohesion, and equality? How could traditional tools of economic progress be changed to help rather than harm the most vulnerable and marginalized people?

Thus one day, in a conference room above West 57th Street in Manhattan, Hinton convened a group of people he respected in his personal network. There was Ruth, a senior adviser to a private equity firm that focused on financial industry investments. She had also put in time at Bridgewater, the massive hedge fund, and other such financial institutions, and had done a two-year stint as chief investment adviser to a large American city. There was Paul, who also worked in private equity, in addition to lecturing at an Ivy League management school. He was a former investment banker and management consultant. There was Aurelien, who led a boutique advisory firm that counseled corporations on strategy amid turbulent market conditions, was a venture partner in several Silicon Valley start-ups, and had earlier been a McKinsey partner. There was Albert, the head of brand and communications for Rio Tinto. There were a pair of World Bank/International Finance Corporation types who had professional knowledge of the topics at hand: One of them, Charlise, had stuck with such work; the other, Juan Pablo, had subsequently put in time with Cisco and the Boston Consulting Group. And there was Hinton, who until assuming this position had been an adviser to mining corporations, banks, and other businesses in China, Mongolia, and Africa.

As the experts sank into red chairs around the leather-covered table, they turned their attention to the three wall-mounted televi-

sion screens, from which beamed a tool that has proven essential to
MarketWorld's conquest of social problem-solving: Microsoft Power-
Point. The questions of justice and equality before these visitors
were among the hardest known to mankind, with the arguments
over them responsible for tens of millions of deaths in the twentieth
century alone. But the discussion would not be built around philosophical insights, or the express desires of the people to be helped,
or an analysis of the power structures that inhibited the pursuit of
justice and equality. Rather, the issues, having been put to a group
of MarketWorld types, would be presented in the business way, in
the form of slides with graphs and charts. The question of building
more inclusive economies would be atomized into endless subcategories, until the human reality all but vanished. The fundamental
problems would grow almost unrecognizable. Justice and inequality
would be converted into problems the private equity executive was
preeminently qualified to solve.

This became especially apparent when, from time to time, as
is common in meetings like this, the discussion became about the
presentation itself. So complicated and attention-sucking are the
waterfall charts, two-by-two matrices, and sub-subcategories that
it all becomes about them. *Move it to that slide. Can we go back to
the previous slide? What is the direction of history in this chart?* It is
like when a couple's fight ceases to be about the issue and becomes
about the conduct of the fight itself, which can be a refuge from
the underlying problem. *Did the chart imply that economic advancement occupied a moderate position in between those pairs of polarities,
or was it really the integration of all four things?* The room begins to
have a proxy discussion about graphic design elements that stand in
only the vaguest ways for human challenges. And the private equity
executive lights up, because now she can not only contribute but
also lead. And the actual experts in the topic and those affected by
these decisions often recede, tongue-tied. The problem has been
reformatted for the operating system of MarketWorld.

These business-trained problem-solvers, having recast the problem to be specially solvable by them, having sidelined those with

more established ways of thinking about it, now stand before a blank canvas that they can paint with their own frameworks and biases. Thus in the Soros meeting, when the talk turned to farm supply chains in a remote region of India, the lingua franca was business language. It was said that there were too many intermediaries in the supply chain: too many traders and brokers and such between the Indian farmer and the Indian dinner plate. The corporate answer was to "disintermediate." What did not appear to cross anyone's mind on West 57th Street was the possibility of being wrong about rural India. What if the intermediaries in that area tended to be women, making the job inefficient but also a beachhead of social progress? What if the intermediaries ensured that fresh produce ended up in villages and hamlets along the route to the cities, whereas large trucks would bypass them and increase their reliance on processed food? What if there were other human facts that the Goldman–McKinsey–Rio Tinto–Bridgewater alumni in this room couldn't see? What if these winners didn't know everything? What if those outsiders who weren't in the room knew a thing or two?

O ver the course of a generation, many people and institutions around the world decided that to make a dent in the problems of the poor and excluded, one needed the advice of the kinds of businesspeople that Hinton had pulled together. The best guides to change, the reasoning went, were those who designed and participated in and upheld the very power structures that need changing. But that view of the usefulness of the master's tools in dismantling his house, to borrow the words of Audre Lorde, had not always reigned.

Long before Hinton learned the protocols of business, he had been on a very different path, as a student at the Guildhall School of Music and Drama in London. He had grown up in an artistic family and in the theater, and he was studying classical music and conducting. Somehow, in his fourth year, he came up with the idea of going to Mongolia. He says the only way he could figure to get into that closed country in the late 1980s was to study ethnomusicology there. So he signed up to do graduate work in the subject at Cambridge, and applied for and won a British Council scholarship to move to Mongolia and study its traditional music. It was meant to be a one-year stint. He would stay, with some breaks, for much of the next seven years.

Hinton moved to Ulaanbaatar in December 1988. Initially, he was forced to live under the tight strictures of the country's authoritarian government. He wasn't allowed to stray more than twenty kilometers out of the capital without minders, which made him a musicologist of limited efficacy. But soon a democracy movement erupted, and before long, seven decades of communist rule ended. The revolution freed Hinton to roam the country. He moved to the farthest western reaches of Mongolia and lived with a nomadic family in the mountains. He focused his research on the love songs and marriage rituals of the western Mongolian tribes.

He liked the country enough to stay after his studies, and the revolution permitted that, too. The burgeoning market economy made it possible to start a business. Tourists were interested in the newly opened country, so Hinton decided to start a travel company to help people have the kinds of Mongolian experiences he had had. There weren't many foreign-owned businesses at the time, and so, Hinton says, he became a go-to expert on the topic. When American embassy officials in Ulaanbaatar received queries about starting a local company, they would sometimes direct them to Hinton. He soon realized he could charge money for this advice-giving and did. He had become a consultant of a particular kind, working not with spreadsheets and PowerPoint, but rather helping people navigate a society in flux.

Seven years after arriving in Mongolia, married, and with his thirtieth birthday nearing, he left Mongolia and went job hunting. "Everybody wanted to take me out for a beer and hear my story about living with the nomads," he says. "But everyone was like, 'Obviously, we can't give you a job.'" The Sydney office of McKinsey was the exception. This was not entirely accidental. Hinton's mixture of intelligence and impressionability made him an ideal McKinsey hire.

Perhaps the most dizzying aspect of the new job was learning an almost opposite way of relating to alien environments. Hinton's task at McKinsey shared a basic commonality with his work in Mongolia: He was to show up as an outsider and try to make good. But the experiences diverged starkly from there.

In Mongolia, Hinton's approach was to learn from the people he was studying by hanging back, observing, realizing all he didn't know. Success required letting other people lead him, as he remembers it: "The tools that I was used to bringing were largely to do with perceiving and sensing; they were largely to do with intuition; they were largely to do with creativity and looking for connections; and they were very much to do with people." For years on end, Hinton had had the experience of resisting easy assumptions, avoiding certitude, hunting for cues, letting others lead. "You turn up in a tent in Mongolia," he said, "and just the whole thing of where you sit, where you put your legs, when you give the gift that you've brought with you—I just became so attuned to all of those things. The body language—am I doing it right? What are other people doing? You become just absolutely, completely attuned to reading those signals from people around you." This approach to an alien environment was what he called humility. "If you think about the skills of living in a tent, in a foreign culture, in a foreign language, in a certainly foreign environment, you don't have a choice but to get taught humility every day," he said. "You're surviving on that, and your very survival is based on recognizing that you don't know, and being absolutely open to everything—being absorptive of every influence around you and listening."

At McKinsey, he realized, he was expected to operate very differently. "Some months later," he said, "I'm sitting next to the chief executive of a very significant business in Australia, and I'm expected to have a point of view and an opinion—a Day One hypothesis about this problem that we're talking about." Instead of listening, absorbing, trying to decipher slowly and respectfully the dynamics of the space one had entered, the high-flying, high-priced consultant was expected to jump in and know things. And even a consultant like Hinton, trained in music and expert in western Mongolian love songs, could be expected to do this, because of the protocols that McKinsey taught its consultants. They offered a powerful way of stepping into a world you didn't know and reconstituting its reality so that the solution became more obvious to you than it was to the client's native executives. The protocols allowed for a strange kind of earned presumptuousness. Equipped with a special way of chopping up problems, parsing data, and arriving at answers, the consultant constructed authority. His job was, as Hinton put it, "the bringing to bear and the championing of the religion of facts—incontrovertible, scientific, unemotional, unencumbered-by-people facts."

The protocols that allowed for this certitude were, as Latin once was, a mother language that had birthed many vernaculars. These vernaculars shared a common purpose: Having arisen not so much within industry as among the insider-outsiders of the business world—consultants, financiers, management scholars—they offered a way to get smart on other people's situations. The banker trying to come up with the initial share price of a soon-to-be-listed chemical company wasn't necessarily an expert in fertilizer. The hired-gun corporate strategist for a pharmaceutical company wasn't necessarily an expert on drug delivery vehicles. The protocols—some specific to domains like finance or consulting, some more cross-cutting—allowed such figures to sweep in and break down a problem in a way that surfaced new realities, produced insight, sidelined other solvers, and made themselves essential.

Hinton learned the McKinsey vernacular of the protocols. In the book *The McKinsey Mind*, by Ethan Rasiel, the firm's protocols are distilled: Consultants first find the "business need," or the basic problem, based on evaluating the company and its industry. Then they "analyze." This step requires "framing the problem: defining the boundaries of the problem and breaking it down into its component elements to allow the problem-solving team to come up with an initial hypothesis as to the solution." This is the insta-certitude at work—hypothesis-making comes early. Then the consultants must "design the analysis" and "gather the data" to prove the hypothesis, and must decide, based on the results, whether their theory of the solution is right. If it is, the next step is "presenting" in a crisp, clear, convincing way that can win over clients understandably wary of fancy outsiders' big ideas. At last, the solution comes to the "implementation" phase, through "iteration that leads to continual improvement."

Hinton's interviews for the McKinsey job had taught him an early and vital lesson about this approach to problem-solving: It was not about drawing on knowledge, and often even sneered at doing so; it was, rather, about being able to analyze a situation despite ignorance, to transcend unfamiliarity. The interview questions that struck him were of this sort: *How many Ping-Pong balls would fit into a Boeing 747? What would you estimate the size of the Bolivian steel industry to be? How many razor blades are sold in Australia every year?* Hinton joked that his instinct, hearing such questions, was to call a friend in this or that job who might be familiar with the relevant facts. But the point in the interviews was not to get the number right. It was to demonstrate how you reason, based on the assumptions you make. The idea, he said, was "if you break the problem down into small enough pieces that are logically related and make educated guesses combined with facts where they're available, or at least you join the dots from the facts that you're able to put together, you can construct a logical and compelling answer to pretty much any problem." In other words, Hinton's initiation into McKinsey and the protocols more generally was being urged to spit out a preternaturally confident answer to something he knew nothing about.

As he adjusted to McKinsey's ways, Hinton picked up the little rules and figures of speech that have become punch lines for many consulting skeptics and yet remain incredibly influential tools in business and beyond. For example, he learned that it was best to speak in lists of three, based on research about how people absorb information. If you have two important points to make, you add a third; if you have four, you combine two or just lose one. Hinton also

learned the commandment against taking on excessively large problems. Do not "boil the ocean," one versed in the protocols might
tell another. The protocols tell you to reduce the scope of what is
considered, limit the amount of data you drink in, to avoid becoming overwhelmed by the volume of reality you confront. And lest
you worry that this shrinking of your purview will harm your ability
to solve the problem, the protocols offer the eighty-twenty rule. In
the early 1900s, the Italian economist Vilfredo Pareto is said to have
noticed that 80 percent of Italy's land was owned by just 20 percent
of its people, and that 80 percent of the peas yielded by his garden
came from just 20 percent of his peapods. These observations had
given rise to the business maxim that 20 percent of many systems
generates 80 percent of the results—one-fifth of one's customers
providing most of one's revenue, to cite the most common example.
The protocols told the problem-solving swashbuckler that it was
possible to swoop in, find that 20 percent, turn some dials in that
zone, and unleash great results. These tricks were not about looking at a problem holistically, comprehensively, from various human
perspectives; they were about getting results without needing to do
such things.

At McKinsey, Hinton learned to make so-called issue trees—
visual maps to help you break down a nicely scoped, eighty-twentied,
pond-sized problem into its elements. It starts with a challenge such
as making a bank more profitable. That increase in profitability can
come through raising revenues or lowering costs, the first layer of
subcategories. Each rung of subcategories must be, in firm par-
lance, "MECE"—mutually exclusive and collectively exhaustive. In
other words, raising revenues must be entirely different from lowering costs, and all routes to the ultimate goal should pass through
them. Now each subcategory can be broken down into sub-subcategories—the increase in revenue, for instance, can either come
from existing businesses or new ones. And so on, until there are
sub-sub-sub-sub-subcategories. To be fair, this kind of exercise can
allow one to see, with a clarity that is impossible when looking at the
whole, the dials that might be turned relatively easily and yet have

outsize effects—for example, closing those three high-rent bank branches in Manhattan might generate 80 percent of the savings required. Yet this schematizing, whether in the McKinsey vernacular or others, can at times be limited by its arbitrariness. Categories are made that may or may not correspond with reality. Divisions are carved between things that may be connected rather than mutually exclusive. Things are broken down in the way that happens to be most obvious or useful for the parachuter, and sometimes this smashing of reality into hundreds of little pieces makes a solution seem apparent while in fact obscuring the true problem. Those who could set the parachuter right, those with valuable traditional and local knowledge, cannot speak the new language of the problem, illiterates in their own land.

Hinton eventually took to the McKinsey way—to declaim. Coming to the firm was, he said, "a shock, but it was thrilling and exciting. And I wouldn't have been there if it hadn't played to many of my own strengths." A second later, he added, "Or weaknesses." All these years later, he was still torn about what exactly he had learned.

Hinton was learning the protocols to work his way into the arena of business. Yet even as he was absorbing them, the protocols were leaping beyond business, conquering domains far afield with their atomizing method. The protocols had grown out of corporate problem-solving, but increasingly MarketWorlders were employing them to elbow into the solution of social problems traditionally considered in other ways, by more public-spirited actors. And the more people accepted the idea of the protocols as essential to public problem-solving, the more MarketWorld was elevated over government and civil society as the best engine of change and progress.

Our age of market supremacy has blessed the protocols with a remarkable change of fortune: They have evolved from being a specialized way of solving particular business problems to being, in the view of many, the essential toolkit for solving anything. The protocols are increasingly seen as vital training for working in charity, education, social justice, politics, health care, the arts, newsrooms, and any number of arenas that used to be more comfortable with their own in-house apprenticeship. Organizations like the Gates Foundation hire the protocol bearers to solve the problem of education for poor children in America. Civil rights organizations put protocol bearers on their boards, taking not only their money but also their advice. As we've seen, young people like Hilary Cohen are persuaded by the surrounding culture that only by learning the protocols can they help millions of people.

Few things better illustrate how far the protocols have spread than the rise of a new kind of consulting firm, dedicated to fighting for the oppressed using the tools of business. One of them, Techno-Serve, founded in 1968, advertises itself as "Business Solutions to Poverty," and offers an example of how the bearers of the protocols elbow their way into the solution of social problems simply by offering their own style of diagnoses. TechnoServe calls itself a "leader in harnessing the power of the private sector to help people lift themselves out of poverty." And right up front, it declares a theory of change straight out of MarketWorld: "By linking people to information, capital and markets, we have helped millions to create lasting prosperity for their families and communities." It is possible to read into this that people are poor because of the absence of these linkages, not because of caste, race, land, hoarding, wages, labor conditions, and plunder; not because of anything anyone did—or is doing—to anyone else; not because of reversible decisions societies have taken.

And while this is highly questionable as social theory, it is a shrewd posture, because if the problem is a lack of linkages, those who are good at making these kinds of linkages are elevated as solvers. Those who propose to solve problems in other ways—especially by looking at power and resources and other things unsettling to winners—are sidelined by this theory. And if TechnoServe has a limited view of what afflicts poor people, it may be because of who leads it. Its managers come, in the main, from corporations, in areas such as investment banking, management consulting, health care, and fund management, and from brand-name companies such as Morgan Stanley, Credit Suisse, Monsanto, Qwest, Cargill, Barclays, and (several times over) McKinsey. Perhaps the clearest signal of TechnoServe's faith in the power of the protocols to cure injustice— rather than, say, life experience—is the constitution of its board. Of twenty-eight board members listed online, twenty-six are white as of last check.

If TechnoServe emphasizes the missing linkages between poor people and the right information, capital, and markets, a rival firm, Bridgespan, argues that too many good solutions are too small— another theory of what keeps people poor that, usefully, does not implicate the rich. If TechnoServe is dominated by ex-McKinsey types, Bridgespan is a landing strip for alumni of another of the Big Three consulting firms, Bain & Company. Its world-changers have a "passion to enhance social mobility and bring about equality of opportunity," the firm says. Bridgespan lays out a theory of change up front: It helps poor people by helping the things that help them grow bigger in scale than they presently are. Its approach "takes on complex problems and identifies practical solutions that can help organizations understand and overcome their biggest barriers to scaling impact." One of Bridgespan's cofounders went to Harvard Business School; the other taught there and is the author of such articles as "Transformative Scale," "Scaling Impact," "Scaling What Works," and "Going to Scale." Doing more of what works was certainly acceptable to MarketWorld.

The bearers of these protocols were, ironically, rushing in to shape the solution of problems that their methods were complicit in causing. Corporate types from the energy and financial industries were drafted into charitable projects to protect the world from climate change, even if their way of thinking about profit, as practiced in their day jobs, was a big part of why climate change was happening. Business leaders were drafted into strategizing for women's rights, even if their tools were to blame for the always-on work culture that made it harder for so many women to claim their rights and for the tax avoidance that made women-friendly policies like universal daycare more elusive. And, as at the Soros event, they were viewed as essential to increasing equality, even if their analytical frameworks and their atomizing of the realities of workers and communities had helped to increase inequality.

The protocols and those who employed them did have a lot to offer the world of social problems: rigor, logic, data, an ability to make decisions swiftly. As they spread into the work of battling disease or reforming education, they could do a great deal of good and allow people's money and time to go further than they could have without it. But there was always a price, and part of that price was that problems reformatted according to the protocols were recast in the light of a winner's gaze. After all, the definition of a problem is done by the problem-solver and crowds out other ways of seeing it. Kavita Ramdas, a longtime nonprofit executive, wrote sharply of the conquest of social change by the "'fix-the-problem' mentality that allowed business people to succeed as hedge-fund managers, capital-market investors, or software-developers." It is an approach, she wrote, "designed to yield measurable and fairly quick solutions." The problem is the often humbler methods that the protocols displace:

> The nuance and inherent humility of the social sciences— the realization that development has to do with people, with human and social complexity, with cultural and traditional realities, and their willingness to struggle with the messy and multifaceted aspects of a problem—have no cachet in this metrics-driven, efficiency-seeking, technology-focused approach to social change.

Even though Hinton could seem to be an archetype of what Ramdas was condemning, he would come to criticize the great business conquest that he acknowledged being part of and at the same time wanted to escape. He called it "the Trying-to-Solve-the-Problem-with-the-Tools-That-Caused-It issue." The spread of these protocols was, he said, a "continuation of the colonial, imperial arrogance of the enlightened white man with money and science, and noble and benevolent intentions, who will solve these problems." The situation was no longer British colonizers helping themselves to your country. It was well-suited people with laptops offering to solve social problems, often pro bono, without needing to know much. Hinton worried that the ascendancy of this PowerPoint-greased "problem-solving" was "slightly more scientific, slightly more rational, but it's an extension of that tradition."

Hinton came to these concerns slowly. He left McKinsey after five years, worked in London for several years after that, running a film studio and starting a boutique investment bank, and then ended up in China, where he fell into stints advising on complex financial transactions. That work led to projects for Goldman Sachs and Rio Tinto, which, seeing a protocol guy who had also once been a Mongolia guy, thought he might help them and their clients navigate the country's political environment. Mongolia was in the middle of a mining boom, with large companies striking deals to extract the country's copper and other resources. Hinton's assignment, as he frames it, was to serve as a go-between for these firms and Mongolia, helping each side understand each other so as to mitigate risks to the project. After all, mining deals gone bad can cost investors enormously.

Hinton's role as a senior adviser to Goldman and Rio Tinto placed him squarely in between the companies he was working for and a country he loved, and the role was full of contradictions that, even years later, he seemed to struggle with. "I was working as a reverse advocate, but I was paid by a mining company; I was paid by an investment bank," he said. "I'm not so naïve as to think that my role wasn't guided by meeting their needs and their interests to a significant degree. Of course it was." It was not yet known, to him or anyone, whether foreign business interests would help the country in the ways they promised, or whether, as had so often been the case in the history of resource extraction, take what they could and run. He was paid to believe, and convince others, that what these companies wanted was the same as what Mongolia needed—a win-win. He had been hired to reconcile what was perhaps irreconcilable. Perhaps he realized that, for at one point some years ago Hinton reached out to an iconic bearer of the protocols who was having his own doubts.

Michael Porter, a Harvard Business School professor who is considered the founder of modern corporate strategy, had seized Hinton's attention with a 2011 essay whose rather modest critique of the prevailing approach to business created a stir in a world not used to such friendly fire. Porter was among the most cited authors on business, and a godfather of theories about how business competition works and what makes societies "competitive" for business, which is to say attractive to it. In addition to his teaching and writing, he had gotten into the protocol-spreading business himself, starting a consulting firm called the Monitor Group and lending his advice to many health care reform efforts. "He has influenced more executives—and more nations—than any other business professor on earth," *Fortune* magazine once proclaimed. And so in 2011, when Porter and a coauthor named Mark Kramer published the essay "Creating Shared Value" in *Harvard Business Review,* it got the business world's attention.

"The capitalist system is under siege," Porter and Kramer wrote, in a fair impression of a nineteenth-century manifesto. Business was being "criticized as a major cause of social, environmental, and economic problems." Companies were "widely thought to be prospering at the expense of their communities." And who was to blame? "A big part of the problem lies with companies themselves," they wrote. And what they blamed in the companies was "an outdated, narrow approach to value creation." Companies had become too focused on "optimizing short-term financial performance." They had acquired a dangerous tendency to "overlook the greatest unmet needs in the market as well as broader influences on their long-term success." Again and again, companies that employed droves of brilliant people and had high-priced outside advisers were making decisions that ignored "the well-being of their customers, the depletion of natural resources vital to their businesses, the viability of suppliers, and the economic distress of the communities in which they produce and sell." Porter and Kramer were critiquing a culture that had overtaken the business world: the culture wrought by the atomizing protocols that obscured context.

Hinton eventually met with Porter to seek his advice on how to structure his companies' deals in Mongolia to be less protocol and more human. Now, several years later, Porter was sitting in a booth at Peacock Alley, in the refined but frenetic lobby of the Waldorf Astoria in New York, explaining how he had come around to questioning the work of the protocols. He had become interested in inequality after the Great Recession, especially after seeing some data on how well many American businesses and individuals had survived it, and how badly the average citizen and worker had done by comparison. He said, "We started really thinking hard about, what are we doing at Harvard Business School? What are we teaching here? Somehow we've missed a big piece of the equation." Those questions led him to his idea of "shared value"—that there were new ways of thinking about business goals and practices that would improve big companies' relationship with their communities.

Porter showed up at the Waldorf that day with an agenda of hopefulness. He didn't want to talk about what people were doing wrong. "My view is that there are now very strong forces which can be tapped into," he said. People knew the old ways of doing business weren't working. People wanted new ways. "So it's a question of articulating what's the 'should' rather than what's the 'not,'" he said. This reluctance toward the "not" was understandable for a man still very much of MarketWorld. But Porter's ideas on the "not" seemed of greater import, because if it was obvious to millions outside Market-World that the business protocols of the last generation had caused so many of the problems the world now confronted, it was, willfully, one suspects, not yet obvious to many within it. Perhaps hearing it from Michael Porter would undercut the plausibility of their denial.

In Porter's careful, methodical way, he began to lay out how the business approach to life had, over a generation, contributed to some of the very societal ailments for which it now offered itself as a cure. At the heart of his account was a critique of the protocols, and how their piecemeal approach to reality, their rejection of the whole, had harmed people.

Porter spoke of how companies over the last generation had pursued a vision of globalization in which they owed nothing to any community. This was simply because those taught by professors like him at places like Harvard Business School, groomed by consulting and Wall Street and other training grounds, tended to be agnostic about place. You analyzed the data, and then you went where the opportunity was; it didn't matter if that chase severed you from your own community and your obligations to it. "There were many things that business traditionally did to support the community, from training people to whole sets of other activities that they sort of took responsibility for, which we call investing in the commons," Porter said. By commons he meant the shared assets of a place—things such as public schools that both industry and average people benefit from. "As people got disconnected from locations, business stopped really reinvesting in that. They thought their job was globalizing."

This disconnection of which Porter spoke was abetted by the decontextualizing, disaggregating, ocean-boiling-avoiding approach of the protocols—by their tendency to atomize. Before the protocols had come to dominate the world of business, a company might have raised its money from not far away, sourced its inputs from not far away, sold to customers not far away, paid taxes to authorities not far away, and, when growth came, parked the profit in a bank not far away or reinvested it in a new venture with a plant not far away. But in recent decades, that began to change, as technology made it easier to do business with faraway entities, as new markets opened, and—importantly—as the financial wizards and management consultants increased their influence over boardrooms. These protocol-equipped figures pressed companies to embrace a new philosophy: Do each of your activities where it can be best done, wherever that might be. You raised money from Korean investors, sourced from Mexico, sold in France, paid taxes in the Caribbean, and, when growth hit, chose a Swiss bank or ethereal Bitcoins to store the proceeds—or reinvested them in whatever venture on earth promised you the most attractive returns. It was an expansion of commercial freedom. Porter suggested, however, that it had disrupted an older pattern of companies behaving with a sense of citizenship. "There is somehow a detachment because of this notion of globalization—that we're no longer an American company," he said. "And the odds are that if you're operating all around the world, then you don't have any special requirement to worry about Milwaukee."

Somewhere on the road to globalization, Porter said, the self-image of business as a pillar of community had yielded to a self-image of "We're global now, and that's no longer our problem." He added, "They started not accepting any responsibility for that community because they didn't think it was their job, and they could always move somewhere else if that community didn't want to do its thing." This was a win-lose: The companies had flourished because of their freedom to escape and the community's lack of leverage.

Porter's second area of criticism regarded "optimization." Thanks in part to the emergent protocols, a new culture of business had developed in which each microscopic element of a company's activities had to be perfectly optimized, and this, Porter said, had made it easier to mistreat workers and ignore questions about one's effects on the larger system. These new protocols had succeeded because the business world they began to conquer in the latter half of the twentieth century was often clubby, provincial, and very unoptimized. Many businesses, even big ones, operated like families (which many were still run by): You didn't sell everywhere you could sell, and at the exact best market price in each place; you sold where you knew someone who knew someone, and charged whatever your best guess was. You didn't pay workers more when demand spiked and less when it sank; you paid them an even salary.

The management consulting firms, leveraged buyout companies, investment banks, and other bearers of the protocols swept into this rather quainter business world over the last few decades and pressed for each of these pieces to be optimized. They did this through some combination of advisory projects the companies paid for, hostile takeovers after which they forced their new wards to straighten up, and shareholder pressure to lift the stock price. A new ethic of optimization spread across the business world, and at first, to Porter at least, it seemed entirely positive. He said, "We have learned a lot about how to run businesses more productively, and how to operate supply chains, and how to better deploy technology, and how to be smarter about procurement and purchasing." Over a generation, these efforts, many of which were incubated at Harvard Business School, made the economy as a whole more productive and competitive. Yet it was not a coincidence, Porter said, that as "this slack got run out," as he put it, over the same period, life grew harder for many workers: "We ended up making business more productive, which allowed wage increases for many, many years, and good things. But we also, without even kind of realizing it, started building a disconnect between the business and their average employees."

He brought up Starbucks. It had, like so many companies, begun to schedule workers using newfangled "dynamic scheduling" tools, which allowed employers to change schedules more often, so as to constantly optimize. It helped a company pay the smallest wage bill it could to service a given amount of demand. This kind of thing made a company more profitable, but it could bring chaos into workers' lives. They no longer knew how many hours they would get in a given period of time, which complicated paying bills and making purchases. They had to arrange child care on the fly. Porter said, "Somehow in being efficient and being clever and being productive, people thought they had the license to just stop thinking about the human beings and the well-being of everybody else in the system." The same shortsightedness, Porter said, could be seen in highly profitable companies' insistence on low wages: "We turn many of these people into commodities and we just kind of optimized it on us rather than optimize it in any way on them. So a lot of the labor practices, a lot of this idea that you should have contract workers and not have to pay benefits—all this stuff was just too clever and everybody sort of justified it in terms of, 'Oh, we're being productive and we're kind of maximizing our returns, and that's somehow our job.'"

Porter was making clear that "business" is not a fixed quantity. It can be done in different ways, following different approaches. It happened in recent decades to have been taken over by protocols that, in the name of making everything optimal, granted a license to neglect and even hurt others. "We sort of created a cartoon," Porter said, "which is this view of, if you can force your employee to work overtime without paying them, then you should do it—that's free markets, and that's profit maximization."

Finally, Porter spoke of how the spread of the financial vernacular of the protocols had caused companies to be run more and more for the sake of shareholders rather than for workers or customers or anybody else. "When I was first teaching," he said, "we didn't talk about shareholder value." What lodestars guided business back then? "I think it was: The business has to earn a good sustained return, and we're in it for the long run, and we're building a great company," he said, "rather than this notion that it's the stock market vote every day that determines whether you're succeeding or not." Back when businesses were run in a more localized and less scientific manner, they were also run for a variety of people. Shareholders were part of the mix, but the micro-movements of the share price were not the be-all, end-all indicator of a company's success, nor the guide to how it should be run. Of course, there was waste involved: A lot of capital was not put to the most efficient use. And then in the 1970s and '80s, as ascendant neoliberalism spawned changes in law and culture, it came to be viewed as the first duty of a business to maximize value for shareholders. "The social responsibility of business is to increase its profits," the Chicago School economist Milton Friedman declared in the *New York Times Magazine* in the fall of 1970. Wall Streeters trained in the protocols saw their influence rise as their way of evaluating a company, and their degree of say in how it should be run, gradually took over.

Porter watched this phenomenon, which is often called "financialization," turn companies into the servants of their owners, to the detriment of other considerations. "The shareholder-value mind-set became very, very strong," he said. People became "fixated" on it; it pulled them into "short-term" thinking; it caused decisions that might raise the stock price temporarily but actually hurt a company's long-term prospects or its workers or customers or community. "I've been on a bunch of boards," Porter said, "and I experienced it when I go to board meetings, and we worry about an hour-to-hour score, and we start listening to that scorekeeper, the capital markets, in what they think we should do."

An argument like "We need to pay workers a steady salary, which will cost us a lot in the low season but will help us retain them over the long term" now could not be justified. An argument like "We need to pay workers a steady salary, which will cost us in both the short and the long term but is the right thing to do" had no chance. "I think we somehow—again, in the pursuit of efficiency, and financial-market sophistication, and modeling and so forth—we found lots of ways to make money," Porter said, "but it's somehow detached from what capitalism ultimately at its core is all about, which is about the real economy." The investing aspect of business had come to dominate those other aspects of it involving building things, serving people, solving problems.

Taken together, these changes had brought a great rationalizing to the business world, in two senses: They were the instruments through which business operations had been rationalized, and, not unimportantly, they were how businesspersons had rationalized their lives to themselves. Much of what Porter described had entered the business world through the atomizing protocols. With their help, businesses had straightened up their act over a generation, analyzing and optimizing everything. Porter was now allowing that some of it had been overdone. "Somehow, many of these generally sensible types of practices in various aspects of business ended up overshooting," he said.

The result was pain and chaos in so many lives. Now the protocols were turning up at foundations and government agencies and antipoverty consulting firms as the solution to these woes.

Some years after his meeting with Porter, Hinton found himself sitting across from another capitalist with concerns about modern capitalism. George Soros needed someone to run his new program on building more inclusive economies—preferably someone who hadn't bought into the protocols entirely. An ethnomusicologist with years in western Mongolia under his belt who had ended up with McKinsey and Goldman Sachs seemed perfect. Hinton knew his rigorous business training was part of his appeal. But, he added, "Presumably, some of why I'm there is because some of those other things that I did and, hopefully, my Mongolian musicologist bit of me can come out a bit as well, occasionally."

He took up the new job, dividing his time between New York and London, and making his first forays into the new world of the social sector. He was surprised that so many of the people now tasked with helping the oppressed—whether at the Gates Foundation or the Omidyar Network or the Clinton Foundation—were fellow ex-consulting and/or -finance types like him. He knew how they operated. "One thing that that approach entirely fails to take into consideration," he said, "is that the people who are the so-called beneficiaries of this help and this insight may themselves have the answer to the problems." Hinton described the assumption that he saw guiding the protocol bearers in their new, public-serving assignments: "If we assemble enough brainpower and enough money, we can crack this, we can solve these problems." Then the solutions can "get scaled." This approach, he said, "just fails to recognize that we are attempting to solve these problems with the very tools and the very minds that constructed the problems in the first place."

Hinton saw how the protocols, redeployed to the war on hardship, could be very useful to MarketWorld. "If we can suddenly be the white knight and ride in as the savior of the rest of the world, maybe it wasn't bad, after all," he said of the system and ideas that

MarketWorld upheld. "Maybe it actually was good, and this is the chance to redeem capitalism."

The protocols' spread to social questions also gave elites a chance to limit the range of possible answers. "You absolutely constrain the solution set that you're prepared to look at," he said. "It's kind of obvious, isn't it? If you only have English speakers in the car, then the solution is going to be done in English." In Hinton's view, it was not a matter of malice. "It's the banality of inattentiveness," he said. "It's not wickedness. It's not conscious self-censorship. It's just habit." He brought up that meeting of nonexpert experts he had hosted in that conference room above West 57th Street. "I'm guilty of that," he said. "I've got a pretty broad Rolodex. But when you reach out, you reach out to smart, articulate people like yourself. I mean, we all do that. So it self-replicates."

He wondered aloud whether the larger project and the foundations behind it could be run differently. If he believed the protocols' spread to be a colonization, what would decolonization look like? "My assumption is that colonization is inevitable," he said. "I think the idea of independence didn't even dawn on me. I didn't even ask the question. I feel foolish. What does decolonization look like? How would you reverse the trend? Well, I think it is necessary but not sufficient to have a dramatic shift in the complexion and the voices that are around the table." By that, he said, he didn't just mean the usual push for ethnic and gender diversity, nor the keeping around of tokens. What about having the kind of people the foundations seek to help as part of the leadership? he asked.

He was presently in the middle of constituting his board of advisers for the new Economic Advancement Program. "I haven't even questioned the assumption that I would be looking for people with depth of experience and elite credentials," he said. But what if he jettisoned that assumption and put, say, a primary school teacher on the board—one from India? "Actually, I'm going to have a go at that idea," he said. He said he would try to put an ordinary person—one of the people on whose behalf those private equity and consulting types had been deliberating—on the board. That meant the nature of the meeting itself might have to change to accommodate a wider array of backgrounds. Maybe it was best to avoid PowerPoint. Maybe he would have to present in the form of a narrative talk or story, or show a film. Ideas were churning.

Hinton is a Bahá'í, and the Universal House of Justice, the high council of the religion, had once put out a statement about the appropriate way to seek the improvement of the world and the lives of other people:

> Justice demands universal participation. Thus, while social action may involve the provision of goods and services in some form, its primary concern must be to build capacity within a given population to participate in creating a better world. Social change is not a project that one group of people carries out for the benefit of another.

Hinton believed in that idea. In his own life, he felt his faith to be one of the few forces strong enough to counterbalance the business way of thinking. The great flaw of that way, he said, is "materialism." The businessperson tended to see work in utilitarian terms, as something people do to feed themselves and acquire things. But there is a spiritual dimension, too: "That work might be the expression of the inner desire to be productive and to be of service to one's community—and that the idea of denying someone the opportunity to fulfill that is like not letting a tree produce fruit." Many bearers of the business mind had, like him, a religious or spiritual life on the side, he said, "but I think that somehow that thinking never overlaps with that mind." He added, "People don't have permission to think about those things in their working life. We've decided that those are separate domains, and it's kind of not really okay in my circles to talk about religious faith."

He had been hired for his skill at solving business problems using the protocols. His values were his own problem. "That wasn't why I was invited to the party," he said.

CHAPTER 6

GENEROSITY AND JUSTICE

Wealth is like an orchard. You have to share the fruit, not the orchard.

—CARLOS SLIM

Darren Walker, topped by a furry drum of a Russian hat, sat in the back of a black Lincoln limousine, inching nervously toward West 57th Street and what he called "the belly of the beast." His limo was heading to the New York office of KKR, the private equity firm immortalized in *Barbarians at the Gate*—a firm that had led the charge of the great rationalizing, one protocol-guided buyout at a time. Walker was the president of the Ford Foundation and thus in the social justice business. He spent his days giving money away.

Walker's assignment—to address a group of private equity executives at a luncheon—was complicated by a much-publicized letter he had written some months before. The letter broke with the pleasantness that tends to prevail in the philanthropy world. It had raised, in sharp and provocative language, the question of what to do about the crisis of inequality. This in itself was disturbing to many rich people, who preferred to talk about reducing poverty or extending opportunity, not about more thoroughgoing reforms that would perhaps require sacrifice. Walker's letter had squarely blamed the very elites who give back through philanthropy for ignoring their complicity in causing the problems they later seek to solve.

Before writing the letter, Walker had been universally popular with the plutocrats, which isn't to say that everyone disliked what he had written. Robert Rubin, late of Goldman Sachs, Citigroup, and the Treasury Department, told Walker he loved the letter, finding it "fresh and different." He said he had "never read anything that did that." But many plutocrats objected to Walker's shining the spotlight on inequality, instead of the issues they were more comfortable talking about, like poverty or opportunity. They disliked that he framed the issue in a way that blamed them rather than inviting them to participate in a solution. They disliked his focus on how money is made rather than how it is given away. "I just think you should stop ranting at inequality," a friend in private equity had snapped at him a few nights before the KKR event. "It's a real turn-off." Walker had broken what in his circles were important taboos: Inspire the rich to do more good, but never, ever tell them to do less harm; inspire them to give back, but never, ever tell them to take less; inspire them to join the solution, but never, ever accuse them of being part of the problem.

The headline above Walker's letter on the Ford website read "Toward a New Gospel of Wealth." He was attempting to revise and update—or perhaps overturn—an old gospel that dates back to an era much like ours, a gospel that had itself transformed earlier American ideas of helping other people.

The late historian Peter Dobkin Hall, an authority on the American giving tradition, traces it back to the late seventeenth and early eighteenth centuries, as the colonial trade in commodities magnified differences in wealth and created "an increasingly visible population of poor and dependent people for whom the public was expected to take responsibility." Before this time, Hall writes, much giving was to the public sphere—to government institutions themselves or to entities like Harvard, which "were regarded as public corporations, subject to legislative oversight and supported significantly in the form of legislative grants of money." But an increasingly complex society and economy—thanks to growing international trade, immigration, a burgeoning market economy, population growth, and outbreaks of diseases like smallpox—inspired Americans to take matters into their own hands, according to Hall. He credits Cotton Mather, the revered Puritan clergyman in New England, with reframing prevailing ideas about charity with his 1710 pamphlet *Bonifacius:*

> The Man who is not Satisfying of the *Wisdom* in making it the Work of his *Life* to *Do Good,* is alwayes to be beheld with the Pity due to an *Ideot.* . . . None but a *Good Man,* is really a *Living* Man; And the more *Good* any Man dos, the more he really *Lives. All the rest is Death;* or belongs to it.

Mather, in Hall's account, had specific ideas about what it meant to do good, "advocating 'friendly visiting' of the poor, the use of voluntary associations for mutual support, and philanthropic giving by the rich to relieve the poor and support schools, colleges, and hospitals."

A marked feature of American giving before the age of big philanthropy was the helping of the many by the many. Groups for that purpose multiplied through the eighteenth and nineteenth centuries. Hall writes of a spreading view that "the hazards and uncertainties of urban life could be mitigated through fraternal associations which helped members and their families financially in times of illness and death. Associations of artisans protected their members from exploitation and sought to ensure that they received fair prices for their work." In the 1830s, when Alexis de Tocqueville made his pilgrimage from Europe to America, he observed that Americans didn't wait for kings and popes to help people. They made "associations"—a phrase he helped make famous—"to hold fêtes, found seminaries, build inns, construct churches, distribute books, dispatch missionaries to the antipodes."

As the nineteenth century drew down, major changes in American life helped to develop these early tendencies into what is today called organized philanthropy. "Acts of human kindness are as old as humankind," the scholars Lucy Bernholz, Chiara Cordelli, and Rob Reich write in a recent book they edited, *Philanthropy in Democratic Societies.* "The modern practice of organized philanthropy, on the other hand, has a much more recent provenance." Around the turn of the century, a new industrial capitalism flourished. Incredible fortunes were made in railroads, steel, oil, and other factors of a booming nation's growth. Much as is the case today, inequality widened as some seized on the new possibilities and others were displaced. Anger bubbled, and populist impulses surged. The money that was being made in this earlier gilded age was, in the view of many, unseemly in its quantities, unjust in its provenance, untenable in the power it conferred over a republic breaking out in new populist sentiments. It was also fuel for new ideas about giving: "Growth in inequality might be a foe to civic comity, but it is a friend to private philanthropy," Reich, a political scientist and a leading authority on charitable giving, writes in the book.

In this moment, out of a mix of altruism and the self-preservational desire to cool public anger, some aging tycoons, notably Andrew Carnegie and John D. Rockefeller, began to give back. Frederick Gates, an adviser to Rockefeller, wrote to him, "Your fortune is rolling up, rolling up like an avalanche! You must keep up with it! You must distribute it faster than it grows!" Which seems to suggest that among the things that distinguished the new philanthropy was an awareness of the age. At least some of the givers knew they had to calm this menacing concern and anger.

The new form of charity birthed by this era was the private foundation, which, Reich argues, was different from the charities of the past, both in scale and in nature. It was

> an entity with broad and general purposes, intended to support other institutions and indeed to create and fund new organizations (e.g., research institutes), seeking to address root causes of social problems rather than deliver direct services (work "wholesale" rather than "retail"), and designed to be administered by private, self-governing trustees, with paid

professional staff, who would act on behalf of a public mission. One other aspect of these foundations was new: their vast resources enabled them to operate on a scale unlike other, more ordinary endowments.

These foundations were, in other words, allowing a small handful of wealthy people like Carnegie and Rockefeller to commit monumental sums of money to the public good and thus gain a say in the nation's affairs that rivaled that of many public officials. Vast new foundations concerned themselves not with niche causes so much as with the general welfare of mankind, much like states. The new philanthropy was professionally managed by an entity analogous to a corporation, and, like governments, it was advised by experts, unlike the more willy-nilly voluntary associations. It was important, Rockefeller wrote at the time, to do "this business of benevolence properly and effectively." This emerging philanthropy would be less and less about the local barn-raising Tocqueville witnessed, the coming together to solve common problems, and ever more about "the private redistribution of wealth—usually first earned through private capitalist profitmaking—through a 'nonprofit sector,'" writes Jonathan Levy, a historian at the University of Chicago.

Despite the scale of the new generosity, there were criticisms. One had to do with how the money being given had been made. The new foundations were troubling, as Reich puts it, "because they represented the wealth, potentially ill-gotten, of Gilded Age robber barons." When Rockefeller proposed to establish his benevolent foundation to deal with his avalanche of money, powerful voices resisted, railing that the money was tainted by its origins. "No amount of charities in spending such fortunes can compensate in any way for the misconduct in acquiring them," said President Theodore Roosevelt. Memories remained fresh of Rockefeller's less-than-benevolent monopoly in oil and less-than-benevolent allergy to labor unions. Charles and Mary Beard wrote of the robber barons' "raw plutocracy," of how they "writhed and twisted, casting about for more respectable mantles of security and atonement." In the muckraking reporter Matthew Josephson's 1934 history *The Robber Barons*, a term he is credited with coining, he wrote of how they "hastened to confer substantial parts of the booty taken in successful raids, as if fearing that God would be angry unless much money was paid."

Other criticism focused on how the new philanthropy not only laundered cruelly earned money but also converted it into influence over a democratic society. Reich writes that the new foundations "were troubling because they were considered a deeply antidemocratic institution, an entity that could exist in perpetuity and that was unaccountable except to a hand-picked assemblage of trustees." He cites as illustration the criticism of the Reverend John Haynes Holmes, a Unitarian minister who was a longtime chairman of the American Civil Liberties Union:

> I take it for granted that the men who are now directing these foundations—for example, the men who are representing the Rockefeller foundation—are men of wisdom, men of insight, of vision, and are also animated by the very best motives. . . . My standpoint is the whole thought of democracy. . . . From this standpoint it seems to me that this foundation, the very character, must be repugnant to the whole idea of a democratic society.

As Reich points out, it is rare to hear such criticisms today. "We have come a long way in one hundred years," he writes. "Philanthropists are today widely admired, and the creation of foundations by the wealthy meets not with public or political skepticism but with civic gratitude." It is hard to imagine an American president or very many influential journalists condemning rich people for giving their money away. Indeed, in cases of exceptions to that rule among journalists, the rule is quickly reinforced by other journalists. When David Callahan, the founder of the website Inside Philanthropy and one of few influential chroniclers of the field with a critical bent of mind, recently published *The Givers*, a book on the subject, the attitude of his *New York Times* reviewer, a fellow journalist, revealed the benefits these givers have reaped from a century of persuasion: "Many readers will be ready to throw up their hands in exasperation. So now we're supposed to fret about rich people being too socially conscious? What exactly does this guy want?"

It might have seemed unimaginable in the early twentieth century, when the concern about philanthropists was common, that by the early twenty-first century journalists could shoot down colleagues for criticizing elite power. But in those days, unlike today, giving back didn't purchase immunity for the giver. It didn't make people smile and bite their tongues about the money's origins. It didn't make journalists feel bad for the rich and rush to their defense. It didn't silence questions about the system in which the wealth was generated. The culture in which giving achieved these things had to be invented and spread. Eventually it was, and among the foundational intellectual contributions to the new culture was an 1889 essay by Andrew Carnegie, a man with a great interest in how philanthropy would come to be seen.

Carnegie's essay, titled "Wealth" and more widely known as his "gospel of wealth," helped to found a new vision of philanthropy that not only rebutted the kinds of criticisms that he and others had faced, but effectively delegitimized critics and questioned their right to question. Carnegie set out to explain away all the grisly things he and other big givers had done to make the money, and to temper the concerns about private power over public affairs in a democracy. What the critics seemed to desire was a world in which the Carnegies and Rockefellers were less extreme in their taking phase, which would leave them with less to give away, and thus limit the amount of authority they wielded. If Carnegie was to counter this, he would have to argue that a time of extreme taking followed by a time of extreme giving was better than the alternative.

Carnegie's gospel, published in the *North American Review*, deftly began by naming the problems on the critics' minds. He argued that inequality was the undesirable but inevitable cost of genuine progress. The "conditions of human life have not only been changed, but revolutionized," he wrote. Inequality is a better thing than it may seem, Carnegie explained: "The contrast between the palace of the millionaire and the cottage of the laborer with us to-day measures the change which has come with civilization. This change, however, is not to be deplored, but welcomed as highly beneficial." Stratification was the price of the onward chugging of progress.

Of course, even if inequality was the price of progress, the rising millionaires of the age didn't have to extract quite so much from their industries, and pay the laborers quite so little. Refraining from such greed would allow the laborers to upgrade from cottages, if not to palaces, then at least to decent houses. Carnegie rejected this. There is no choice, he said, but to operate in the most aggressive, if miserly, way, lest you go out of business:

> Under the law of competition, the employer of thousands is forced into the strictest economies, among which the rates paid to labor figure prominently, and often there is friction between the employer and the employed, between capital and labor, between rich and poor.

This is the first step of Carnegie's intellectual two-step: If you want progress, you have to let rich people make their money however they can, even if it widens inequality. Businesspersons deserve this permission, he said, because "this talent for organization and management is rare among men." Its methods aren't to be questioned. Carnegie wrote:

> We accept and welcome therefore, as conditions to which we must accommodate ourselves, great inequality of environment, the concentration of business, industrial and commercial, in the hands of a few.

Lest there be doubt that these industrial stewards know best, Carnegie said their talent is "proved by the fact that it invariably secures for its possessor enormous rewards." In other words, rich people must be freed to make money however they can, because when they are, they tend to make a lot of money, which in turn brings progress for all.

In this way, Carnegie effectively declared the economic system that generates wealth off-limits for the discussion. It was now time to turn to the giving half of the gospel:

> The question then arises,—and, if the foregoing be correct, it is the only question with which we have to deal,—What is the proper mode of administering wealth after the laws upon which civilization is founded have thrown it into the hands of the few?

Considering various ways to give away wealth, Carnegie derided the two most common approaches: giving to descendants and giving after death. The former approach bred feeble children. The latter wasted many years of potential helping while a benefactor waited to die. Carnegie, in fact, unlike many rich people then and now, believed in a punitive estate tax that would encourage philanthropy: "Of all forms of taxation, this seems the wisest." If the rich knew that much of the money would vanish upon their deaths, they might be persuaded to donate it to good causes during their lifetimes.

Actively giving one's own wealth away was the only approach Carnegie supported, because wealth, in his view, belonged to the community. Keeping was hoarding. A rich man should practice "modest, unostentatious living, shunning display or extravagance." Of what wealth remained, he was "the mere agent and trustee for his poorer brethren." Hoarding was thus akin to thieving the public:

> Men who continue hoarding great sums all their lives, the proper use of which for public ends would work good to the community, should be made to feel that the community, in the form of the state, cannot thus be deprived of its proper share.

Here the justifier of extreme taking had laid out a doctrine of extreme giving. It isn't just good to give to the public. Money that you don't need and that the public could employ *isn't really your money*. Carnegie was proposing an extreme idea of the right to make money in any which way, and an extreme idea of the obligation to give back. "It is a strange, seemingly contradictory picture," writes Levy, the historian. "Carnegie at his desk, writing one letter to his lieutenants at the Carnegie Steel Company, imploring them to slash wages, then writing another to one of his philanthropic lieutenants, giving his wealth (the profits earned by slashing those wages) away at his own discretion."

For Carnegie, then, inequality was a brief state between the taking and giving phases. Giving back, he wrote, is "the true antidote for the temporary unequal distribution of wealth, the reconciliation of the rich and the poor—a reign of harmony." This idea of temporary inequality is vital: For Carnegie, inequality is transitional—a necessity for progress, but soon reversible thanks to the fruits of that progress.

Carnegie seemed to anticipate the objection that the poor might not need so much help had they been better paid. Dripping with paternalism, he defended the necessity of temporary inequality. "Wealth, passing through the hands of the few, can be made a much more potent force for the elevation of our race than if it had been distributed in small sums to the people themselves," he wrote. By "small sums," he makes clear in the ensuing sentences, he is referring to wages. Citing the case of Peter Cooper—industrialist turned philanthropist and the founder and namesake of Cooper Union in Manhattan—Carnegie wrote:

Much of this sum if distributed in small quantities among the people, would have been wasted in the indulgence of appetite, some of it in excess, and it may be doubted whether even the part put to the best use, that of adding to the comforts of the home, would have yielded results for the race, as a race, at all comparable to those which are flowing and are to flow from the Cooper Institute from generation to generation.

Carnegie believed that he could not pay workers well, could not be sentimental about how many hours of work were too many, for that would hurt the public interest. But he could give back to the workers. He financed libraries, museums, and other public amenities for the eventual pleasure and edification of his underpaid workers. He wrote:

> Thus is the problem of Rich and Poor to be solved. The laws of accumulation will be left free; the laws of distribution free. Individualism will continue, but the millionaire will be but a trustee for the poor; intrusted for a season with a great part of the increased wealth of the community, but administering it for the community far better than it could or would have done for itself.

This is the compromise, the truce, distilled: Leave us alone in the competitive marketplace, and we will tend to you after the winnings are won. The money will be spent more wisely *on* you than it would be *by* you. You will have your chance to enjoy our wealth, in the way we think you should enjoy it.

Here lay the almost constitutional principles that one day would govern MarketWorld giving: the idea that after-the-fact benevolence justifies anything-goes capitalism; that callousness and injustice in the cutthroat souk are excused by later philanthropy; that giving should not only help the underdogs but also, and more important, serve to keep them out of the top dogs' hair—and, above all, that generosity is a substitute for and a means of avoiding the necessity of a more just and equitable system and a fairer distribution of power.

One hundred twenty-seven years after Carnegie's essay was published, everyone at a charity gala in New York seems to have internalized its core principles. The organization raising money helps troubled, vulnerable, and poor New Yorkers find work, housing, skills, companionship, and safety. The whole night is divided into two types of performances from the stage. The young and the helped, mostly black and brown, repeatedly dance for their donors. Then, between performances, older white men are brought up to praise them and to talk about, and be applauded for, their generosity to the program.

Most of the men work in finance. They include the corporate raiders who, seeking to raise profits by cutting costs, have helped to do away with stable employment. They are the gentrifiers who have pushed real estate prices through the roof and made it harder for families like those of the young dancers to maintain a livelihood in the city. They are the beneficiaries of tax laws that give carried interest a major break and help to keep the public coffers low and the schools attended by the city's poor underfunded, thus driving them into the streets and occasionally, when they are lucky, into the charity's arms. But these men have been generous, and in exchange for their generosity, these issues will not come up. No one will say what could be said: that these precarious lives could be made less precarious if the kind of men who donated to this program made investments differently, operated companies differently, managed wealth differently, donated to politicians differently, lobbied differently, thought differently about pretending to live in Florida to avoid a minor New York City tax—if, in other words, they were willing to let go of anything dear. It is one night in one city, but it speaks of a broad, unstated immunity deal: Generosity entitles the winners to exemption from questions like these.

On his way to the top of the philanthropic world, Darren Walker had attended more galas of that type than he could count, and had endured his share of wealthy white people saying nice things about him while refusing to see a connection between their lives and the nearly inescapable life that he had escaped. And this was one way to explain the letter he wrote challenging the immunity deal, to explain how he mustered the gall to break the taboo.

"Look at Darren," he mimicked his admirers cooing. "Why can't they all be like Darren? I mean, look at Darren. He had a single mother. He put himself through school. You know, he never had a father. He didn't even know who his father is." The question that his life raised for them was: Why couldn't all poor people end up like Darren Walker?

"Part of my job," he told me one day in his Ford Foundation office, "is to remind them why they can't all be like me—what we have done to make it harder for people like me, with my background, with my heritage, to be able to end up with my story—and how, systematically, we are completely making it impossible for stories like mine to continue to emerge in the years ahead because we're doing horrible things now. And I feel like I need to do that. I just feel like I need to do that."

This impulse had taken a long time to develop, though, because at first Walker was not a natural critic of the philanthropic complex so much as a natural poster child for its good works. He was born in Louisiana, at the Lafayette Charity Hospital. The rich families had their own hospitals and clinics, and the poor whites and African Americans were tended by institutions of charity. Walker's mother found herself in a harsh predicament: a black mother "in this small town, not married, had two babies with this man, and, obviously, he's not going to marry her," Walker said. His mother, "who was wonderful, and perhaps challenged in many, many ways, had the foresight and the ambition" to realize: "I need to get out." She moved the family to Liberty County, Texas, to the town of Ames—the county's "Negro town," as Walker put it.

Walker's mother studied to become a nurse's assistant and soon earned her certificate. She always worked, but it was not enough to keep poverty at bay. Walker remembers being at their tiny house and the electric man or the telephone man coming by to cut off service on their past-due account, and he would negotiate with them, ask for a grace period or at least enough time for his mother to go out, cash her check, and return.

One day, a woman showed up at the home asking if she could register Darren for something called Head Start. His mother agreed, not knowing much about it. Here was charity again blessing Walker, but charity that functioned as a humble complement to government action. Starting in the 1920s, the Rockefellers and other donors had funded research on children. Much of it was based at the University of Iowa's Child Welfare Research Station, where scholars established the then-controversial idea that children's success depended more on the opportunities given to them than on heredity. These researchers had made their case quietly and in the shadows of politics over decades. Then, what began as charity became public policy when, on May 18, 1965, President Lyndon B. Johnson stood in the Rose Garden of the White House and announced a new initiative to ensure "that poverty's children would not be forevermore poverty's captives." Within weeks, the government would open 2,500 preschool programs, aiming to reach 530,000 children. The goal was to prepare them to attend school in the autumn, and to treat the tens of thousands of them who had health impediments. One of the first half million enrollees would be Walker.

He also benefited from the kindness and wisdom of a schoolteacher named Mrs. Majors, who told Walker he was talented but that his behavior risked his being placed in special ed, where the system sent too many black boys, who from there traveled with near inevitability down a pipeline into prison. Mrs. Majors's sociological insight was sound: "Six of my cousins, my male cousins, have been in prison," Walker says. "One of them committed suicide in prison. All of them were in this pipe." Mrs. Majors's warning helped him turn himself around.

His path showed him the power of interventions large and small to transform individual lives. But there were moments along the way which reminded him that nothing changed if you didn't change the system as a whole. For example, when he was twelve, he worked as a busboy out of necessity—to supplement his mother's paycheck in order to keep their household afloat. (Years later, he would tell the trustees of the Ford Foundation, who were considering him as a potential leader, that the restaurant job had prepared him for the role more than any of the others he had had.) Given his age, he might have been working illegally, and he felt something visceral and dark in the job. He felt what it was like to live on the margins of human society. The restaurant took the long-standing but abstract facts of his life and staged them as a vivid performance. "You walk around a room where there is excess and plentifulness and people of economic means who actually have the disposable income to go out and eat and pay more than what the food actually cost to have a meal and drink nice wine," Walker said. "And you walk around on the periphery of that room, and you are invisible. You're invisible even when you are taking away the plates and cleaning up after people. You're invisible. No one says, 'Thank you.' No one acknowledges your presence. And that experience, for me, remains the most profound and the most important."

Still, he bought into the American story that exceptional individuals can work, and buy, their way out of powerlessness. As his cousins circulated in and out of prison, he made it to the University of Texas at Austin, where he earned undergraduate and law degrees. He joined the international law firm of Cleary Gottlieb Steen & Hamilton. He moved to UBS, the financial services firm, where for seven years he worked in the capital markets division. He quit and took a year off to volunteer in Harlem, feeling the pull of social uplift. The experience of helping families like his own moved him. He joined the Abyssinian Development Corporation, a community development organization in Harlem, and focused on the building of public housing and a public school. Then he moved on to the Rockefeller Foundation, where he was told by a colleague that he wasn't the usual "Rockefeller type," not because he was black—it was a new day—but because he was gay. Finally, he landed the Ford job, overseeing a multibillion-dollar investment portfolio.

In keeping with his official position and his own joyous magnetism, his careful irreverence, his attention to everyone in a room, he soared into the upper echelons of New York society. He was a member of the Council on Foreign Relations. He was on the boards of the city's ballet, of Rockefeller Philanthropy Advisors, of Friends of the High Line. He began to be first-name-dropped. *You know, Darren was saying the other day . . . Darren and I were on a panel, and . . .* One day he would be at a White House state dinner for the Chinese president; another day he would be in Silicon Valley helping Mark Zuckerberg reflect on his giving.

Even as he was establishing himself in big philanthropy, there were constant reminders of what his and his colleagues' efforts were persistently failing to change. He was at a gala one night when he received a text from his sister with photographs from the funeral of his aunt Bertha. In one of the pictures, Walker noticed a cousin of his. He was wearing a prison jumpsuit, and an unknown white man was standing behind him. Walker texted back: "What is with that?" She answered that in Louisiana they sometimes let you out of prison for a relative's funeral. You pay a service fee, and a police officer comes with you. On another day, another message, another funeral. A different cousin of his had died. The cousin's family had no money, and so Walker's mother covered the cost—using the credit card that Walker pays for her.

The dissonance with his own life grew louder with time, as did his questioning about his complicity. His compensation was to be $789,000 that year; he wore fabulous clothes, had billionaire friends, attended lavish galas, dined at sumptuous restaurants, lived in a luxurious condominium on Madison Square Park, which was sweetened by a tax abatement that he did not need. The tax abatement bothered Walker; it played into his guilt. He lived among millionaires and billionaires who had secured for themselves a tax break for their apartments and his—money that could have been invested in his cousins and all those others he had left behind in Texas. Would he or anyone else, however principled, renounce the tax break? Of course not. That's why he had begun to feel a need to talk about systems. "Why do we live in a society where that can happen?" he asked. "And what do we need to fix that? And we who are privileged ought to be engaged in that, because we can't say, on the one hand, 'Isn't it horrible, this affordable-housing crisis we have in New York?,' and then, by the same token, accept a system that is essentially corrupt."

He mused, "I really wonder about my own privilege, and am I too comfortable in it?" He said his guilt "definitely nags at me on a daily basis."

Social scientists speak of "idiosyncrasy credits," a kind of resource that a leader earns, which allows him or her from time to time to innovate on, or even defy, group norms. Walker had been working hard at racking up credits. "As you're working your way up, you have to be nuanced, and you have to pick those battles," he said. Now, at Ford, he had reached that pinnacle. "People return my calls. I don't have to go to see Bob Rubin and Roger Altman. They come to the Ford Foundation." In fact, the two men, who had rotated in and out of the highest levels of government and finance for decades, had just walked out of his office.

Walker's new status made him ask himself what he could do with it, how he could "leverage" his position on the inside of the circle to help those he had left behind on the outside. That was what he meant by his answer to one of the trustees' questions during his interview for the Ford role. He was asked, "What kind of president will you be?" To which he answered, "I would want to use the platform of being president of the Ford Foundation to really deeply interrogate the structures and systems and cultural practices in our country that increase the likelihood of more inequality in our society and of more exclusion and marginalization of people, particularly low-income people, people of color."

Walker knew the kind of world he wanted to fight for, and knew there were many different ways to go about it. One was to drop out of the stratosphere into which he had risen, to quit what he called the "globetrotting jet set of people going from Davos to Bellagio to Aspen, talking about solving poverty." Walker did struggle with the "contradiction in that," and yet he was also realistic about who he was, which was some combination of the angry busboy and the UBS banker. What he could do, he concluded, was persuade winners who had let him inside their gates. He could convince them that many of the stories they told themselves and others weren't true, and that these false stories had dire consequences. When stripped of those stories, perhaps a new conversation about equality, and a fair society, would be possible. Perhaps they would see the self-preservational quality of so many of their approaches to social change. Perhaps.

Walker's letter went online in October 2015. It began to ricochet around the philanthropic world, some people receiving the same email from three or four different people. It shook up the giving universe and got people talking.

Walker's new gospel began where he had to begin, with Carnegie. That text was, Walker said, "the intellectual charter of modern philanthropy, and its basic precepts remain the underpinning of U.S. giving and, in turn, have greatly influenced an era of burgeoning philanthropic enterprise around the world." At the heart of Carnegie's essay, as Walker read it, was the idea of extreme inequality as "an unavoidable condition of the free market system" and of philanthropy as an effective remedy.

You can picture an executive at KKR reading this and nodding. *Yeah, exactly, unavoidable.* But then Walker began to go off script. The giving world, he wrote, needed "to openly acknowledge and confront the tension inherent in a system that perpetuates vast differences in privilege and then tasks the privileged with improving the system." Here Walker was already breaking the Carnegie pact. He was questioning the idea of the rich as the best and rightful administrators of the surplus of the society. He was refusing to confine his analysis to what happens after fortunes are made in the marketplace. He was interested in how those fortunes are made and what choices have occasioned them. "What underlying forces drive the very inequality whose manifestations we seek to ameliorate?" he asked.

Walker suggested that "we are crashing into the limits of what we can do with a nineteenth-century interpretation of philanthropy's founding doctrine." And he said Martin Luther King Jr. might offer a useful complement to Carnegie's encrusted ideas, with his call to laud philanthropy while not ignoring "the circumstances of economic injustice which make philanthropy necessary."

King had argued that the circumstances of economic injustice, when examined, had something to do with the people in power, and that true generosity might mean restrained taking, not just the belated shedding of some of what had been taken. Inequality, by Carnegie's lights, was a natural by-product of progress. The economy changes, a new technology is invented, and some figure out how to seize on it, and their wealth surges, and others are left in their humble cottages. Walker complicated this picture by arguing that "inequality is built on antecedents—preexisting conditions ranging from ingrained prejudice and historical racial, gender, and ethnic biases to regressive tax policies that cumulatively define the systems and structures that enable inequality to fester." He was suggesting that people aren't left behind and left out because they fail to take advantage of change. Many are born doomed because of who they or their parents or great-great-grandparents were, because of where they live, because of their color or disabilities—and because of the political choices the society has made about how to treat them. This, in Walker's view, made it important to go beyond Carnegie's idea of temporary inequality as the price of progress. Wealthy individuals needed to ask themselves, "Is the playing field on which I accumulated my wealth level and fair? Does the system privilege people like me in ways that compound my advantages?" Were the rich, as Carnegie had presented them, the transitory guardians of progress's fruits, or were they hereditary hoarders of that progress?

Walker was arguing that the society must have a say not only in what happens to great wealth, but also in how great wealth comes to be. Without that, in his telling, the philanthropist is fighting against himself: perpetuating, even worsening, by day the very suffering he seeks to soothe after dusk.

The privileged, Walker went on, now benefit from the further advantage of having their language and mentality dominate other domains, including the giving world. They no longer just enjoy the privilege of nice homes and cars; they also now have a say over how so many public problems are solved. "When we talk about economic inequality," he said, "we might acknowledge an underlying, unspoken hierarchy, in which we relate everything back to capital. In most areas of life, we have raised market-based, monetized thinking over all other disciplines and conceptions of value."

Walker was presenting the power of the big giver as dangerous. Foundations like his were hobbled by "inherited, assumed, paternalist instincts." Western givers tended to treat recipients in poor countries as subjects to be ordered around, as implementers rather than partners. Big philanthropy needed to get better at "modeling the kind of equality we hope to achieve by listening, and learning, and lifting others up." Walker wrote that foundations—built, like Ford, on the fortunes of powerful people, often wielding enormous power themselves—needed to ask hard questions about their own authority and remove from reality: "How does our privilege insulate us from engaging with the most difficult root causes of inequality and the poverty in which it ensnares people?"

In two thousand words, Walker had shaken the intellectual platform on which MarketWorld philanthropy had long stood. The publication of the letter marked a reconciliation of his long dissonance. Like Hilary Cohen and Amy Cuddy, he had both worked the system and worried about it, had grappled with how to position himself relative to it, whether to be quiet, or walk away, or challenge it. The letter only mattered because he had worked the system long enough and well enough to rise to the presidency of the Ford Foundation. But the letter could perhaps only have been written by a man who had known the wrong end of that system before he ascended it, and who refused to let himself enjoy the climb without also making it useful.

.   .   .

The Lincoln wormed up Third Avenue in thick midday traffic as Walker thought through the proper approach for KKR. The nature of his burden had been inverted by the issuance of his new gospel. Now that he had spoken one of the more uncomfortable truths in his arena, his task had changed: It was to stay in the game, to keep the powerful listening, to challenge his plutocrat friends without scaring them away.

As the Lincoln surged some inches and halted and surged again, Walker pondered the pushback he got from these friends—the pleas to "stop ranting at inequality," to speak of "opportunity" instead. He wondered what the criticism was telling him. Were these rich people aligned with his ideals deep down, wanting the same kind of society he wanted but preferring gentler, more inviting language for it? Or did he and they want fundamentally different things?

At first he defended them, revealing the openheartedness that had won their confidence over the years. They may not use his language of inequality, he said, but "they actually would say, 'No, I *do* want a world where there's opportunity.'" He understood their uneasiness about the word "inequality," and why some of his friends felt he was "hassling" them. It was because, for so many of the winners he had come to know, their narrative of themselves was not of privilege but struggle. "I'm not some privileged kid," he imagined them saying. "I'm working my ass off. I'm busting my ass out here pitching to these jerks, trying to raise money from them or trying to sell my widgets or whatever it is. So don't tell me I'm privileged. I'm getting up every day at four o'clock and on the train from Rye and coming to New York, da-da-da."

A moment later, he reconsidered his own magnanimity. "I think it's hard, often, for them to want what I want," he said. "It's hard to reconcile, because what I want means they would have to give up something. And so the crux of it is, in order to reduce inequality, we actually have to talk about redistribution. We have to talk about equity. And that will impact them." What he wanted, and what he had spent a long time earning the chance to call for, was a reining in of the power of people like them. He wanted them to pay higher taxes. He wanted them to give up their legacy preferences at the leading universities. He said, "All my friends who want to talk about education, you say, 'Let's talk about legacy programs. Do we really think legacy preferences, when we're getting rid of affirmative action—shouldn't we be getting rid of legacy?' Oh, hell no. People will be like, 'Oh, absolutely not.'"

What might have worried his critics the most was Walker's view that moneymaking had to change. It was one thing to say that rich people needed to pay higher taxes and stop sneaking their children into Harvard; it was another to suggest, as he now did, that the very industry he was about to visit was predatory. "One of the fundamental challenges of private equity is so much of what they are about is efficiency and extracting value from their portfolio companies. And what that translates into is generating more productivity with less expense. So, basically, firing people, laying people off," he said. "We know the productivity of the last twenty years has been not to the benefit of workers. Workers' income is flat." Those resources were "extracted," he said, and now show up as returns for firms like KKR. Some of that money will end up in charity, soothing the wounds it helped to cut.

If this was what Walker planned to say at KKR, it would surely be one of the more lively of their guest-speaker luncheons.

In spite of these ideas, Walker had a chance that few did to persuade an audience like this, because he knew how to talk to them and because he didn't believe they were bad people. He did not malign them. He thought that they were trapped, as so many people in MarketWorld are, in a false dogma. He distilled the dogma thus: "You go out there and you make as much money as you can in the world, and you do all you can to make our capitalist system work—and then you're a philanthropist. It's phased, and it's compartmentalized."

What he had learned from observing the rich was how the dogma made it easier to feel like a good person. "Compartmentalizing is a means of coping," he said in the back of the limo. "And so, sure, there are things that they know, they see, on a daily basis that must, if they've got any morality, appall them." But they tell themselves that "in my spare time, I'm going to be on that board in that school up in Harlem; or I'm going to mentor these three black boys in Bed-Stuy, and I'm going to get them to Yale." It makes them feel like decent citizens. "The problem with it," Walker said, "is that it allows you to park the part of your brain and your morality and your humanity that would make you demand something else of yourself and of the system."

There are few families in modern American life who embody everything Walker was discussing as well as the Sacklers. They are one of the country's richest families, and their lives intersected with Walker's at various points in the philanthropic galaxy: organizations he and they have donated to; an award he had received from a museum of which Elizabeth Sackler was a trustee. The Sacklers were Carnegie's old gospel incarnate: Give and give, honorably, thoughtfully, abundantly, and expect in return that questions will not be asked about the money's origins and the system that let it be made.

The Sackler brothers—Elizabeth's father, Arthur; Raymond; and Mortimer—were doctors and cofounders of a pharmaceutical company that would come to be called Purdue Pharma. The brothers made large gifts to the Metropolitan Museum of Art (which opened a Sackler wing as a result), the Guggenheim, and the American Museum of Natural History in New York; the Smithsonian Institution's Asian art museum in Washington, D.C., which boasted "some of the most important ancient Chinese jades and bronzes in the world"; the Tate Gallery and Royal College of Art in London; the Louvre in Paris; the Jewish Museum in Berlin; Columbia, Oxford, Edinburgh, Glasgow, and Salzburg universities; and the medical school at Tel Aviv University.

The brothers gave not only in their personal capacity; their company was also admirably generous to the communities in which it operated. It offered grants to local groups to "encourage the healthy development of youth by reducing high-risk behaviors, such as substance abuse." It supported organizations that "improve quality of life at a national level and in our own communities." It funded education programs to "help medical professionals recognize and reduce medication abuse." In the shadow of its headquarters in Connecticut, it funded the Stamford Boys & Girls Club, a provider of services to the homeless, a library, the Stamford Palace Theatre, the Connecticut Ballet, the Stamford Symphony, the Stamford Chamber of Commerce, the Business Council of Fairfield County, the Stamford Museum and Nature Center, the Maritime Aquarium, United Way, and Making Strides Against Breast Cancer.

In the hubs of power and influence in America and around the world, it was difficult to avoid the generous legacy of the Sacklers. But Walker had now raised the question of whether the givers were obliged not only to contribute to solutions but also to answer about their role in causing the problems.

In business, the Sacklers had engaged in practices that at first raised eyebrows and eventually summoned serious legal problems. Arthur Sackler was, according to the *New York Times*, "widely given credit (some would say blame) for creating many of the drug industry's more aggressive marketing techniques—for example, holding conferences for doctors in which attendees learn about the efficacy of the sponsoring company's drugs." That legacy of aggressive drug marketing affected the promotion of many different medicines, but it was particularly consequential for Purdue Pharma and its affiliated companies, and for American society, in the case of a painkiller called OxyContin, which it began to sell in 1996. OxyContin is a forceful narcotic that provides up to twelve hours of respite from serious pain. At first it was marketed as a breakthrough, with a time-release formulation that made it less likely to foster addiction and abuse.

"That claim," the *Times* reports, "became the linchpin of the most aggressive marketing campaign ever undertaken by a pharmaceutical company for a narcotic painkiller." In addition to the wining and dining at conferences, the marketers of OxyContin, including

Purdue's partner Abbott Laboratories, were ingenious in their pursuit of doctors—including in the case of an orthopedic surgeon who wouldn't give the drug reps his time, until they discovered his weakness, according to *STAT,* a medical publication. "We were told by his nurses and office staff that the best way to capture his attention and develop our relationship was through junk food," the drug reps noted in a memo disclosed by *STAT.* The reps were swift to act on the advice. An Abbott rep showed up the following week, according to *STAT,* bearing a box of donuts and other treats. The sweets had been specially arrayed to spell the word "OxyContin." This time, the reps got the ear of the doctor. "Every week after that, the Abbott sales personnel visited the doctor to ask him to switch at least three patients to OxyContin from other painkillers," *STAT* reported.

Purdue also pursued a strategy of promoting OxyContin to general practitioners, who tended to have the disadvantage (or advantage, depending on your viewpoint) of less training than specialists such as orthopedic surgeons in treating serious pain and in detecting signs of painkiller abuse by patients. There are also, of course, many more general practitioners than there are such specialists. This huge marketing blitz for OxyContin took Purdue from being a small drug maker in the mid-1990s to earning nearly $3 billion in sales in 2001. Four-fifths of that was from OxyContin.

Oxy, as it came to be called, was a powerful new weapon against pain, but it also swiftly became a widely abused street drug. It was meant to be swallowed, which allowed for the extended release. But, the *Times* wrote, "both experienced drug abusers and novices, including teenagers, soon discovered that chewing an OxyContin tablet or crushing one and then snorting the powder or injecting it with a needle produced a high as powerful as heroin." And so Oxy-Contin began to be implicated in a growing number of overdoses and deaths, concentrated in rural areas down on their luck. These deaths around the turn of the millennium turned out to be early signs of what years later would come to be called a national "opioid epidemic." As the *New Yorker* reports, "though many fatal overdoses

have resulted from opioids other than OxyContin, the crisis was initially precipitated by a shift in the culture of prescribing—a shift
carefully engineered by Purdue." Eventually, the Centers for Disease
Control and Prevention would report that overdose deaths from
prescription opioids quadrupled between 1999 and 2014, claiming
fourteen thousand lives in that last year. That same year, nearly two
million Americans "abused or were dependent on prescription opioids," and a quarter of patients who used the drugs for noncancer
purposes battled addiction. The opioids were sending more than a
thousand people a day to emergency rooms. And in online forums,
people traded notes about the best ways to get the best highs without
killing themselves:

RE: CHEW OR SWALLOW WHOLE?

just keep in mind your tolerance will grow very very quickly!!!
    I ate 2 x 80;'s today since 10am and snorted 1 as of 10pm.
    Thats with 3 yrs experience and I suffer from 2 major
conditions that require pain treatment, but 2.5 or 2.25 could do
it. I let loose on weekends. and it also varies with how much I
am active. Walking, etc . . .
    Be careful. I started with 4 x 20mg per day. . . . . . and now @
300mg / Day.
    You dont wanna go through withdrawals if you run out man.
if you could have been with me December 24th last year I was
out 1 week early at this level and had to suffer bad. You dont
wanna know.

Sometimes no one sees a massive social problem like this coming. This was not one of those times. In 2001, as sales of OxyContin
and other opioids soared, officials at the state employee health plan
in West Virginia noticed something strange. As the insurer for state
employees, it received paperwork when they died, including the
coroner's account of the cause of death. Officials at the insurer took

note of a rising number of deaths attributed to something called oxycodone, the active ingredient in OxyContin, according to *STAT*. The officials were familiar with the drug, because prescriptions for it were exploding among their clients, who ingested $11,000 worth of it in 1996 and $2 million worth in 2002.

The officials were quick to speak up. They pushed for regulations that would require doctors to secure prior authorization before prescribing OxyContin, which was intended to confine usage of the drug to people who genuinely needed it and to keep it away from known addicts and others with a record of abusing it. But these efforts met furious resistance from Purdue Pharma. *STAT* reported that beating back any attempt to limit OxyContin prescriptions became a "top priority" for Purdue in 2001. A memo obtained by that news outlet, describing the annual goals of the company's West Virginia operation, found "Stop any preauthorization efforts for OxyContin" prominent among them. Another memo mentioned a meeting with officials in West Virginia to "interrupt" any efforts on their part to slow the prescription of OxyContin.

As a former Purdue official explained to *STAT*, "We like to keep prior authorization off of any drug." The official was casting these efforts as flowing from a generic aversion to regulation. Purdue found a clever workaround, using third-party companies known as pharmacy benefits managers to ensure that West Virginians could receive OxyContin without prior authorization. It made an arrangement to pay the benefits managers a "rebate" if they prescribed the drug without that additional safeguard.

Publicly, Purdue worked to project an image in keeping with its charitable spirit and that of its owners—that it existed to help people and was as keen as the state to prevent abuse or harm. Still, according to motions filed by the state's lawyers:

Contrary to the picture of helpfulness and cooperation Purdue attempts to paint, Purdue's employees were actively and secretly trying to prevent West Virginia from imposing any control on the sale of OxyContin.

McDowell County, West Virginia, turned out to be "a proverbial canary in a coal mine when it came to the emerging national opioid crisis," *STAT* noted. Back in 2001, when officials at the insurer first spoke up, the state as a whole was still at 6 deaths per 100,000 residents from opioid overdoses. McDowell was already at 38 per 100,000, however, and its fate foreshadowed West Virginia's, which would see its death rate more than triple in the ensuing decade, giving it the country's highest rate of deaths from overdoses and of painkiller prescriptions in general. Many of those deaths might have been prevented if state officials had not faced the opposition they had to regulating OxyContin prescriptions. The McDowell sheriff, Martin West, said to visiting reporters, "Listen to the scanner here every night. It's first responders out every night going up and down hollers for an overdose. It's pitiful what is going on."

Meanwhile, as other public servants around the country began to worry about the drug's propensity for addiction and abuse, Purdue pushed back, according to the *Times,* "claiming that the drug's long-acting quality made it less likely to be abused than traditional narcotics." The U.S. Department of Justice disagreed: "OxyContin was not what Purdue claimed it was," in the words of John Brownlee, who was then the U.S. attorney in Roanoke, Virginia. "Purdue's assertions that OxyContin was less addictive and less subject to abuse and diversion were false—and the company knew its claims were false. Purdue's misrepresentations contributed to a serious national problem in terms of abuse of this prescription drug." The drug's fraudulent promotion, he added, had "a devastating effect on many communities throughout Virginia and the United States." Brownlee brought charges against Purdue, which in 2007 agreed to settle. It acknowledged that it had marketed OxyContin "with the intent to defraud or mislead," and it agreed to pay $635 million in fines and other outlays.

It was one of the largest fines ever paid in such a case, but only an inconvenience when compared to how lucrative OxyContin was becoming. In 2015 *Forbes* declared the Sackler family the "richest newcomer" to its annual list of wealthy families, with a net worth

of $14 billion. Noting that the family had edged out "storied fami-
lies like the Busches, Mellons and Rockefellers," it asked, "How did
the Sacklers build the 16th-largest fortune in the country? The short
answer: making the most popular and controversial opioid of the
21st century—OxyContin."

Another answer to that question might be: by thwarting the
guardians of the public good every time they tried to protect citizens.
It was later reported that Brownlee had received an unusual phone
call the night before securing Purdue's guilty plea. A senior Justice
Department official, Michael Elston, had called Brownlee on his cell
phone and "urged him to slow down," according to the *Washington Post*. Brownlee rebuffed his superior. "Eight days later," the *Post*
said, "his name appeared on a list compiled by Elston of prosecutors that officials had suggested be fired." It was part of a larger
attempted purge of prosecutors by the administration of George W.
Bush. Brownlee kept his job; Elston lost his amid the controversy of
the list's becoming public. And what had occasioned the phone call?
According to Elston, his boss, a deputy attorney general named Paul
McNulty, had asked him to place the call to Brownlee after receiving a request for more time from a defense lawyer representing a
Purdue executive.

The Sacklers were just one family out of many in America who
might have been inspired by Walker's essay to look at the past. What
Walker was drawing their attention to was not just their own conduct, but the playing field on which they had played, the system in
which their advantages had formed.

Despite the easily available knowledge about Oxy and the Sacklers, MarketWorld embraced the family's do-gooding and kept mum
about the harm. The most common single-word descriptor for
members of the family became "philanthropist."

Generosity is not a substitute for justice, but here, as so often
in MarketWorld, it was allowed to stand in. The institutions that
benefited from the Sacklers' largesse have shown little interest in
demanding that they atone for any role they might have played in
fomenting a national crisis. The generosity tended to be in places

where influential people gathered, whereas the injustice tended to happen out of view, in places like McDowell County, whose storytelling apparatus had little chance of competing with a headline about a gift to the Metropolitan Museum of Art. The generosity was in the millions; the injustice had helped to build a $14 billion fortune. According to the *New Yorker,* "two hundred thousand Americans have died from overdoses related to OxyContin and other prescription opioids" since 1999.

In his letter, Darren Walker, paraphrasing Dr. King, called for givers like the Sacklers not only to give but also to "bend the *demand curve* toward justice." It wouldn't be easy.

The Lincoln was at 49th Street and Third Avenue. Walker was talking about how he tries to reach people—be they philanthropists like the Sacklers, executives like those at KKR, or any of the other wealthy and powerful people among whom he moves.

The key, he said, adopting a pair of beloved modern phrases, is to "meet people where they are" and "not be judgmental." Here he made an analogy that was revealing about Walker's own way of looking at things. When he worked in Harlem, it was hard getting parents to bring kids to medical appointments. There was a temptation to judge and criticize: *Here we are trying to help you, and you can't even get up off your couch.* Walker said he knew that was not the right approach. He knew they would have their own logic, their own story. "You don't knock on the door and say, 'You're a loser. You're a bad . . .' You've got to meet people where they are."

"That's my view writ large," he continued. "And so where we're meeting them"—he was now speaking of the highly privileged—"is where they are, which is they actually believe that they are doing good, they are contributing to our economy. They're contributing to the tax base. They are contributing to philanthropy through their own personal giving and commitments to boards and whatever. So that's where they are."

The analogy is telling, because it illustrates how an ethic of not judging that had developed to protect the weak could serve just as well to guard the strong. Meeting people where they are means one thing when applied to a mother with mental health issues in Harlem, juggling three jobs, two kids, and their appointments. It is quite another thing for the private equity tycoon to enjoy that same suspension of judgment. Should he, like the subaltern, really be met wherever he is?

Ensconced in the Lincoln, Walker said that the concentration of wealth and power in our time was causing "a hollowing out of the middle class" and a "huge blowback of populism, of nationalism, of xenophobia." Around the world, the politics of anger and revenge were on the rise, he said, "because people are truly feeling the pain in a way we have never felt in modern times." Rich people didn't want to talk about that, though. They wanted to talk about opportunity. "Okay, I'll meet you there," Walker said. "Let's talk about opportunity."

Still, it irritated him to sit in a boardroom or living room and hear yet another elderly white tycoon who inherited much of his money explain why "it's not about inequality." He said in the car what he doesn't say to those tycoons but seemed to fantasize about telling them: "You are allowed to live in a world where you don't have to deal with reality." Yet, Walker said again, gearing up for KKR, "I'll meet you where you are."

Many in MarketWorld have no interest in asking themselves Walker's questions about how their money was made. But there are others who are inclined to ask those questions, and yet struggle to let themselves truly go there and escape their own web of justifications.

Kat Cole is the chief operating officer of Focus Brands, the private-equity-owned company behind Cinnabon, Auntie Anne's, Moe's Southwest Grill, Carvel, and other food purveyors. Unlike many philanthropists whose fortunes were already amassed, Cole is an operating businesswoman who still has a chance to follow both the taking and giving aspects of Walker's new gospel. At the same time, her life offers a case study in the reasons and rationalizations that the gospel finds itself up against.

Cole started working at Hooters at seventeen. She joined a business that has long been morally controversial to some for the same reason so many people do: survival. She grew up in Jacksonville, Florida, in a family that was at first middle class. Her parents' household was the only one in the extended clan with two cars. They worked white-collar jobs. Many of their relatives lived in trailer parks and revolved in and out of work (junkyards, factories, trucking), of jail, and of addictive substances. Cole's father was an alcoholic. He was gone all the time, she said, and was no longer a reliable husband or father, leaving his wife miserable and the family unstable.

When Cole was nine, her mother came to her and said, "That's it. I don't know how we're going to do it, but we got to go." As Cole, who prides herself on her pragmatism, remembers it, she didn't even become upset: "I just thought, 'What took you so long?'" Her mother soon headed a much poorer household, with a $10-a-week food budget for herself and three daughters. Their diet was heavy on Spam, potted meat, Beanee Weenees, and sloppy joes. Cole's mother continued to work as a secretary, and took on side jobs nights and weekends. Within a few years, she would remarry and the home would gain some stability. But the years of living close to poverty shaped Kat, who would spend her career wondering about her responsibilities to others without a surfeit of luck or good options.

Cole began selling clothes at the mall when she was fifteen. In her junior year of high school, she took the Hooters job. The following year, she was promoted from hostess to waitress, and in this new role was earning enough to drop the retail job and still save up for college. Though the restaurant promoted its servers' breasts as a selling point, and boasted of being "delightfully tacky, yet unrefined," Cole found it empowering. Here she was, as a high school and then a college student, making as much as $400 a shift. (For the record, Cole insists, against all odds and ads, that "the chain has never promoted breasts," but rather sells "overall sex appeal.")

She was a good and versatile waitress. If someone was needed to come off the floor and sling wings, she could do it. If a bartender went missing, she could tend bar. These skills got her noticed by managers, and when Hooters corporate came looking for talent, her name surfaced. At twenty, she switched to management at head-quarters. She traveled the world opening up new franchises. Her pay and duties grew swiftly year by year. She became a star.

In the roles she would later come to occupy, she would serve as something of a role model for aspiring female leaders, asked to mentor young women and to speak to them at conferences. She was a complicated role model, since she was doing it all for Hooters.

At first, she had seen no contradiction between her own empow-erment through Hooters and the fact of what Hooters was. The chain was part of the Jacksonville landscape. "In Florida, that just wasn't that big of a deal, really," she said. That location had been around since Cole was very young. In high school, it was where everyone ended up on Saturday nights—the baseball guys, the foot-ball guys, the cheerleaders. "It didn't feel foreign, it didn't feel shady, it didn't feel that it was exploiting women, because you'd go in and the girls were having so much fun. And when you're a high school girl and you see these beautiful women that are having fun, they are very much in control in their roles, they're almost little celebrities in their own way, that seemed really aspirational, actually." They also seemed a lot happier than the servers at Applebee's.

Moreover, the company put women in leadership positions, and as it grew, often promoted from within, which much of the time meant turning skimpily clad waitresses into managers. "So my immediate view from the inside was, 'This place is awesome for women,'" Cole said. There were moments when men got drunk and hit on Hooters girls. Cole had friends who worked at Applebee's, though, where the same thing happened, if not as often. "I saw nothing but women's empowerment all around me," she said.

She was enormously grateful for all Hooters had done for her, and defensive on its behalf. When she moved to management and gave out her business cards at a conference, she would watch people look down at that owl logo, and she would see the judgment fill their eyes. She still remembers the woman who said, "How dare you not just work for but be a part of the growth of a company that exploits women!" Cole answered her by telling her something she had come to believe: "We don't exploit women. We employ them."

Cole was laying the foundation for the system of rationalizations that so many businesspeople must construct to quiet their own doubts and the doubts of others. There was tangible good that she could see, and that was enough for her. She did not open herself to questions about her company's negative contributions to a larger system that was abstract and hard to make sense of.

Cole eventually became an executive vice president at Hooters. And when she reached those heights, she rationalized that whatever harm people might perceive was offset by good deeds. She worked on a tuition reimbursement program that helped put women through college. She created a résumé-writing program to help people who were leaving the chain to "articulate the experience they had in the best way that would minimize the judgment we knew they would get."

Eventually, though, Cole decided that she didn't want Hooters to be her "only story." She went back to school, earning an MBA (despite not having a bachelor's degree) on evenings and weekends. She was recruited by a private equity firm and named president of one of its portfolio companies, Cinnabon. Later, she was promoted to a senior executive role at its parent company, Focus Brands. For the Cinnabon job, new rationalizations were needed. Cole was responsible for putting out into the world many food items that people were probably better off avoiding. She rationalized this by insisting on calling Cinnabon a "bakery." She said, "It's literally a bakery, which has been around for centuries." She seemed to hear herself, and she added a point: "We're just adding a shitload more sugar. And that is a meaningful change from the bakeries of two hundred years ago."

This rather audacious rationalization mingled with other, more plausible-sounding ones such as that if there were going to be bad industries, good people should run them. "If in a free-market society there will be demand, whether it's for sugary products or alcohol or scantily clad waitresses in a restaurant concept, then it will exist," she said. "And so if it exists, what matters is the *how*." This rationalization was important, because it suggested not only that it was acceptable for someone like Cole to devote her talent to an organization like Hooters or Cinnabon, but also that it might be preferable to using it somewhere nobler. If places like these were going to exist in a free market, and what mattered was how they were run, then not working there would solve nothing; it would in fact increase the likelihood that the wrong leaders, pursuing the wrong *how*, would end up there in your stead.

Cole also told herself that she had done her duty by leveling with the public about Cinnabon's rolls. She said, "We call it what it is. We tell you it's made full of sugar and fat. It's marketed as an indulgence, and even when I would do media, I would say you shouldn't eat this for breakfast, lunch, and dinner." Once again, it was important to zoom in and ignore the issue of systems and structures, the larger, more complicated issues of poor dietary habits, nutrition options, and obesity.

Cole regarded her attempt at transparency about a harmful product as a more authentic form of corporate virtue than the moral offsetting that Carnegie promoted. She said she steered her brands away from giving back to the very problems they may have helped to cause. Doing that wouldn't be right, in her view: "What is probably disingenuous is to go support the juvenile diabetes foundation." She suggested that telling customers your product is potentially harmful to them and not intended for regular consumption is a better way to "outweigh," in one's moral calculus, the effect of advertising it and selling it to them.

Cole's rationalizations were strongly and sincerely held. If Darren Walker wanted to change the moneymaking system itself, to change how business is conducted, he was not only up against powerful corporate interests and their lobbyists. He was also up against the psychologies of thousands of people like Cole, and a way of looking at life that didn't require cynicism or callousness to commit harm. It was a way of viewing things that inured the viewer to the larger systems around you, that made those systems not your problem.

Some months before Walker's visit to KKR, he was sitting in his office thinking about the award the philanthropist Laurie Tisch would be giving him that evening at the Museum of Modern Art. Tisch would also be "doing a little dinner for eighty afterwards at the St. Regis." And Walker was excited, because, as with the KKR luncheon, he felt that events like this were "opportunities to be disruptive." "Not to say, 'Shame on you, rich people,'" he said, "but to just ask questions and to interrogate and to talk about things that make people uncomfortable like wealth and race and privilege and justice, and the role that we all play in having more or less justice."

Walter Isaacson, the president of the Aspen Institute, one of the temples of MarketWorld, would be interviewing him onstage, and Walker knew exactly what Isaacson would want: Darren Walker's improbable life story. "I can assure you Walter will prompt that, and he always does, and that's fine," Walker said. "That's the idea. And so part of my approach is to give him what he wants. It's to give him the story to remind people that we have lived in a country where people like me can realize their dream." But this was only half of the cocktail Walker wished to deliver: "At the same time, we have to say, 'All right, so you believe in the story, right?'"—he mimicked the coos of the adoring, mostly white crowd—"*Yes, we believe in the story. We believe in* your *story.* And then you have to help people paint a picture that stories like mine won't be nearly as achieved, as realized, in the future. My journey, my story, could never be possible today because of all the things we know. When I got on the mobility escalator, all the things along that journey that helped propel me forward in many ways either aren't there anymore, or are weaker, or in fact they would push me backwards." The delicate art of a night like this, he said, was to make the plutocrats "feel good about America" and make them "feel good about themselves," and, having softened them with those feelings, persuade them that their America has to change.

Tisch is a philanthropist who was already warm to Walker's call for fundamental change and a new conversation about justice—but who also struggled with how to get there. She was an heir to a family fortune that estimates put at $21 billion. Her late father, Preston Robert Tisch, was a founder of the Loews Corporation, where the family made most of its money. It was one of the more visibly generous families in America, especially in New York, where the Tisch name is ubiquitous on the edifices of good causes. Thanks to this giving, Laurie was cochair of the board of trustees of the Whitney Museum of American Art, vice chair of the board of trustees of Lincoln Center, a trustee of the Aspen Institute, and former chair of the Center for Arts Education and the Children's Museum of Manhattan. She was also a co-owner of the New York Giants football team.

By the standards of her fellow plutocrats, Tisch was ambivalent about her fortune. Late one morning not long ago, she sat in a banquette corner at the Regency Bar & Grill at a Loews hotel in New York, talking of why she had always seen herself as an "outlier" in her family. Maybe it was because she grew up the lone female in her generation of Tisches, encircled by two brothers and four male cousins. She was, she said proudly, the first woman born a Tisch, which was a watered-down version of a name too alien-sounding for the America of the early twentieth century, when her grandparents emigrated from Russia, setting down fresh roots in Bensonhurst, Brooklyn.

Tisch, now in her middle sixties, recalled her days as a student at the University of Michigan in the final years of the Vietnam War. She was involved in what she hedgingly called "kind of radical politics"—think campus rallies, "no bomb throwing." She and her comrades tried to bar ROTC from recruiting at Michigan. Although she came from one of the great new fortunes of the era, she says she thought capitalism "was a bad word." One day midway through college, she informed her parents that she was planning to drive to

Washington for a big protest march. "Let me just get this straight," she recalled one of them answering. "So you're going to go to Washington to yell 'Smash the corporations' in the car that we bought? Just sayin'." A car bought thanks to the money from their growing corporation. She ended up not going.

To be Laurie Tisch back then was to be both against the system and the embodiment of the system you were against, and, she said with a laugh, it meant "having a headache all the time." And while her ideas and tactics have evolved over the years, that basic conflict and that headache have never left her.

The conflict filled her with a guilt that grew over the years. It was a guilt that her rich friends seem not to feel or even understand when they tell her to get that facial, jet over to that spa, acquire that painting—"Of course you should do it. You deserve it," she says they tell her. The guilt made her say to herself, "I deserve it because . . . ? Because I inherited a lot of money?" She once mentioned the guilt to Darren Walker, who in fact thought such guilt was justified and had bet his career on the idea that giving isn't enough, but he was too gallant to tell her that. "He kind of talked me down from it," she said. To rebut her sense of complicity in injustice, he praised her generosity: "That's ridiculous. Look at what you're doing!" But even Walker wasn't charming enough to wash the guilt away. Tisch said she has spent most of her life racked by it—"being at war with myself or being a little bit schizophrenic, a little bit tortured." She likes to joke that nonprofits that want to raise money from her should track her credit card bills, because when her spending surges, her guilt rises in tandem, along with her inclination to give back.

For Tisch, though, the guilt was not just an emotional problem to manage. It was also a spur to believe and do the right things, as she saw them. "When are you ever going to get rid of the guilt?" a friend of hers asked long ago. After all, she had given so much. "Hopefully, never," Tisch replied. "It's my compass." The guilt doesn't absolve her of benefiting from a system that she thinks unjust, but it does keep her from forgetting that fact, and it inspires her to do what she can. Among her reasons for starting her personal foundation was, she said, "taking it away from guilt and turning it into something more useful. But it will always be there a little bit." It is there in part because she knows that the giving she does is "not institutional change or systemic change," she said. "I'm going to leave that to my kids."

But if she was being honest, the guilt also gives her something she is reluctant to part with—a sense of superiority over rich people less guilty and more indulgent than she is. Tisch's guilt and feelings of complicity could make her a good target for Walker's new gospel—a gospel centered on a fairer, less guilt-inducing economic system, not just latter-day giving. But when actually confronted with what a different system might mean for her, her instincts of self-protection begin to overwhelm those of guilt.

Does she believe that inheritances should be taxed more heavily than at present—as is the case in many other countries? She squirmed. "I mean, ideally, definitely, there shouldn't be such a gap between the rich and the poor. There shouldn't," she said. But did she believe that the society would have been better off had she not been able to inherit as much as she had? That was harder for her. "I'm lucky that I can do what I can do," she said of the philanthropy that her inheritance has allowed her to engage in. "But do I think it's the most fair system? Probably not."

So, then, should she have been taxed more? Should her children's inheritances be taxed more? "You'd have to be a better student of history than I am," she said. "I mean, that's kind of the aspirational dream." What she seemed to be suggesting was that higher taxes on people like her family were the right idea in theory, but maybe only in theory. And sometimes she was unsure even of that: If rich people's children didn't inherit large fortunes, wouldn't they continue chasing money, going to Wall Street or wherever, and having less time to spend on helping people?

Did she believe that a society with less hereditary wealth would be better? "Would it be better?" she said. "I mean, it's probably better not to be poor."

Could she, then, support such changes? "That's why I said I'm not a student of history, because that's kind of aspirational," Tisch said. In other words, it is a utopian idea that perhaps sounded good, but she maintained that she didn't know enough to embrace it. "But," she added a moment later, "in countries where they're closer to that, is that a better society? Probably."

But places like Scandinavia, where there is less poverty, had, it should be noted, less money lying around for people like Tisch to give away. "You don't need to give away as much," she said. You don't need to treat so many symptoms when the diseases are fewer.

Yet while we have the system we do, was there any way she saw to reconcile her abstract positions with the way she actually lived? She didn't seem to think so. "I guess it's the same, on some level, as our last president or any president being very pro–public education and sending their kids to private school. I don't have an easy answer," she says.

Her life and ideals similarly collide over the question of the influence of wealthy people like her on politics. Does she believe such influence should be curbed? "You think it's great in theory, but you don't want to be the only schmuck doing it," she says. She believed the campaign finance system to be unjust, and understood the link between that injustice and the drowned-out voices and social exclusion that she later seeks to alleviate through philanthropy. And yet when it came to supporting Hillary Clinton's presidential campaign, she said, "how many fund-raisers did I go to at $25,000 and $50,000?" Tisch's ex-husband, Donald Sussman, has been very public in making the case for what may appear to be the twisted logic of the anti-mega-donor mega-donor. Sussman, a hedge fund manager, reportedly contributed $40 million to Democratic super PACs and other outside groups, making him by some accounts Clinton's biggest supporter in 2016. He told the *Washington Post* he was inspired by his wish to remove the influence of big donors like himself. "It's very odd to be giving millions when your objective is to actually get the money out of politics," he told the *Post*. "I am a very strong supporter of publicly financed campaigns, and I think the only way to accomplish that is to get someone like Secretary Clinton, who is committed to cleaning up the unfortunate disaster created by the activist court in *Citizens United*." In order to change the status quo, you have to give in to the status quo.

This difficulty in escaping the status quo was especially evident in Tisch when it came to the aspect of her fortune that gave her the greatest guilt: her cigarette money. In 1968, Loews had "capitalized on growing public health concerns over smoking by buying a cigarette company at a bargain price," as the *New York Times* put it. Its acquisition, Lorillard, produced Newport cigarettes, which were controversial for targeting African Americans with a product more alluring and more lethal than most: laced with a menthol flavor that made it easier to start smoking and a higher-than-average nicotine content that helped keep one hooked. When seven tobacco executives famously sat side by side in Congress in 1994 and denied cigarettes' harmful effects, Laurie's cousin Andrew was one of them. When asked if he thought that smoking and cancer were connected, he said, "I do not believe that." The following year, Laurie's uncle Laurence, then the chairman of CBS, aroused anger when his network killed a *60 Minutes* segment about the tobacco industry whistleblower who would eventually be portrayed in the movie *The Insider*. (The segment ran only after Loews announced its intention to sell the network.)

Laurie Tisch knew these things, and she had to know that people had died because of those cigarettes and those self-serving deceptions. She sometimes thought about the cigarettes when people thanked her for promoting the arts, or investing in young lives, or giving grants to support more healthy food in African American communities like Harlem. It was hard to know whether the debt would ever be repaid, whether the lives saved would ever catch up with the lives that were stolen. But Tisch said she had this guilty reaction when the people thanking her didn't know about the cigarette money. On other occasions, she said, "they do know it, and I get defensive." She wondered aloud, "Are cigarettes worse than alcohol? Is alcohol worse than sugar? So I also get defensive when I get criticized for it—that my family shouldn't give to the hospital

or do this or that." It bothered her when she heard people say that
tobacco money had no place in a hospital dedicated to saving lives.
Why should her family be the only schmucks singled out for harmful products?

Still, Tisch, outfitted with that compass of guilt, ventured past her
own defensiveness. "I do think that good, solid people can generally
rationalize taking advantage of the system," she said. And how do
they rationalize it? By telling themselves that this is the system we
have. "That's how it is," she said. "Why should I be the only fool?"

In her reluctance to be the only fool, Tisch was revealing the
hold that the status quo had on her. Again and again, she had voiced
an ideal for which in the end she was unwilling to sacrifice. It was
important to her to feel superior to her rich friends, but she was
unwilling to rush out in front of them and be the only one not to
take advantage of a system she knew to be wrong. Her repeated
confessions that she will not be the one to bring about the world
that she swears she believes in sent a message to Darren Walker:
If he wants a fairer system, he is going to have to seek it in spite of
people like her, not with them at his side; he might have their moral
support, but he could not count on them to make the decisions to
change the system that made them everything that they are.

"The people who get to take advantage of the system, why would
they really want to change it?" Tisch said at one point. "They'll maybe
give more money away, but they don't want to radically change it."

Was there anything she could imagine that would convince them
otherwise—that could inspire them to pursue a fairer system?

"Revolution, maybe," she said.

At last, Walker's limousine pulled up to 9 West 57th Street, and
he was whisked upstairs. A cheerful receptionist took custody
of his camel overcoat and furry hat. Janice Cook Roberts, who led
investor relations at KKR and is the daughter of the legendary Washington power broker Vernon Jordan, exchanged pleasantries with
Walker about her father. Then Walker ran into another executive,

Ken Mehlman, who helped to advance the Republican Party's anti-gay agenda as its chairman until he came out as gay a few years after stepping down and began to fight for gay rights. Like Carnegie, he had done what he had to do, and was now in the redemption phase, albeit one pursued while working at KKR.

The session was held in a large room with a buffet off to one side. The room was filled with elegant white leather chairs. The crowd was young, mostly junior employees. They had the look of people who are living without rising to the level of being alive. Walker had said that in his experience, many such employees show up at these events because they nurse dreams of quitting and becoming doers of good. Yet for now they carried themselves with a boredom and alienation that was a high-end analog of what one detected in the workers at Walmart. You got into this room by making the right, careful choices over and over again. Like Kat Cole, you learned to zoom in and not ask questions about what larger things you were abetting. And because the firm knew at some level what psychological sacrifice all this demanded, it had the decency to put on a speaker series for you, where museum chieftains and health care experts and this foundation president—people living closer to their truths than you—could inspire you a little. Walker, visibly exuberant about his mission, offered a striking contrast to his audience.

Was he going to tell them they were responsible for the rise of nationalism globally, that the world he wanted would lower them a few pegs? Was he going to say that their business practices were part of the problem, or that they needed to pay higher taxes? Would he "meet them where they were"? Was it possible to do all these things?

On that day, at least, no. Walker, in his opening remarks, referred a few times to Henry Kravis, one of KKR's founders, as "a philan-thropist." He was no longer a corporate raider, a pioneer of the kind of value extraction Walker deplored in the limo. Walker spoke highly of his own experience in the financial services industry. It had given him "skills"—some of which, presumably, were the protocols that he could now tell himself he had redeployed in service of the weak. It taught him how to multitask, manage a complex portfolio of projects, assimilate data and turn it into insight, have discipline. He wasn't flattering his audience. He was reciting the reasons why so many people like Hilary Cohen, who aspired to help millions of people, went to places like KKR before embarking on their work of changing the world.

Walker tried to keep the room comfortable by turning philanthropy into a relative concept. "If you say philanthropy in America, it means a lot of different things," he said. "It means individual philanthropists like Henry, and many people who you know and many of you, because many of you are also philanthropists, even though you may not call yourself a philanthropist."

Eventually, he got to the subject at hand. "We have in America and in the world a level of extreme inequality that—I don't mean to be hyperbolic—but I think really threatens our democracy. Because at the core of the American narrative, in our democracy, is a very simple idea of opportunity." That's how he did it: poking them with a thought that might not have been their favorite, and then quickly meeting them where they were, with the language of opportunity, that MarketWorld staple.

And then, unsurprisingly, he told the story of the charity hospital in Lafayette and all the rest of it. He talked about how there "was a mobility escalator that I could get on," about "the leverage of opportunity in American society." In the car, he had said that the wealthy, believing that America has an opportunity problem but not an inequality one, "are allowed to live in a world where you don't have to deal with reality." Now, in front of a new generation of the "barbarians at the gate," he was meeting them where they were. "The more inequality we get in our system, the less opportunity there is," he said. He closed in more personal terms:

I challenge myself about my own privilege every day and say, "You know, you're incredibly privileged. You have cousins who were definitely as smart as you and they ended up in prison. Why did that happen?" And so everything is a conversation in my own little head about privilege and about being in places like these with people like you, who are clearly smart, ambitious, and want to make a difference in the world and are privileged.

It was not, in fact, evident that the people in the room wanted to "make a difference" in the way that Walker suggested. That became clear when question-and-answer time came. The first question was about his leadership style and how he motivated employees: a businessperson trying to learn from him how to be better at business. The second was about global security. The third was about whether there was too much charitable money chasing too few capable do-gooders. Walker had been subtle, verging on silent, about what he said in the car about private equity's complicity in inequality, about what they needed to do less rather than more of. And his subtlety and their imperviousness had conspired to ensure that he was not really heard.

Back in the limo, Walker said he could tell the group hadn't really grasped or connected with his new gospel material. He had found solace, however, in two women toward the back of the room who were "nodding on all of those issues." He said, "The white guys at the front table, they were, like, sort of motionless." They had been, except when one of them heard a variant of the phrase "paid no taxes," which came up a few times in describing the setup of the Ford Foundation. Then he had nodded.

Walker knew of course that he had been speaking to the associates of the firm, not its "rainmakers." He had been addressing people still in the fearful, climbing season of their lives. To get the rainmakers, he said, you had to be in more private settings. "You get the people like that in one-on-ones or at an event, you know, like the one where I was the other night where there was a bunch of very rich white guys," he said. "And so they're all together at somebody's house for a drink, whatever. And it's safe." He added a moment later, "These people don't sit around and go to a talk at the library."

This thought led Walker to the observation that America was becoming privatized now. The American public had their big conversation out there in the messy democracy, and the elite had its own ongoing intramural chat. He mentioned the proliferation of idea salons in his social universe. He brought up the people who spend tens of thousands of dollars on a batch of theater tickets, and have the director come to their home to give their guests a little preview lecture before the show. It reminded him of a trip he had taken to Brazil. He had met someone who grew up in a tightly secured gated community—nothing unusual in that country. What struck him was that, as children, the man and his friends had had their own disco within the building. "They couldn't go into town to disco because it was too dangerous," he said. "So they created their own little disco."

Walker looked at America today and saw his rich friends building their metaphorical buildings with gates on the outside and discos indoors. Gated communities. Home theaters. Private schools. Private jets. Privately run public parks. Private world-saving behind the backs of those to be saved. "Life goes more and more behind the gate," he said. "More and more of our civic activities and public activities become private activities."

Inequality gave some the resources to build their own discos and sequester themselves indoors. But it took the further ingredient of culture to make this way of life desirable. People chose to live in this way when they lacked faith in what lay beyond their gates—in the public. They felt this way when "public" had been allowed to tumble to lower status than "private" in our imaginations, in a reversal of their historic rankings: There was a time, as the legal scholar Jedediah Purdy has observed, when we loved "public" enough to place our most elevated hopes in republics, and when "private" reminded us of its cousins "privation" and "deprived." An achievement of modernity has been its gradual persuasion of citizens to expand the circle of their concern beyond family and tribe, to encompass the fellow citizen. Inequality was reversing that, eating away at Walker's beloved country. Government still had the responsibility, but, more and more, the wealthy made the rules.

One had to wonder if Walker had the stamina and the ability to make the Sacklers and Coles and Tisches and KKRs of the world think more like him. Almost a year after his new gospel came out, it was announced that he had joined the board of PepsiCo. The move attracted some criticism, in part because this warrior against inequality would now be earning more than a million dollars a year from the Ford presidency and this new, very occasional role, and in part because he now bore formal responsibility for what Pepsi did, including the company's continuing choice to sell its harmful sugary drinks. The critics could console, or depress, themselves with the thought that he was far from alone: Several of his counterparts at the major foundations served on the boards of firms like Citigroup and Facebook. The fear was that, yet again, MarketWorld would infiltrate and win. "The best tactic is to bring your critics into the fold," a former Ford Foundation executive told the *New York Times*. But Walker promised and seemed to believe that he would change them, not the other way around. "I will bring my perspective as the leader of a social justice organization," he told the *Times*. "I will bring my perspective as someone who is deeply concerned about the welfare of people in poor and vulnerable communities." His only compromise so far had been to switch his habit from Diet Coke to Diet Pepsi.

CHAPTER 7

ALL THAT WORKS IN THE MODERN WORLD

Many of these people had been coming to Bill Clinton's conference for years. Though they tended to label themselves such things as givers, philanthropists, social innovators, impact investors, and the like, recent political upheavals had given their tribe a new name that was sticking. They were coming to be known, by their friends and enemies alike, as globalists. Those arriving at the Clinton Global Initiative on that September morning in 2016 were looking forward to a week that had become a kind of family reunion for the globalists. And yet they were aware of gathering at a time when they were ever more despised. Around the world, a suspicion seemed to be taking hold that jet-setters solving humanity's problems in private conclaves was as much a problem as it was a solution.

The conference was one of many events taking place during what was known, somewhat anachronistically, as UN Week. The week got its name from the convening of most of the world's heads of state in the city of New York. They went before the UN General Assembly one by one and there, standing before its famous green backdrop, sought to speak to the world. Because of their presence, the security in New York on this September morning was virtually militaristic, provided by darkly clad men whose scowling eyes presumed guilt. Every few minutes, a motorcade sped past in a coned-off lane reserved for heads of state and ministers. Here on Second Avenue, a group of protestors was seeking to warn the visiting dignitaries to keep their "Hands Off Syria." On another corner, a pair of women in West African robes stood with clipboards, seeking signatories for a petition about health. They were positioned strategically close to the United Nations. Perhaps no one had told them that, thanks in large part to Bill Clinton, the United Nations was no longer where the action was during UN Week.

Clinton had left the American presidency in January 2001 as a late-middle-aged man needing redemption. He had survived two terms haunted by scandal, an impeachment vote by the House of Representatives, and an exit marred by dubiously given pardons and claims of stolen White House furniture. In *Man of the World,* an inside account of Clinton's post-presidency, the journalist Joe Conason portrays the former president as anguished and under siege in the first months of his new life. The talk of scandal continued— first the fallout from the pardon and furniture affairs, then from the former president's bid to set up his taxpayer-funded offices in a midtown Manhattan building whose rent would exceed that of the offices of the four other living ex-presidents combined. Clinton recovered from the outcry by instead setting up his office on West 125th Street in Harlem, where he tried to help the surrounding African American community by enlisting protocol-bearing business consultants to help shopkeepers pro bono. Still, the negativity was hard to escape. Clinton's new speaking agent booked him gigs for up to $250,000 each, only to see many canceled thanks to what Conason calls "the deluge of public scorn." Few foreign invitations were rescinded, though. There was a lesson in that for Clinton. "Soon he and his staff came to realize that however diminished his popularity might be in his native land, much of the rest of the world was ready to welcome and even celebrate him," Conason writes.

Guided by this insight, Clinton began to make his first post-presidential forays overseas, which would set him on a path to becoming an icon of global philanthropy and the eventual subject of a made-for-television documentary titled *President of the World: The Bill Clinton Phenomenon.* He raised money for the earthquake in the western Indian state of Gujarat. He brokered complex deals to lower the costs of HIV/AIDS drugs in developing countries. Then, in 2005, attuned to the currents of his time, Clinton decided that if you wanted truly to change the world now, you needed the help of companies and plutocrats, and thus you needed your own conference on the MarketWorld circuit.

The idea that formed was to host a conference during UN Week in New York, to take advantage of all the world leaders in town, who could perhaps serve as lures to attract the rich and generous to the city. Clinton credited his longtime aide Doug Band with the idea of this timing. Clinton later recalled his own reaction: "I said, 'Yeah. And everybody would have the exquisite joy of driving in New York City during the opening of the UN.' Then I did probably an impulsive thing and said, 'I'll try this.'"

In January 2005, on a stage at the World Economic Forum in Davos, one of the original conferences on the MarketWorld circuit, where corporate types paid vast sums of money to mingle with political leaders and others of similar social position, Clinton announced the Clinton Global Initiative. It would, he said, be like Davos, except it would require the rich and powerful people it brought together to commit, as a condition of showing up, to tangible projects for the global good. "I'm a big supporter of Davos, but the world leaders of the rich and the poor countries and everybody in between come to the UN every year in September," Clinton said, according to Conason, adding, "So what I thought we would do this year is to have a somewhat smaller version of what we do at the World Economic Forum, but that it would be focused very much on specific things all the participants could do." Decisions and actions, the actual solving of problems, would be the distinguishing feature of CGI. "Everybody who comes needs to know on the front end that you're going to be asked your opinion about what we should do on AIDS, TB, malaria; what the private sector can do about global warming," he said. Moreover, "you're going to be asked to participate in very specific decisions about that and to make very specific commitments."

The first CGI got many warm reviews. Tina Brown, the veteran magazine editor, wrote, "Clinton seems to have found his role as facilitator-in-chief, urging us to give up our deadly national passivity and start thinking things through for ourselves." She made a pointed comment about CGI as an alternative to the public, governmental way of solving problems, in light of the colossal state failure exposed by Hurricane Katrina the month before. "Commandeering the role of government through civic action suddenly feels like a very empowering notion—the alternative being to find oneself stranded in a flood waving a shirt from a rooftop," she wrote. Indeed, as CGI developed, it brought together a growing number of people interested in "commandeering the role of government": investors, entrepreneurs, social innovators, activists, entertainers, philanthropists, nonprofit executives, protocol-equipped consultants, and others, who came to brainstorm new double-bottom-line funds, plot against malaria, and also, since they were in town and so was everyone else, cut their own deals. And with every passing year, their growing presence seemed to shift the center of gravity of UN Week.

As CGI developed, two words came to define it: partnerships and commitments. Clinton invited people from various sectors— entrepreneurs, philanthropists, political leaders, labor unions, civil society—to work together on initiatives for societal betterment, and to make public promises about what they planned to achieve. This approach spoke of an emerging view of how progress is made that Bill Clinton hugely endorsed and actively evangelized. Clinton had as a young man gone to Yale Law School, and for decades afterward he pursued the improvement of the world through the instrument of politics and the law. He had embraced a liberalism that was, in the words of the writer Nathan Heller, a "systems-building philosophy," whose revelation was "that society, left alone, tended toward entropy and extremes, not because people were inherently awful but because they thought locally." Private individuals couldn't be relied on to see the big picture of their society, Heller writes, but "a larger entity such as government could." When he started in public office, Clinton believed public problems were best solved through public service and collective action. During his White House years, though, and even more decisively afterward, he had been won over by the theory that it was preferable to solve problems through markets and partnerships among entities private and public, which would find areas of common cause and work together on win-win solutions.

Early on, Clinton wondered if people would pay money to attend an event whose purpose was to get them to contribute more money, and volunteer on top of that. "I mean, who's ever heard of paying a membership fee to be asked to spend more money or spend more time?" he joked.

He underestimated himself. The commitments brought rewards. If you worked for a consumer products company and committed to making water filters available to millions, or a foundation that committed to restore some hearing to hundreds of thousands, you might be invited to come up to the CGI stage. There Bill Clinton would stand beside you and read your commitment to the room and praise you. This moment would become, among the doing-well-by-doing-good set, the coveted capstone to a career: People who were influential and/or rich but relatively unknown would bask in the celebrity-like glow. It was also a good way to get your face before a lot of rich and powerful people if, say, you were seeking investors for your new fund. If you owned a plane and had a lot more money where that charitable commitment came from, as the Canadian mining magnate Frank Giustra did, you could soon find yourself trotting the planet with Bill Clinton as your door-opener and bro. You would help him with his foundation, and he might let you into his inner circle, and being in his inner circle might benefit you the next time you bid on a mining project.

By Clinton's count, the twelve CGI meetings had inspired some 3,600 commitments. The organization claimed that these commitments had improved more than 435 million lives in 180 countries—a figure that was as impressive as it was hard to verify, since this new mode of world-saving was private, voluntary, and accountable to no one. One commitment, titled "Creating Prosperity with Major Corporations," was put forward by TechnoServe, the antipoverty consulting firm, in partnership with companies such as Walmart, Coca-Cola, Cargill, McDonald's, and SABMiller; it later submitted a progress report claiming to have implemented a "business plan competition program for entrepreneurs at the 'bottom of the pyramid.'" Another commitment was titled "WeTech." Drawing on partners such as McKinsey, Google, and Goldman Sachs, the initiative promised education and mentoring programs for girls and women seeking careers in science and technology.

This general approach to change jibed with what Clinton had stood for while in power: the championing of globalization, the embrace of markets, compassion, the declared end of labor/capital conflict, the promise of the rich and poor rising together—the insistence that loosened regulations good for Wall Street would also be good for Main Street; the marketing of trade deals craved by large corporations as being ideal for workers. The country was two months away from a referendum on Clintonism. Hillary Clinton had beaten Bernie Sanders, who spoke of putting the "billionaire class" in their place in order to make the working class thrive, whereas Clinton had spoken of wanting everyone to do better. Now she found herself up against the ultimate win-losey opponent, though this time of the race-baiting, authoritarian, ethno-nationalist sort. Donald Trump had harnessed an intuition that those people who believed you could crusade for justice and get super-rich and save lives and be very powerful and give a lot back, that you could have it all and then some, were phonies. He had harnessed these feelings, to the bafflement of many, despite embodying the pseudo-concern he decried.

The criticism of what CGI did and represented had been building over the years, fueled by never-ending questions about whether the philanthropy was an end in itself for many of the attendees or rather a means to more self-serving ends. "It's Davos for the social do-good set," Darren Walker said one morning that week, sitting in his Ford Foundation office. The new UN Week lived at "this intersection of doing well and doing well by doing good." He credited Clinton, whose event Ford was sponsoring, with the change. "It really was through the vehicle of CGI that so many new actors were mobilized and so many different modalities like impact investing—all of these other things started." Clinton had used his extraordinary powers of convening to bring improbable partners together, and creative solutions to poverty and suffering had been born. However, Walker said, it was also the case that "philanthropists and commercial enterprises saw in CGI a platform that they could leverage for both doing good and building their brands." As a result, self-service flirted dangerously with altruism at CGI, in Walker's view. Why were all these CEOs flying in? "They fly here because they see investment opportunities; they see branding opportunities," Walker said. Clinton's brilliance had been in using his gathering "as a way to give people a profile" if they agreed to help people. But this had, by Walker's lights, clouded the motives of the giving that CGI unleashed. Now others were following its example of barnacling themselves onto UN Week, and "hundreds of side events," as Walker put it somewhat exaggeratedly, had come into being. "The risk in this is the potential canceling out," he said. "It's this idea that you can support a health initiative in Nigeria on the Niger Delta to reduce disease or diarrhea or whatever, and you can also make an investment in a company that is a polluter in the Niger Delta."

The blurring of public good and private desire during UN Week, if seeded by CGI, was no longer confined to it. Indeed, other public-private world-changing events in its mold, if not remotely at its scale, had sprouted across the city, growing more numerous every year: a meeting called Make a Difference, Invest with Impact; the GODAN Summit, inviting you to "Join the Open Data Revolution to end global hunger"; another called Leveraging the SDGs for Inclusive Growth at George Soros's foundations (the SDGs being the new Sustainable Development Goals); a meeting on "sustainable finance" at HSBC; the Concordia Summit, where "thought leaders and innovators" meet to "examine the world's most pressing challenges and identify avenues for collaboration," sponsored by Coca-Cola and J.P. Morgan; and, courtesy of sponsors Citi, Mars, and SABMiller, an event called Business Collaborating to Deliver the SDGs; the Africa Alternative Investment Intensive Forum; Catalyzing Climate Change Innovation Through Charitable and Impact Investment; a networking event called Scaling the Clean Economy, hosted at the international law firm of Baker McKenzie; the U.S.-Africa Business Forum, convened by Bloomberg Philanthropies; and the Every Woman Every Child Private Sector-Innovation high-level luncheon.

The Social Good Summit was another of these private world-changing conclaves, a two-day conference bringing together "a dynamic community of global leaders and grassroots activists to discuss solutions to the greatest challenges of our time." Held at the 92nd Street Y in Manhattan, it promised that its attendees would "unite to unlock the potential of technology to make the world a better place." The mingling of public and private was everywhere at this event, as at so many others. The summit was sponsored by Target, Nike, and the Taco Bell Foundation, but the M&M's found in the Digital Media Lounge were emblazoned with little icons repre-senting the UN's Sustainable Development Goals—a major theme of UN Week that year. Before things got under way, there was a brief moment of silence to reflect on Alan Kurdi, a drowned Syrian boy who had seized the world's attention: a spur to recall the refugee cri-sis. Then there was a flurry of business-speak: "In order to reach the world that we want by 2030, collaboration and co-design are key." One also learned that "the Taco Bell Foundation believes that young people need to dream big."

These various events—Bill Clinton's and the raft of other corporate-sponsored world-saving gatherings that benefited from his example—amounted to a kind of parallel UN Week, centered on MarketWorlders. Just a few miles from CGI stood the Langham building, on Central Park West, built in the style of the French Sec-ond Empire. In a high-up apartment owned by one of the barons of private equity, some Africans had been invited to talk to people with money about investing in Africa, at a dinner cohosted by one of the McKinsey-but-for-poverty consultancies. Over chicken curry and salad, there was talk of what deal possibilities there may be in Africa and of the stupidity of regulation and the importance of scale. Then the revelers boarded a black party bus waiting downstairs.

The bus ferried its passengers downtown to a party in honor of

Africa. On board was a tall, lanky executive at Uber who said he was responsible for opening up African markets for the company. It went to show how inclusively humanitarian efforts were defined in the new, enlarged UN Week. The bus pulled up to the Gramercy Park Hotel. The lobby was abuzz with word of a sighting of President Obama dining at a restaurant nearby. He was in town for UN Week, but he would also address the U.S.-Africa Business Forum. The party bus squad marched up to the rooftop, for a do organized by the new Africa Center on Fifth Avenue.

The party was full of the kind of people who say they "live between" two places. Chicken sausages and deviled eggs swirled around. A prominent executive at Google could be seen making a Nigerian woman laugh. The vice chairman of one of America's great newspapers was tapping the host of the party on the shoulder to ask where her father was. She was Hadeel Ibrahim, and her father, Mo, was said to be Africa's richest man. Her cohost for the party was Chelsea Clinton, who didn't show. Mary Robinson, the former president of Ireland, walked by. There was a brief toast to the Africa Center and Africa. Then back to business. Someone was whispering that one ought to get to know the man standing behind her, because he had an amazing place on Martha's Vineyard, and it was actually not one house but three separate houses, and he liked to have interesting people there.

Several of the people at the party that night worked for Dalberg, one of the antipoverty consulting firms, for which it was also, naturally, a big week. Dalberg disseminated a list of the side events at UN Week (or main events, depending on your view). On its calendar, the right-hand column noted whether and how one might join each event. Eight events had free registration, eight sold paid registration, and forty-eight were invitation-only. The ratio told a truth about the new, MarketWorld-led UN Week: When private actors move into the solution of public problems, it becomes less and less of the public's business.

The privateness of the Clinton Foundation's endeavors had attracted criticism over the years. Who exactly was giving money?

What exactly were their motives? Were they giving at least in part to secure influence or jobs in a future Hillary Clinton administration? Thanks in part to these criticisms—and to the expectation that Hillary would soon win, making the criticisms even more menacing— the conference that had done so much to transform UN Week was meeting for the twelfth and final time. And so there was nostalgia in the air at CGI that week—but also worry. A seething rage was engulfing many societies, fed by the perception that the kind of world-traveling elites meeting at this conference had done a better job of protecting their own interests in recent years than of making the world a better place.

MarketWorlders were waking up to the anger. The events of 2016 had made it "the global elite's annus horribilis," in the words of Niall Ferguson, a Harvard historian, a preeminent and lavishly paid thought leader, and an esteemed member of the globalist tribe. He wrote in the *Boston Globe* of how he and his peers had laughed at Donald Trump in January in Davos, only to see him claim the Republican nomination; and then, some months later, ricocheting among Aspen, Lake Como, and Martha's Vineyard, had failed to take seriously the campaign to sever Britain from the European Union, only to see it succeed. The world's elites were being revolted against, and the revolts perhaps had something to do with how disconnected they were from the realities of others. Ferguson argued that his tribe of "rootless cosmopolitans" had no choice but to agree with this comment from the German finance minister: "More and more, people don't trust their elites."

In New York in the run-up to UN Week, this mistrust had hung over a number of dinners, salons, panel discussions, and board meetings in preparation for the upcoming confabs. At these occasions, the question being asked was: Why do they hate us? The "they" were the rootless cosmopolitans' less-rarefied fellow citizens, who in one place after another were gravitating to nationalism, demagogy, and resentful exclusion—and rejecting some of the elites' most cherished beliefs: borderlessness, market cures for all diseases, inevitable technological progress, benign technocratic stewardship.

Some of the elites believed that their beautiful dream had to be reexplained to the people. The vision of One World, open borders, technological progress, rule by data, MarketWorld supremacy—this was all part of the right vision wrongly sold. They hadn't marketed globalization and open borders and trade with enough passion. They hadn't properly sanded the rough edges of change, with things like job retraining for those displaced.

There was another camp of MarketWorlders who had taken to wondering whether the globalist dream itself was problematic. It wasn't that the members of this camp were nationalists; they, too, tended to be steeped in the doing-well-by-doing-good, globalist way of seeing. But the anger on the streets, in so many places at once, was starting to hit home. They were realizing that they and their fellow elites had failed to see mounting frustration, over decades, about the agonies of change that were only now becoming front-page news. They were acknowledging that the protesters also wanted the world to be improved—but they wanted more of a say in how; people believed the promises democracies told them about caring what they think, however poorly they had been fulfilled. That autumn, when MarketWorlders found themselves in heated discussion about the anger, some suggested to others: *Maybe the problem is us.*

And what exactly was the nature of that problem? Many MarketWorlders were exploring that question in public.

For Ferguson, he and his fellow MarketWorld elites had been drafted into a new class war. It was no longer rich versus poor but rather people who claimed to belong to everywhere versus people stuck somewhere—echoing his colleague Michael Porter's notion of somewhere people and everywhere companies. In Ferguson's telling, from the same essay as earlier, what went wrong was that the Somewheres were simply no longer fooled by the Everywheres' performance of concern and charity, and the numbers finally caught up with the Everywheres: "No prizes for guessing which group is more numerous. No matter how many donations the global elite made, philanthropic and political, we could never quite compensate for that disparity."

Like the protocol-guided companies that Michael Porter criticized, MarketWorld's winners had, in Ferguson's telling, surrendered any loyalty to place. The trouble was that the world was still governed by place, and so elites whose loyalties and projects focused on the global level were essentially pulling away from democracy itself. And some of the most militant globalists were now admitting as much. Lawrence Summers, the economist who formerly ran the U.S. Treasury and Harvard University, wrote his own apologia in the *Financial Times,* calling for an end to "reflex internationalism" and for a new, "responsible nationalism":

> A new approach has to start from the idea that the basic responsibility of government is to maximise the welfare of citizens, not to pursue some abstract concept of the global good. People also want to feel that they are shaping the societies in which they live.

Dani Rodrik, a colleague of Summers at Harvard, published a piece in the *New York Times* on the Saturday before UN Week admonishing the MarketWorlders against the assumption that what was good for them was good for everyone. Globalization, he argued, needed to be rescued "not just from populists, but also from its cheerleaders." He wrote, "The new model of globalization stood priorities on their head, effectively putting democracy to work for the global economy, instead of the other way around."

Jonathan Haidt offered another theory of what went wrong in an essay that year. "If you want to understand why nationalism and right-wing populism have grown so strong so quickly, you must start by looking at the actions of the globalists," he wrote. "In a sense, the globalists 'started it.'" They started it, in his view, because the "new cosmopolitan elite," as he called it, "acts and talks in ways that insult, alienate, and energize many of their fellow citizens, particularly those who have a psychological predisposition to authoritarianism." For Haidt, globalists were utopians. They believed in change and in the future. They were "anti-nationalist and anti-religious" and "anti-parochial," believing that "anything that divides people into separate groups or identities is bad; removing borders and divisions is good." Their opponents, Haidt went on, could be understood as possessing an intuition about roots that Émile Durkheim helped to confirm with his landmark book *Suicide:* that "people who are more tightly bound by ties of family, religion, and local community have lower rates of suicide," as Haidt voiced it. "But when people escape from the constraints of community they live in a world of 'anomie' or normlessness, and their rate of suicide goes up."

In Haidt's analysis, globalism and antiglobalism are both cogent worldviews with valid concerns and data behind them. There are advantages to a world of free and rampant human mingling and motion, and there are different advantages to stable, tightly bound communities. But according to Haidt, the globalists had so convinced themselves of the moral superiority of openness, freedom, and One World that they were unable to process the genuine fear these things aroused in millions of people.

What these confessions sometimes passed over was the immense amount of racism, xenophobia, anti-Semitism, male chauvinism, and slandering of immigrants undammed and even stoked by the populists. Those sentiments were real and played an important part in the story of the political turmoil. Yet it could also be argued that MarketWorld's sins—those being apologized for by Ferguson and the others—were partly to blame for giving the right-wing populists, ethno-nationalists, and others their opening.

In an interview by email some days after CGI but before the presidential election, Clinton offered his own estimation of what lay behind the surge of populist anger. "The pain and road rage we see reflected in the election has been building a long time," he said. He thought that the anger "is being fed in part by the feeling that the most powerful people in the government, economy, and society no longer care about them or look down on them. They want to become part of our progress toward shared opportunities, shared stability, and shared prosperity." But when it came to Clinton's solution, it sounded a lot like the model to which he was already committed: "The only answer is to build an aggressive, creative partnership involving all levels of government, the private sector, and non-government organizations to make it better." In other words, the only answer is to pursue social change outside of traditional public forums, with the political representatives of mankind as one input among several, and corporations having the big say in whether they would sponsor a given initiative or not. The swelling populist anger, of course, was directed in part at the very elites he had sought to convene, on whom he had gambled his theory of post-political problem-solving, who had lost the trust of so many millions of people, making them feel betrayed, uncared for, and scorned.

What people were rejecting in the United States, Britain, Hungary, and elsewhere was, in their view, rule by global elites who put the pursuit of profit above the needs of their neighbors and fellow citizens. These were elites who seemed more loyal to one another than to their own communities; elites who often showed greater interest in distant humanitarian causes than in the pain of people ten miles to the east or west. Frustrated citizens felt they possessed no power over the spreadsheet- and PowerPoint-wielding elites commensurate with the power these elites had gained over them—whether in switching around their hours or automating their plant or quietly slipping into law a new billionaire-made curriculum for their children's school.

What they did not appreciate was the world being changed without them.

The organizers of this final CGI, held in the throes of the antiglobalist revolt, decided that a panel on the topic was a must. And the organizers evidently concluded that the panel should consist entirely of globalists, with no one representing the other side. (This was not the only exclusion on display: Those inspired by the topic to come toward the front of the room would find the first several rows of seats mostly empty but reserved for deep-pocketed sponsors, including McDonald's and the Rockefeller Foundation.)

The formal title of the session was "Partnerships for Global Prosperity." A more fitting title would have been "Why Do They Hate Us?" Bill Clinton was moderating this panel. On it were Mauricio Macri, a former businessman who had defeated Argentina's entrenched populists to become president; Matteo Renzi, the Italian prime minister, who styled his own career on the pro-market progressivism that Clinton called the "Third Way"; Ngozi Okonjo-Iweala, a former Nigerian minister and World Bank official, often seen in Aspen and at TED and elsewhere along the MarketWorld circuit, who had recently joined the investment bank Lazard; and Sadiq Khan, the first Muslim mayor of London and a champion of the doomed Remain campaign to keep Britain in the EU. The panelists represented the left and the right, and everybody onstage was part of the globalist, cosmopolitan, technocratic, win-win consensus, promoted and sponsored by MarketWorld, that had come under fire of late.

Clinton praised Macri for bringing common sense to a country afflicted by what he called "a totally discredited economic and political situation." Then he invited Macri to share with the audience "what you found, what you're trying to do, and how others can support this, particularly people from the private sector and NGO sector."

"Argentina, as you know, President, has suffered decades of populism," Macri began. He framed the victory of his pro-business campaign as a collective decision that Argentines "deserve to live better. We wanted to be part of the world. We wanted to cut with isolism." He knew his audience was interested in making the world a better place, so he decided to focus his remarks on his plan to reduce poverty in Argentina. Even so, he came nowhere near the concepts of equality and justice and power; he didn't broach a topic like land reform or the concentration of wealth in a handful of families. Instead, he spoke of making it easier to do business. "We know—we all know—that to cut poverty, you have to create good jobs, quality jobs," he said. "And for that you need to create an environment of trust, of confidence. You have to assure the investors you will be attached to the rule of law, that you will be reliable."

What he was arguing was classic MarketWorld win-win-ism, inflected by globalism: The best thing for the worst-off people in Argentina was to do whatever made foreign investors and international agencies feel at home. That is why, he said, he was making "tough decisions": to unify the country's exchange rate, release the payment of dividends abroad, settle the country's disputes with foreign bondholders. He was proud to have brought an International Monetary Fund delegation to Argentina not long ago. He was excited to have hosted a business and investment forum the previous week, drawing a few thousand businesspeople from several dozen countries. "We need all global companies coming to Argentina, so as to help us developing our country," he said. His vision of the good society as a place reassuring to foreign capital was a curious solution to the problem of publics swimming in resentment against the globalists and the winners from change.

Clinton moved on to Renzi, whom he praised for having the courage to bring pro-market policies to Italy—to reform its labor market and to put up a controversial (and ultimately doomed) referendum to reduce the number of legislators and consolidate his own power. Renzi was exactly the kind of Moody's-approved politician the room loved, and he said all the right things, which again had a theme of economics superseding politics. Italy, he said, couldn't just be about masterpieces and culture anymore. It had to accept the "challenge of change."

Renzi dropped a casual aside in talking about his labor-market reforms that reflected another aspect of the globalist consensus. He said Italy's rewriting, the previous year, of its hiring-and-firing laws had finally caught the country up to the standards of Germany and Britain. He added, "Obviously, U.S.A. arrived to this point twenty years ago." The globalists believed that there were "right answers" in public policy—answers that made a place safe for the foreign investors that Macri had been worried about—and having a very flexible labor market, in which it is easy to hire and fire people, is one of those right answers. The right answer, then, was not arrived at democratically: It was not the answer the people of Italy had chosen, by action or inaction, during those twenty years of "delay." It was a globalist truism that hovered over the country, waiting for it to get with the program and accept the prudent way of the world. And when at last it did, the nation's prime minister could describe those earlier years, defined by other choices, as a delay. Italians, not famous for punctuality, were late in arriving at the globalists' "right answer." Leaders like Renzi saw the checklist program pushed by multilateral agencies and foreign investors as possessing a moral validity that democratic choices by his citizens lacked, because they were bad for efficiency and growth.

Now Clinton turned to Mayor Khan, whom he praised as "a great example of positive interdependence." MarketWorld believed in interdependence, because it reflected how the world was one, and also because it translated into more markets for companies to enter. (One often finds nationalistic people, but one rarely encounters nationalistic businesses.) Clinton recognized that this vision was under threat, for now "the intensity of the feelings of people resisting our being pulled together outweighs the intensity of those who are winning from this," as he put it.

It would have been useful to have onstage someone who actually felt some of the resentment that was roiling the world. Instead, it was left to Khan to explain it. He was asked, "What did the Brexit vote mean in terms of what's going on all over the world?" "During the referendum campaign," Khan responded, "people who have challenges getting their children into good local schools, people who worry about health care, people who worry about getting genuinely affordable homes were led down a path of the politics of fear. They were told the reason for your challenges and your issues is because of the EU, is because of the Other." In other words, the people who voted for Brexit were easily misled sheep.

Clinton piled on to this idea of false consciousness. "All these English counties voted to give up economic aid from the EU," he said. "And they needed it, but they had no idea what they were doing. They just wanted to come inside and close the door. There is a kind of a visceral us-and-them mentality developing." This was the diagnosis of the former president of the United States a few months after Brexit's unexpected success, and two months before his wife's unexpected defeat to a populist demagogue who allied himself with the Brexit campaign. The people setting themselves the task of understanding the anger around them were precommitted to the idea that the anger had no possible basis in reason or conscious choice. They could not process people who saw the world fundamentally differently than MarketWorlders did and, misguided or not, wanted to be heard.

"I'm really proud that London was the one region of England to vote to remain in the EU, decisively so," Khan said. "In my view, it's not a zero-sum game. And London doing well is not at the expense of the rest of the UK. If London does well, the rest of the country prospers."

The idea that what was good for a prosperous, globally networked megalopolis full of bankers and other well-educated professionals who could afford to live there, and overrun by Saudi, Russian, and Nigerian absentee princelings who pushed up rents without contributing much to the economy or tax base or the communities they lived in—the idea that whatever was good for such a metropolis was automatically good for all of Britain was part of the conceit that some voters understandably rejected when the Brexit choice came before them. To cite one counterexample, Britain had in recent years been engaged in a political argument about austerity. The kind of fiscal "discipline" favored by City of London banker elites translated directly into the cuts to education and health and the reduced social mobility that left people angry and caused them to wonder how there was money to help foreigners. But there was no space in Khan's vision for the idea that millions of ordinary people, in Britain and around the world, had suffered because things were too good and easy for, and too rigged in favor of, elites. He was offering another version of what Macri and then Renzi had voiced: The winners of globalization were in no way part of the problem; if we help them win, everyone will win.

Here was represented the complex of CGI values in a single panel: doing the market-friendly thing instead of the idealistic thing; elevating what the people supposedly needed economically over what they wanted politically; believing that the right, data-driven, technocratic answers speak for themselves; judging politicians' success by investors' returns; thinking of market forces as an inevitability one must give in to, make way for, adapt to.

The four panelists and Clinton speculated about "these people," as Okonjo-Iweala called them. They mused about the anger on the other side and came up with convenient theories. Clinton offered that "the conflict model works better at a time of economic distress." Okonjo-Iweala suggested that making vaccines more accessible— her bailiwick as the leader of a global vaccine alliance called GAVI— might help to reduce anger. (She didn't mention the bankers for whom she now worked, and how it might also reduce anger if they were punished for their sins, if they compensated the public for the bailouts they got, if they had the humility to stop thwarting regulation of their conduct.) She plugged vaccines to the Market-World crowd in language they would understand: They didn't just save lives; they were an investment, for healthy citizens mean more growth and taxes paid and companies started. Vaccines, she said, are "one of the best buys in economics today," since "$1 invested in vaccines returns $16." She gushed, "The rate of return on that is very high."

A moment later, Okonjo-Iweala said the globalist tribe represented in the room needed to "debunk those who are trying to use them as a platform"—the "them" being the angry voters. The people were being used; they were rubes. There was a total refusal to accept that angry people were actively, concertedly trying to tell their fellow citizens something, however flawed. And they weren't here to tell them what it was in person.

The panel members saw themselves as above and apart from fearful, conflictual politics. Their politics was technocratic, dedicated to discovering right answers that were knowable and out there, and just needed to be analyzed and spreadsheeted into being. Their politics had borrowed from the business world the pleasantness and mutualism of the win-win. It was striking to have five political figures share a stage and have not one moment of real argument. They all seemed to suppose that the good society was the society of entrepreneurs, whose success was tantamount to that of the society itself. That the weaving of the world was among the most vital human strivings. That government should work as a partner to the private sector, not a counterweight to it.

One could forget, watching such a civilized group, that traditional politics is argumentative for a reason. It isn't that politicians don't know how to be nice, but rather that politics is rooted in the idea of a big, motley people taking their fate into their own hands. Politics is the inherently messy business of negotiating and reconciling incompatible interests and coming up with a decent plan, designed to be liked but difficult to love. It solves problems in a context in which everyone is invited to the table and everyone is equal and everyone has the right to complain about being unserved and unseen. Politics, in bringing together people of divergent interests, necessarily puts sacrifice on the table. It is easier to conjure win-wins in forums like this one, where everyone is a winner. The consensus was a reminder of all the kinds of people and perspectives that had not been invited in.

The panelists, though, knew they lived amid great anger, and they seemed to be groping for ways to respond to it. "What's more important is, rather than playing on people's fears, address them," Mayor Khan said. Clinton confessed his fear that the winners of MarketWorld, confronting the rage all around them, would pull away from it. "One of the things that I think we really have to work on all around the world is not to let our urban, diverse, young, economically successful areas just basically say, 'This is too exhausting. I'm gonna run away from the rural areas, I'm going to run away from all that.'" Would the anger over elite secession simply inspire more elite secession? Would the corporate escapism that

Porter chastised and the cosmopolitan escapism of Ferguson's fellow winners, having frayed the relations of so many communities and fueled so much discontent, reverse themselves as a result—or rather feel more justified now? Clinton said, "This is a big test for all of us."

The dream of borderlessness pervaded CGI. Consider the panel moderated by David Miliband, the former British foreign secretary who now ran the International Rescue Committee. The topic was refugees. This kind of complex global problem gave Market-World types a straightforward way to condescend to national democracies. Hikmet Ersek, the chief executive of Western Union, sitting beside his fellow panelist the prime minister of Sweden, said, "One of the issues in the politicians, with all respect, Mr. Prime Minister, is that you guys are voted by local people, but you're responsible for global issues." Hearing this, Queen Rania of Jordan, a regular at these MarketWorld gatherings, added, "One thing that I find frustrating is that, looking around the world, most leaders are stuck in linear modes of thinking and in traditional approaches. Or they're consumed by very urgent issues, like votes and short-term politics, that they don't think of the disruptions that are happening in the world and the effects they're going to have on us in the future."

This was very CGI. Here was a CEO lamenting that a politician represented an actual group of people from an actual place. This naturally stood in contrast to a money-transfer CEO, who represented the here-there-everywhere flow of capital itself and had a strong financial interest in borderlessness. But did that make an elected leader representing a specific group of people myopic? And then there was a queen suggesting that politicians are too consumed by the search for votes to think clearly about the world. For Queen Rania, the voting public wasn't something that she and her husband, who was also at CGI, had to worry about—nor for the Western Union man, for that matter. Not worrying about votes was among the advantages of being a monarch or CEO. Here was globalism's antidemocratic streak in open light. Globalists were boosting a way of solving problems above, beyond, and outside politics. They weren't interested in making politics work better, but insisting on their own proprietary power to give the world what it needed, not necessarily what it wanted.

Had the organizers of CGI truly been interested in why people resented the globalists, they could have invited Dani Rodrik, a Turkish-born economist at Harvard and author of several books on globalization. Rodrik's bicultural life bespoke their One Worldism, but he had become one of the more incisive critics of how the globalists' noble intentions undermine democracy.

"There's no more global citizen than I am," he said on the phone from his office at the Kennedy School. "I know more about the rest of the world than I know the United States. I carry the passports of two countries, and most of my friends here are non-U.S.-born." So one might have expected Rodrik to recoil, as so many of the globalists did, when Theresa May, the British prime minister, smeared "citizens of the world" shortly after coming to power in the choppy wake of the Brexit referendum. "Today," she said,

> too many people in positions of power behave as though they have more in common with international elites than with the people down the road, the people they employ, the people they pass on the street. But if you believe you are a citizen of the world, you are a citizen of nowhere. You don't understand what citizenship means.

Rodrik observed a swift and fierce reaction to those words among his fellow well-educated and world-traveling elites. The near-universal globalist reaction was that the statement was wrong and malicious: "It was just trying to appeal to the basest instincts within people." What struck Rodrik was that "the reaction was so predictably negative to something that seems to me to be so patently obvious on the face of it." What May was suggesting was perhaps problematic in its attempt to pander to the rising tide of xenophobic feeling. But it was also, Rodrik felt, referring to a real problem: that so many elites—often well-meaning—who speak grandly, airily of improving the world as a whole have rarely attended a community meeting; that so many elites who claim to feel linked to all humanity have chosen to live sequestered from anyone not of their class. "The people around the Clinton Global Initiative or the liberal globalist establishment have told themselves a story about how they're really working for the world," Rodrik said. "But they are not really a part of a political process. A political process requires that you're competing with and you're testing ideas against other citizens. Citizens are defined as being members of a preexisting political community. We obviously don't have that at a global level." In other words, politics is about actual places, with actual shared histories. Globalism, chasing a dream of everyone, risks belonging to no one.

For Rodrik, it isn't just that solving things at the global level (which, in the absence of world government, often means privately, which often means plutocratically) lacks legitimacy. Pushing things up into that realm gives globalists "moral cover or ethical cover for escaping their domestic obligations as citizens in their own national setting." It is a way of doing good that allows them to ignore the fact that their democracies aren't working well. Or, even more simply, it allows them to avoid the duty they might otherwise feel to interact with their fellow citizens across divides, to learn about the problems facing their own communities, which might implicate them, their choices, and their privileges—as opposed to universal challenges like climate change or the woes of faraway places like Rwandan coffee plantations. In such cases, diffuseness or distance can spare one the feeling of having a finger jabbed in one's face.

The globalists, Rodrik said, have embraced a theory of progress that is out of step with the facts of the age. "There's a general understanding of how the world works that lies behind those kinds of initiatives, which I think is false," he said. "And that understanding is that what the world suffers from is a lack of true international cooperation." This understanding is right on some issues, such as global pandemics and climate change, he said. "But in most other areas, when you think about them, whether it's international finance, whether it's economic development, whether it's business and financial stability, whether it's international trade—the problem, it seems to me, is not that we don't have sufficient global governance, that we don't have sufficient global cooperation, that we're not getting together enough. It's just that our domestic governance is failing us." He added, "Many of the problems that the world economy faces—whether it's trade restrictions or financial instability or lack of adequate development and global poverty and all those things— many of these problems would in fact become much less severe if our local politics were working right.

"And the idea that you could just either develop these solutions from outside," he continued, "or you could parachute them in, or you could bypass local politics through these transnational kinds of efforts—it seems to me it's well-meaning; it's definitely worth doing as complementary efforts. But when it becomes a substitute, when it starts to replace the hard work that we should get engaged in, in terms of our domestic political processes, then I think it becomes potentially quite perverse." Rodrik saw a "direct link" between this doing-well-by-doing-good antipolitics peddled by the globalists and the chaos of 2016. "The world's financial and political and technocratic elites," he said, were "distancing themselves from their compatriots. And then what that results in is a loss of trust."

C. Z. Nnaemeka wrote a prescient essay about this distancing in the *MIT Entrepreneurship Review* a few years ago. It criticized elite twenty- and thirtysomethings' neglect of what she called "the unexotic underclass"—people neither rich enough to be global elites themselves nor poor enough to get the global elites' attention. "Chances are there are more people addressing the Big Problems of slum dwellers in Calcutta, Kibera or Rio, than are tackling the big problems of hardpressed folks in say, West Virginia, Mississippi or Louisiana," she wrote. This preference for distant needs and transnational problem-solving can deepen the feeling that all those globalists are in cahoots with one another and not attentive to their compatriots. This feeling is puffed up by a vast and cynical complex that produces conspiracy theories and fraudulent news to this effect. The feeling is also given air by very real changes in the world over the last generation that have meant more decisions that affect people's lives being made in nations not their own, more of their children's toys being made in cities whose names they cannot pronounce, more of the decisions about what they read being made by algorithms whose creators stay invisible.

These changes help to explain the sense of disorientation that many people feel in this era, and why it would have been an especially good time for elites to be trusted by their fellow citizens— and why it is so destabilizing when they aren't. Rodrik brought up Hillary Clinton. "Her proposals would have done a lot more for the middle classes, and lower-middle-income classes, than Trump's," he said. But "she wasn't getting traction, and I think it's the sense of this loss of trust—that they're associated with a group of globalist elites or just hanging out with Goldman Sachs and so forth. And it doesn't matter how good your proposals are. Basically, if these are proposals that come from people whom you don't trust fundamentally, if you don't think that they have your interests in mind, then these proposals are not going to be taken seriously."

Because the globalists tended to hang out with other globalists, they were at risk of trapping themselves in an echo chamber. "There were a certain number of tales about how globalization was supposed to work, and these people kept telling these tales to each other," Rodrik said. "This was the tide that was going to lift all boats. And this tale kept being told, and then it got reinforced, and anybody who rejected this tale was basically just a self-interested protectionist."

Rodrik asked, "If you have an understanding of the world that's currently faulty, how are you going to find that out?" He answered his own question: "In an ideal democratic world, where citizenship is fully exercised and participatory, it's a process of domestic deliberation where you're testing your idea against other domestic citizens, and you're seeing that, 'Well, hold on; I thought that was a good thing, but what's been happening in North Carolina, where these people have lost their jobs because of NAFTA?' Maybe we didn't put in place the kind of protections that were needed, and I can understand that. But that kind of exposure and that kind of challenge has not been truly provided."

Any position critical of globalization has had to contend with globalism's One World moral glow, Rodrik said. Unity always sounds better than division, and engagement better than line-drawing. Bill Clinton himself had been the master of framing globalization not as something to be chosen, not as a particular arrangement of policies and incentives that could be done in various reasonable ways, but as an inevitability of moral progress. "I respect the antiglobalization people, and I think a lot of their criticisms are valid. But they want to take us back to a time that never was," he once said in a speech, adding, "Human history is the journey of going from isolation to interdependence to integration. A divided world is unsustainable and dangerous. Antiglobalists want to go from interdependence to isolation, and it's not possible." What was sometimes a rather narrow vision of globalization, centered on what would allow businesses to expand most easily and protocol-optimize most seamlessly, was gussied up by such rhetoric into moral evolution. Which made it easy to cast criticism as hatred, even when it had nothing to do with it. You want to restrict some area of trade with Mexico? *What, do you hate Mexican people? Don't you believe that we're all God's children?*

For Rodrik, the dream of global harmony is admirable, and there is undeniable virtue in the philanthropy and social concern galvanized by an event like CGI. What worried him was that at the very same time, the globalist sphere of which it was part was continuing to undermine the idea of politics as the best way to shape the world. "The locus of politics, I think, is the key issue here," he said. "What is the right locus of politics, and who are the decision-making authorities? Is it these networks and these global get-togethers? Or is it at the national level?" Who should make change, and where should they make it?

As he said this, he could already hear the globalists' objection: *But we aren't engaging in politics when we come to CGI or Davos or the*

Aspen Institute or Skoll. We are just helping people. "Probably people who get together in these congregations don't think of what they're doing as politics," Rodrik said. "But of course it's politics. It's just a politics that has a different locus and has a different view of who matters and how you can change things, and has a different theory of change and who the agents of change are." To put it another way, if you are trying to shape the world for the better, you are engaging in a political act—which raises the question of whether you are employing an appropriately political process to guide the shaping. The problem with the globalists' vision of world citizens changing the world through partnerships, Rodrik said, is that "you're not accountable to anybody, because it is just a bunch of other global citizens like you as your audience." He added, "The whole idea about having a polity, having a demos, is that there's accountability within that demos. That's what a political system ensures and these mechanisms don't."

The political system that Rodrik speaks of is not just Congress or the Supreme Court or governorships. It is all of those things and other things. It is civic life. It is the habit of solving problems together, in the public sphere, through the tools of government and in the trenches of civil society. It is solving problems in ways that give the people you are helping a say in the solutions, that offer that say in equal measure to every citizen, that allow some kind of access to your deliberations or at least provide a meaningful feedback mechanism to tell you it isn't working. It is not reimagining the world at conferences.

The breakout session was called "Beyond Equality: Harnessing the Power of Girls & Women for Sustainable Development."

"Welcome to our sunrise service here at CGI," the panel moderator, Melanne Verveer, said in opening. Her panel was, she said, emblematic of what lay ahead that day, for it brought together diverse stakeholders from multiple perspectives on the topic of women's equality. The diverse stakeholders turned out to be three corporate executives and one UN man. There were no feminist thinkers, activists, lawyers, elected leaders, labor organizers, or other varietals of women-savers on the panel. Serious feminists might have found this slate of experts problematic, but it was not, by CGI's standards, a poorly formed panel. On the contrary, much like the panel on globalism and its haters, it was a panel that could be counted on to provide the right amount of stimulation while worrying absolutely no one.

A panel like this was a perfect place to explore a question that Rodrik raised: Did this well-meaning, if democratically dubious, globalist private sphere "complement" nations seeking to solve their own problems, or did it inadvertently serve as a "substitute"?

On the surface, the answer might seem obvious: How can a group of private people getting together substitute for democracy? Sure, they're rich and powerful, but congresses and parliaments still do their work. Surely, they're the ones setting the agenda.

It isn't necessarily that simple. A pair of Stanford sociologists, Aaron Horvath and Walter Powell, investigated the question and came up with a surprising answer. When elites solve public problems privately, they can do so in ways that contribute to democracy, and they can do so in ways that disrupt it. The former occurs when elite help "contributes to and enlarges the public goods provided by the state, and attends to interests not readily provided for by the state." But the same elite help, backed by the same noble intentions, can instead "disrupt" democracy when it "replaces the public sphere with all manner of private initiatives for special public purposes." These latter works don't simply do what government cannot do. They "crowd out the public sector, further reducing both its legitimacy and its efficacy, and replace civic goals with narrower concerns about efficiency and markets."

Horvath and Powell's most interesting analysis is about *how* elites can pull off this crowding out of vast machineries of state. How can private hotel ballroom hangouts have their way with democracies in possession of their own standing armies? The seasoned and astute private world-changer seeks to alter "the public conversation about which social issues matter, sets an agenda for how they matter, and specifies who is the preferred provider of services to address these issues without any engagement with the deliberative processes of civil society." The savviest of these elite saviors recognize that they live in democracies and respect that. They don't ignore public opinion, but that doesn't mean they base their help on that opinion. The disruptive approach to private helping, Horvath and Powell write, "in lieu of soliciting public input, seeks to influence or change public opinion and demand."

So one could ask about a panel like this: Was it merely seeking to supplement the public solution of public problems? Or was it engaging in the art that Horvath and Powell lay out, of seeking to bend an issue and the possible solutions to it in a direction favorable to elite interests, by tweaking how people think and talk about it?

Right up front, the choice of moderator offered a clue to anyone seeking to answer that question. Verveer was a prudent selection by MarketWorld standards. She had been the first U.S ambassador for global women's issues, and before that Hillary Clinton's chief of staff during her husband's White House days. Verveer was the kind of safe, corporate-sponsor-compatible feminist who got invited to conferences like this. (You didn't run into feminist legal scholars like Catharine MacKinnon or feminist writers like Virginie Despentes in these halls.) Verveer had been active in the civil rights movement a generation ago. If one of the corporate panelists had looked her up before the talk and been concerned about a potentially political orientation, they would have been reassured by the website of her strategic advisory group. It featured a quote, from the CEO of Coca-Cola, about how "women are already the most dynamic and fastest-growing economic force in the world." (MarketWorld being a small world, he was also the father of a cofounder of the Even app.) Verveer's firm called itself a "center for thought-leadership," offering advice and organizing "impact convenings" for clients. It made clear that it was not in the business of real, structural change. Its mission, borrowing a concept from Michael Porter, was "to create shared value—advancing women and girls while driving sustainable results." In the age of markets, if feminism didn't also fatten the bottom line, certain feminists appreciated that equality was an ask too hard.

Verveer's panelists on women's equality were Bob Collymore, chief executive of Safaricom, a Kenyan mobile phone provider; David Nabarro, a special adviser to the UN secretary-general on sustainable development and climate change; Carolyn Tastad, who was in charge of North America for Procter & Gamble; and Jane Wurwand, the founder of Dermalogica, which sells skin products. They made opening speeches, and before long the conversation had pulled into the port where so many of them eventually dock—the idea that the solution to the problem (in this case, women's equality) was entrepreneurship. "For me, it's all about jobs," said Wurwand. She noted that the beauty industry generates a disproportionate number of jobs for women. The best way to empower women, the thing it was "all about," was getting them jobs in the beauty industry and helping them own salons. What would most liberate women happened to be the growth of Dermalogica's own sector.

"Excellent! Entrepreneurship!" Verveer responded. They were talking about the equality of women, but now, already, they seemed to be limiting the topic to jobs and the growth of their sectors. They were talking about feminism on the condition that they stick to the profitable wing of it.

MarketWorld's ideas weren't promoted through propaganda and falsehoods so much as through this kind of confinement. Its weapon was not utterance but silence, the people it did not invite, the way it hemmed in a conversation. This approach eliminated the kind of expertise that could cogently and persuasively formulate a less MarketWorld-friendly response. In the absence of diverse voices, any criticism of such a panel might attract easy putdowns: *What, you don't think women can own their own beauty salons? What, do you think it's better for women not to have jobs?* This is why it was important not to have people sympathetic to such criticisms sitting on the panel.

For example, what you didn't hear asked at CGI was: Didn't the beauty industry fuel the very commodification of women that sustained gender inequality? In a world of true gender equality, might not the beauty industry shrink? Isn't it possible that there would be millions fewer nails done and heads blow-dried and bottles of foundation sold in the egalitarian world the panelists claimed to want? Naomi Wolf writes in her book *The Beauty Myth* that "whatever is deeply, essentially female—the life in a woman's expression, the feel of her flesh, the shape of her breasts, the transformations after childbirth of her skin—is being reclassified as ugly, and ugliness as disease." This perceived ugliness is, she notes, good for business, because industries like retail and advertising—not to mention salons and plastic surgeons—are "fueled by sexual dissatisfaction." Wouldn't true equality for women be a win for women but a loss for Dermalogica?

You did not get into testy structural things like that here. That was getting into the zone where someone's progress comes at a cost to someone else's business—someone who is a speaker at and/or sponsor of this gathering. And because the staff had done each part of their job right—from the selection of a moderator to the choice of the panelists to the framing of the topic—there was little risk of such questions. The panel itself was an endlessly sunny, conflict-free zone. It was rare to have a genuine, full-throated philosophical disagreement, which was remarkable given the topic of women's equality. Sometimes, when a hairline fracture opened between two panelists, a skilled moderator could, as Verveer did in this very panel, rush to say, "I don't think Bob and David are in conflict with each other."

To keep disagreement out of one's panels was not just an aesthetic decision. In some small way, it changed how the world operated, because it shaped what ideas got talked about, and what solutions got acted on when people left this room, and what programs got funded and didn't, and what stories got covered and didn't, and it tipped the scale in the direction of the winners once again, ensuring that the friendly, win-win way of solving public problems would remain dominant. People asking big questions about the underlying system and imagining alternative systems would not be attending.

The market consensus also served to elevate certain kinds of solutions over others, to give them a kind of Good Housekeeping seal. For example, the panelists spoke of diversity, and the moderator told everyone what her consulting firm made good money telling people: that diversity wasn't only just but also profitable. "The diversity advantage is truly an advantage," she said. They turned to the United Nations' Sustainable Development Goals. Tastad, of P&G, tried to give these a boost by saying, "The SDGs are fundamentally consistent with our company's core purpose, which is empowering lives." Good to know.

Then the moderator came at the same concept another way by asking whether the panelists saw women's equality becoming a fundamental part of business strategy, or whether it would continue to languish as a priority mostly of philanthropists and corporate social responsibility departments. Wurwand thought it was a competitive advantage. "Empowering girls and women is the hot new branding thing!" she explained. In MarketWorld, this was important to underscore to the audience. "So it's not just the right thing to do," Verveer said. "It's the business-smart thing to do." This was the highest praise a cause could receive.

Women's equality, it was now said, was a $28 trillion opportunity. This had become a near-constant refrain in MarketWorld—some permutation of the words "women," "equality," and "trillion." If the logic of our time had applied to the facts of an earlier age, someone would have put out a report suggesting that ending slavery was great for reducing the trade deficit. "Of course, you should do it because it's the right thing to do, but there's a strong business case," Collymore, of Safaricom, now said. In other words, of course you should do it because morality is enough, but since we all know that morality isn't actually enough, you should know that the business case is fantastic.

Now it was Q-and-A time, and the cult of consensus continued. Only once did the pleasantness break. A woman with a German accent, who said she was from Healing Hotels of the World, rose to make a comment. Speaking of the women the panel had spoken of helping, she said, "Sometimes I think that, with all our ideas, we victimize them."

That simple statement suggested a range of possibilities. What if they in the doing-well-by-doing-good set were wrong? What if their exclusions and noninvitations and silences were mistakes? What if those omissions, with the enormous financial backing that they enjoyed, had real consequences in people's lives? What if the reason much of the world had in recent centuries turned away from closed-door conclaves of unelected, unaccountable people making decisions for humanity is that they could do more harm than good? Didn't democracy arise because of a wise wariness of such rooms? What if it was unfair and illegitimate for an unelected body to have any errors they make so widely influence societies and ramify into the lives of millions of people without the power, connections, and platforms to register their interests and talk back? What if reimagining the world in such rooms was, in fact, the business-smart thing to do but not the right thing to do?

The Healing Hotels woman's comment was the only one the panel ignored. The moderator listened, nodded, moved on.

These questions of anger and participation and democracy had hovered over the conference, and they hung in the air in the final session of the final day of the final Clinton Global Initiative. The session title was "Imagine All the People." Its centerpiece was a much-anticipated valedictory address by Bill Clinton. He wanted to lay out his own first draft of CGI's legacy.

He spoke for more than an hour, perhaps one of his last major speeches to a world that still loved him, reciting the history of the CGI model and celebrating its accomplishments. The central thrust of that success had been the luring of private-sector actors into the public problem-solving arena. But it wasn't always clear which had influenced which more. Clinton spoke of constant innovation, of impact, of scalability, of margins, of volume. This had not been his language coming out of Yale Law and campaigning around the state of Arkansas. One of the major cultural developments during his adult life had been the growing pressure on political leaders to tone down the political language and amp up the business jargon if they wanted to be taken seriously and get MarketWorld's help. Clinton, like so many leaders, had accepted the bargain. It was another way in which the new philanthropic model that he had promoted was disruptive of, rather than contributory to, public life: The private sector didn't merely add to the public sphere's activities. It got to change the language in which the public sphere thought and acted.

Of course, no one at CGI would be caught denigrating democracy. The alternative mode of problem-solving that Clinton promoted was not intended to be in tension with democracy; it was meant to bolster it. He described CGI's model of extrademocratic partnership as "living proof that good people, committed to creative cooperation, have almost unlimited positive impact to help people today and give our kids better tomorrows." Then he added an astonishing aside: "This is all that does work in the modern world."

According to the former leader of the most powerful country in history, a centrist but from the political left, whose wife hoped she was just a few months from her own long-sought turn at its helm, all that worked in the modern world was private, donor-financed world-saving, full of good intentions, unaccountable to the public, based on win-win partnerships initiated by companies and philanthropists and other private actors, blessed (sometimes) by public officials. All that worked was projects cooked up out of public view at a forum underwritten by Cisco, Diageo, Procter & Gamble, Swiss Re, Western Union, and McDonald's. The only problem-solving approach that worked in the modern world, according to Clinton, was one that made the people an afterthought, to be helped but not truly heard.

Clinton now voiced the sense of besiegement that the globalists had been feeling. "This is a time when this sort of talk is not in fashion all over the world," he said of their ethos. "Everywhere today," he said, "there's a temptation to say to everything I just told you,

'No. You're wrong; life is a zero-sum game, and I'm losing. You're wrong; our differences matter more than our common humanity. To hell with the findings of the Human Genome Project, that we're all 99.5 percent the same. No. Choose resentment over reconciliation; choose anger over answers; choose denial over empowerment; and choose walls over bridges.'

These are not the right choices. The choices you have made here, for eleven years, are the right choices."

Was this the only way of framing the choices? Was there a case to be made for communities wanting to resist the globosphere— a case that deserved to be heard on its own terms, and not emptily smeared as favoring resentment and difference? Clinton's globalist dream was admirable, but it was also intolerant of other dreams. It sought to make hard choices seem inevitable and uncomplicated. It sought to blur what happened to be good for the plutocrats in the room with what was good for ordinary people. It promulgated another inspiring vision of changing the world that left the underlying systems untouched. Clinton was right that his philosophy was meeting resistance, but he did not take much responsibility for why it was being resisted. The win-win doctrine upon which he had built his foundation was more than unfashionable. It was among the things inspiring the revolt by making so many people feel barred from decision-making about the future of their own world.

Eight months later, Clinton was walking his dog near his home in the New York City suburb of Chappaqua. He ran into one of his neighbors, a "zany" right-winger who was a fan of Donald Trump and who, several weeks after the final CGI, had gotten his way with his neighbor Hillary's electoral defeat. The neighbor and Bill had a tradition of bantering across the chasm between them. So that day, Clinton recalled, he was "ragging with him," when at one point the neighbor said, "Obama and Hillary started the second Civil War."

Clinton told this story sitting forty stories above Manhattan in his foundation office, sipping milkless tea. He had had half a year to digest the defeat that plunged America into the Trump era. If his wife had suffered most as the candidate whose platform failed, Bill had suffered in a different, more abstract way: Trump had defeated Hillary, but the ideas that propelled his "America First" campaign were a repudiation of the globalist consensus of which Bill had always been the louder and more unreserved champion.

"My whole life in politics was marked by a political version, on a small scale, of the epic global contest that is now under way between inclusive cooperation—involving networks and diverse people working toward a common goal—and the reassertion of tribal nationalism," he told me. With the world aflame and even some in posh Chappaqua feeling the country to be in a kind of civil war, Clinton could not escape the possibility that his side was losing the "epic global contest" that had defined his career. His neighbor, if zany, had recently been backed up in his analysis by the writer Pankaj Mishra, who said of this explosive global moment of terrorist violence, raging xenophobia, and political upheaval, "Future historians may well see such uncoordinated mayhem as commencing the third—and the longest and strangest—of all world wars: one that approximates, in its ubiquity, a global civil war."

The world was in "a period of intense resentment," Clinton said. "In a time of extreme resentment, it's more important to people that you hate the same things and the same people that they do." He looked not only at the U.S. election but also at Brexit, at frothing far-right populist movements in Europe, at the unhinged antidrug crusader who now ran the Philippines, and beyond, and he concluded that despite the prosperity and promise that his new philosophy had spread, "You still have this enormous zero-sum bloc in the world. Win-lose"—people who believed that their progress could only come at the expense of someone else's. He continued to believe in the linearity of progress and growing borderlessness; he assumed the world would come to its senses. He figured, to paraphrase an old line of his, that there was nothing wrong with the world that couldn't be fixed by what was right with the world.

This faith reflected the standard MarketWorld response to what Mishra dubbed the "age of anger": that, yes, the winners of the age had to do a better job of extending victory to others. But this was a facile answer. It avoided the harder, more urgent question facing the winners, which had to do with their culpability for what had happened, and whether they, and the system they oversaw, would have to change. It was admirable that some of the elites had contributed to Clinton's causes. But didn't those elites bear responsibility for the anger, fueled by mistrust of elites, that was bubbling in America and internationally? "Yes, absolutely," Clinton said. "But."

The "yes" part of that was the overconfidence of the winners in globalization as a win-win. "I think a lot of people who lived in comfortable circumstances in theory knew that there were some dislocated people," he said, "but thought there were always going to be more winners than losers." That assumption had not necessarily aged well. As for the "but" part, Clinton blamed his political opponents on the right. "I also believe that when the difficulties became apparent, at least in America, people on our side, whether they were rich or middle class, were much more willing to do something about it," he said, "whereas the people on the other side realized that if they didn't do anything about it, they could blame us and be rewarded for their misconduct." He added, "So we're responsible, but the people who didn't want to respond are more responsible."

In hindsight, Clinton said, he and his fellow globalists could have done more to help ordinary people absorb the shocks of change. He could have insisted, when signing the North American Free Trade Agreement as president, on more restrictions on that freedom. He wondered if he should have imposed a tariff on firms that moved their factories overseas, leading to job losses, and then sought to export products to American consumers—and whether he should have linked his support for NAFTA to such a tariff. He imagined what that position might have been: "Look, I'd be happy to sign this, but I want a fee on the exporters sufficient to take care of the people that they dislodged." He could have fought harder for job retraining monies to be allocated before trade agreements were signed, and for more corporate incentives to keep jobs in the country. He added that when President Obama had brokered the global climate accord, he, similarly, could have offered more of a plan to coal miners and others who would be displaced by change. Clinton took a measure of responsibility for failing to do these things, but he noted, reasonably, that he had been blocked by his Republican opposition on virtually everything. So these regrets might have been moot.

Still, his political opposition as president does not tell the full story of why recent decades have been so grueling for millions of Americans. Clinton, like Obama after him, was up against militant conservatives and libertarians, backed by plutocratic donors, who loathed the very idea of public, governmental problem-solving. To be clear, that is the movement chiefly responsible for market supremacy's takeover of America and the bleak prospects of millions of Americans. Yet the Republican Party represented less than half of the nation, and the Democratic Party had a chance to stand for a robust alternative to market hegemony. And you could say that it did to an extent—but it often did, under Clinton, and Obama, in a tepid, market-friendly, donor-approved way that conceded so much to government's haters that the cause lost the fire of purpose.

Jacob Hacker, the Yale political scientist, who was once described as "an intellectual 'It boy' in the Democratic Party," said in an interview, "Many progressives still believe in a role for government that is pretty fundamental, but they have lost their faith in the capacity to achieve it, and they've in many cases lost the language for talking about it." Republicans, he said, are straightforward in their contempt for government. Democrats, especially those of the Clinton school of centrist, triangulating, market-friendly politics, don't counter the contempt with a vigorous embrace of government. Rather, Hacker said, candidates like Hillary Clinton speak in a "gauzy" language about "bringing people together across lines of race and class" and "solving problems together in some vague way," but remain "understandably reluctant to talk about the use of government itself." They campaign like this in spite of policies that remain committed to government action. Even their proposed policies, though, reflect ambivalence: health care for all, but not through public provision; help paying for college, but not free college; charter schools, but not equal schools. Bill Clinton had distilled this hesitancy when he famously declared, in a passage whose second sentence is rarely included in quotations, "The era of big government is over. But we cannot go back to the time when our citizens were left to fend for themselves."

Hacker argues that this hesitancy and "loss of faith in government" has "hugely asymmetric effects on the two parties." He said, "For Republicans and the right, it is—for the most part, though not always—conducive to their aims, because if government doesn't do things, it can often be consistent with what they would like to see happen. But for the left and for Democrats, it's a huge loss, because their vision of a good society is one in which a lot of valuable public goods and benefits have their foundations in government action."

To illustrate Hacker's point: Bill Clinton's heart disease had led him to experiment with healthier diets. Because of this, he decided to address the problem of childhood obesity, which is of course abetted by processed food and soft drink makers with great political clout and a knack for insinuating their products into public schools.

It was to be expected that the right's answer to this problem would be a hymn to the free market. The left, though, might instead propose to marshal government and the law to protect children from companies they can neither vote against nor easily organize to thwart on their own. From an ex-president without legal power but still with the ability to galvanize a movement, one could imagine a campaign, modeled on those of the Progressive Era, to pressure the government to put an end to this abusive profiteering. Yet his proposed answer was to make it easier for the offending companies to make money selling healthier products.

"If you want to get them to do less harm, it requires innovation, because they still have to make money, especially for publicly held companies," Clinton said. This was, quite literally, the bottom line.

The needs of the market came first. Even a man who had spent his lifetime in politics felt a duty to be solicitous of the businessperson's concerns. Rather than insist that the companies stop shaving years off of children's lives, especially poor ones', we had to make sure they had a better business model waiting on deck to replace the current, noxious one.

Clinton recounted the double-barreled argument he made to the companies: "We know you don't want to give all these schoolchildren Type 2 diabetes. We know you don't want to do it because it would hurt your heart, and because when they're in their mid-thirties, in wheelchairs with their legs cut off, they ain't gonna be drinking a lot of soda pop." Not harming children was not only the right thing to do but also the business-smart thing to do. Otherwise, Clinton said, "their own business model will devour itself." He had worked with the companies to reduce voluntarily, as a group, the calories in their products. They had done so, and children were better off, and government hadn't had to be bothered. "The best government looks for ways to make things work more in the private sector," he said. And he was proud that he had helped children in a way that preserved the companies' ability to make a reasonable return. "They're all still making money, because they did it together," he said.

In this embrace of making things work in the private sector, even when big business is harming children, Clinton revealed how he had made peace with market supremacy. At one point, he used a phrase that captured this acceptance. When faced with a bad system, knowing it is flawed, and wanting to change it, but not wanting to overplay your hand, what do you do? "How much do you do the right thing?" he asked. "How much do you feed the beast?" Perhaps Clinton, like many of his fellow win-win globalists, had, on the question of how to confront the influence of plutocrats over the last generation, overfed the beast. What did he make of the criticism that the private-sector-led approach to social change undermined the habit and idea of governments taking the lead in solving problems? "I think there's some truth in that," he said. And he said that he tried wherever possible in his philanthropic efforts to work with local governments, and "to reach out to the NGOs in the area, and to be open to the suggestions of people."

Such attempts to work with government, though, were not the same as a conviction in the power of government, the supreme power of government, to better people's lives. Clinton seemed to acknowledge this when he said that some globalist do-gooders, whether at home in America or in their work abroad, had at times neglected the duty to make democracy stronger. "If you do this at any scale at all, you have an obligation to build the capacity of the governments to solve the problems of the people and to fight corruption," he said. Yet so many globalists who pursue change today overlook that idea, and Clinton did worry about that. He said, "What I've tried to do is to say to, like, the founder of Toms Shoes—who gives shoes away; he's a good man—or any number of these other younger entrepreneurs, who I think are wonderful, is that, whenever possible, the most positive and lasting impact will be if you do this in a way that increases the capacity of the local officials, both the administrative, public servant types and the elected officials, to take care of themselves."

Accordingly, Clinton proposed a test for do-gooders to judge whether their help is actually improving things: "When you get done, will it be sustainable, and will the people be governed by more effective, more responsive, more honest government?" Yet it was easier to apply that principle to a project in Africa, perhaps, than it was to deploy it in America when taking on the problem of soft drinks, juice boxes, and childhood obesity. One's American plutocrat friends didn't necessarily have a problem with more energetic government in Africa. But they preferred win-win solutions in their own backyard, where energetic government sounded like it could end up being expensive.

Clinton didn't like to think that his connections to, and enrichment from, the super-wealthy had changed him in any way, or shaped his manner of thinking about things. Yes, he had become, in a sense, one of the worldwide chieftains of thought leadership, charging as much as a few hundred thousand dollars a speech. Yes, he reportedly lunched before some of these speeches with smaller groups of plutocrats who paid, say, $10,000 a head to eat with him and hear his take on the world. But, Clinton argued, "When you can't make decisions which benefit them anymore, it's less of a concern." He said this as though it were impossible to imagine how the opportunity to earn tens of millions of dollars after a presidency might affect a president's fight-picking decisions while in office.

In our present age of anger, so many people seemed to intuit that their leaders becoming fellow travelers of billionaires and millionaires *did* have some effect on what they believed. That intuition had hamstrung his own wife's campaign. It had helped Bernie Sanders's unlikely primary challenge, and then Donald Trump's unlikely election victory—made all the stranger by the fact that Trump incarnated the very problem he named. Was it inevitable that the leaders of a democracy should affiliate mostly with plutocrats after their time in public office? Was that not related to the problems of mistrust and alienation and social distance that lurked behind the anger now confronting elites?

Clinton said he had made 649 speeches for money, by his last count, and paid nearly half of the income in taxes, and donated some of it to charity, and helped aging friends and relatives with medical bills. (He pointed out that you don't owe any gift tax if you pay the health care provider directly.) "If somebody wants to think I was corrupted by that, I largely took money from rich people and gave it to poor people," he said. "And, unlike Robin Hood, I didn't have to hold an arrow on 'em."

Was there really no validity to the anger?

"Keep in mind, we are living in a period of extreme resentment," Clinton said. He argued that part of that feeling was over the financial crisis: "The public's anger over what happened to them was insufficiently sated by the number of rich people that went broke and by the number of people who went to prison." Part of the feeling was over the dislocations of globalization, technology, and other changes. In other words, he didn't think there was anything wrong with what he and others had done. He just thought that people were bitter and seeking scapegoats because their own lives had been hard. "These people," as his Lazard panelist had called them, were, after all, being "led down a path of the politics of fear," as Sadiq Khan had put it; and as Clinton himself had said, a lot of the angry people these days "had no idea what they were doing" and were succumbing to a "visceral us-and-them mentality."

Clinton knew, however, that the bitterness toward the globalists threatened their One World dream. One possible response was to be educated by such widespread bitterness and rewrite the dream—to reverse the long-standing habit that Dani Rodrik described of "putting democracy to work for the global economy, instead of the other way around." This was not Clinton's favored approach. The One World dream was nonnegotiable for globalists. The challenge, Clinton said, was to figure out how "to take care of America first, but don't run away from the rest of the world." It could be, he was sure, a win-win. The anger had not deterred his modus operandi.

Clinton had been one of the great shapers of an age defined by globalization and rapid change and market hegemony, and he was also a product of that age. He had long believed in the pursuit of reform, and he was also a pragmatist who was said, by friends and critics alike, to know which way the wind was blowing. And over the course of his political career, the wind had blown in an ever more market-friendly way. In 1964, the year he graduated from high school, 77 percent of Americans reported a high degree of trust in government, according to the Pew Research Center; that number had since fallen into the teens. Clinton, believing in the power of politics to improve lives, having shown the possibilities of politics with his own life, had accepted the shift. He had accepted that businesses must make their returns, and that children must at times have their interests balanced against the imperative of those returns. He had in his post-presidency done more real good and saved more lives than perhaps any of his predecessors; and at the same time he had accepted certain limitations on how good is done nowadays. MarketWorld had so triumphed that even a man who once led the most powerful machinery of state in the history of civilization could now say of private, plutocratic social change, "This is all that does work in the modern world."

For people to question this view is not to deny the good it is capable of doing, any more than to question monarchy is to say that kings always botch up the economy. It is to say that it does not matter what kind of a job the king is doing. It is to say that even the best he can do is not good enough, because of how it is done: the insulation, the chancing of everything on the king's continued beneficence, the capacity of royal mistakes to alter lives they should not be touching. Similarly, to question the doing-well-by-doing-good globalists is not to doubt their intentions or results. Rather, it is to say that even when all those things are factored in, something is not quite right in believing they are the ones best positioned to effect meaningful change. To question their supremacy is very simply to doubt the proposition that what is best for the world just so happens to be what the rich and powerful think it is. It is to say you don't want to confine your imagination of how the world might be to what can be done with their support. It is to say that a world marked more and more by private greed and the private provision of public goods is a world that doesn't trust the people, in their collective capacity, to imagine another kind of society into being.

Through it all, Clinton saw truths in the anger bubbling up around him. He saw how MarketWorld-style change crowded out the habit of democracy. He genuinely worried about young people seeing social problems and, unlike in his activist-prone generation, confining their questioning to what socially minded business they could start up. He accepted that the comfortable had oversold their definition of progress in our globalizing, digitizing age. He had regrets that the winners from change had not invested enough in the losers.

Clinton could see and admit all these things. But he would not call out elites for their sins; or call for power's redistribution and fundamental, systemic change; or suggest that plutocrats might have to surrender precious things for others to have a mere shot of transcending indecency. Someone will have to.

"OTHER PEOPLE ARE NOT YOUR CHILDREN"

Two months after Clinton's CGI swan song and just three weeks after the victory of Donald Trump, in an august apartment tower twenty-six blocks north of the president-elect's Fifth Avenue penthouse, a gathering of people who loathed him were toasting the holidays over cocktails and Peking duck rolls. A woman whom we will call Nicola hovered in the living room, surrounded by elegant dresses and crisp suits, prominent editors and chief executives and even the television doctor Mehmet Oz. Nicola was depressed. Everyone at the party seemed depressed. Everyone was wondering what they could do.

Nicola sensed a great, dangerous turning in the world against everything her life had stood for. She was Mexican, and the new American president wanted to build a wall to keep her compatriots out of the United States. Her past work as a journalist made her an "enemy of the people" in the view of the new administration. She was a proud globalist: She had been a foreign correspondent; she had studied in London back when it was unthinkable that Britain would vote to secede from the European Union; she had spent years working for one of the major MarketWorld conferences; and now she worked for an international organization that the president-elect regularly deplored. Nicola was anguished by the spreading politics of anger. She and many other people at the party wanted to do something about it. Nicola said that globalization and trade and openness and "everything we all believe in"—she gestured at the MarketWorlders circling the buffet—must be explained to those mobs. Nicola said she could start a new initiative, which could be housed at the World Economic Forum, the organization behind the annual plutocratic reunion in Davos. In this thinking she was not alone. All across MarketWorld in that winter of revulsion, people were plotting solutions to the revolt against them that doubled down on the approaches that had gotten us here.

If anyone truly believes that the same ski-town conferences and fellowship programs, the same politicians and policies, the same entrepreneurs and social businesses, the same campaign donors, the same thought leaders, the same consulting firms and protocols, the same philanthropists and reformed Goldman Sachs executives, the same win-wins and doing-well-by-doing-good initiatives and private solutions to public problems that had promised grandly, if superficially, to change the world—if anyone thinks that the Market-World complex of people and institutions and ideas that failed to prevent this mess even as it harped on making a difference, and whose neglect fueled populism's flames, is also the solution, wake them up by tapping them, gently, with this book. For the inescapable answer to the overwhelming question—Where do we go from here?—is: somewhere other than where we have been going, led by people other than the people who have been leading us.

Late at night, Andrew Kassoy sits in the living room of his Brooklyn town house, thinking about the limits of his widely admired approach to changing the world. Is there another way? he wonders. And would another way have room for him?

Kassoy is a poster child for the MarketWorld method of social change. He is one of many people in our age who graduated from a long and successful career in business to a career in seeking to make the world more just and equal—and doing so using the tools and mentalities of his former life. He had spent sixteen years in what he calls "totally mainstream private equity"—DLJ Real Estate Capital Partners, Credit Suisse First Boston, and MSD Capital, where he helped the technology magnate Michael Dell invest his multibillion-dollar personal fortune. It was the kind of career people dreamed of, though Kassoy thought of it as a strange happenstance. "I came from a super-liberal, social justice, academic-oriented family and sort of accidentally ended up on this career," he said. He had been ensnared, perhaps, by a dominant story of his age.

In 2001, he was chosen for the Henry Crown Fellowship of the Aspen Institute. The fellowship is a prestigious finishing school to assist the transition from making it in business to making the world a better place. Its mission is to mobilize a "new breed of leaders" to "tackle the world's most intractable problems." But it defines leader in a particular way: "All are proven entrepreneurs, mostly from the world of business, who have reached a point in their lives where, having achieved success, they are ready to apply their creative talents to building a better society." Fellows meet for four one-week sessions over two years. They read and discuss important texts, debate what makes for a "good society," and develop side projects to do good in ways that generally avoid denting their opportunities to do well. Kassoy attended his first fellowship meeting in Aspen that summer, and the readings and discussions cracked him open. The experience awakened him to his latent discontent with private equity. "It was quite an intense experience because it caused me to say, 'I've been at this for ten, eleven years. It's time to pick up my head and actually think about what my life is actually about,'" he said. "And then I came back, and 9/11 happened."

Among former financiers, stories like this are not unusual: It can take some force majeure (cancer, divorce, death), and sometimes more than one of them, to be jolted out of a comfortable life. Yet, as Kassoy learned, even that jolt may not be enough. He began to think about what else he could do. "Frankly," he said, "I lacked the courage to go do something about anything that I was actually interested in."

The word "courage" suggested that Kassoy's initial thinking about what he might do involved trading in his privilege for another kind of life. He assumed that any doing of good, to be genuine, would have to come at a cost to doing well—perhaps a legacy of his family's politics. In other words, his early instincts defied the messages of MarketWorld—above all, that he could have his cake and give his cake back, too. That assumption came to chill him. "I pretty much ended up putting my head back down," he said. Private equity would remain his meal ticket, and he would help others, at no risk, on the side. He came upon an organization called Echoing Green, which gave seed money to social entrepreneurs. "I ended up on the board because they were looking for people with money to be donors," he said.

After his other flirtations, Kassoy found himself in familiar territory. Echoing Green was built by another private equity firm, General Atlantic. That firm's leadership, according to Echoing Green's website, "predicted that the venture capital investment model they employed so effectively at General Atlantic could also be utilized to drive social change." The revolution would be leveraged; perhaps the master's tools *could* dismantle the master's house, after all. General Atlantic birthed Echoing Green in 1987, "naming it after a William Blake poem about creating a better world."

Kassoy began to moonlight as an adviser to Echoing Green fellows, who tended to be social entrepreneurs seeking to scale their ideas. He began to notice a common problem afflicting them. Some people start businesses to make a big profit. But others, of the bent of mind that Echoing Green sought out, "were creating a for-profit business because they recognized it was a better way to scale a solution to a problem that they were interested in." He gave the example of his advisee Sara Horowitz, who founded the Freelancers Union, which represents independent workers such as Uber drivers and magazine writers. She originally wanted to serve as a broker to help these workers buy health insurance as a group. Then she realized it would be easier and more effective if she simply created the health insurance company herself. But the economy wasn't set up for people like Horowitz. A company not run purely in shareholders' interests risked lawsuits from its investors. The dominant interpretation of corporate law, as we've seen, has since the 1970s come to regard companies' first duty as being to earn a profit for shareholders. A company that put social goals ahead of business ones had no clear place in this regime.

Thus Kassoy came to be interested, as he put it, in "how you build the market infrastructure for people to be able to do business in a different way." This interest began to occupy more and more of his time, at Michael Dell's expense. "I started to realize I was pretty much spending half my day, every day, sitting in my office meeting with these people and not really doing my day job, which didn't seem like a very good thing for me or for my employer or my partner," he said. Kassoy had gone from the "head down" pursuit of private equity success, to an awareness of his duties to others, to the discovery of safe, Wall Street–backed ways of fighting for social change—and now he was ready to do MarketWorld-style change full-time.

He had remained close to a pair of friends from his days as a Stanford undergraduate Jay Coen Gilbert and Bart Houlahan, who were wrestling with the same problem. They had built a footwear company, in which Kassoy had invested, and were selling it after several years. The company had distinguished itself with socially responsible production methods. Now, though, the venture capitalists who had backed the company wanted their payout, and that risked destroying the responsible practices. "Time to sell," the investors effectively said, according to Kassoy. "Seven years is up, and you're going to sell to the highest bidder." The problem, he said, was that the buyer "who was willing to pay the most for the business was the person who saw the most opportunity to get rid of all of those things"—the responsible practices—"in order to make more money."

The trio batted around ideas for addressing this problem, and at last alighted on the vision of creating a parallel capitalist infrastructure, next to the traditional one, in which companies could be more responsible and conscious, and nonetheless raise money from capital markets and comply with the law. Thus was born the B Corporation or benefit corporation, as it is also known. The three men started a nonprofit called B Lab, which gives better-behaved businesses a certification based on a rigorous analysis of their social and environmental practices. Kickstarter, King Arthur Flour, Ben & Jerry's, and the Brazilian cosmetics company Natura are all B corps.

Kassoy and his cofounders wanted to make the world a better place, and they found a way of doing so in line with MarketWorld values. They made it easier for companies that were willing to do good, while all but ignoring the companies that wanted to do harm. "The basic theory was 'make good easy,'" Kassoy said. "Make it easy to identify what's a good business, codify that with a brand that people will understand, and then get the leaders to adopt that brand and speak loudly about their values. And, somehow or other, in doing that we will create a new sector of the economy. And, eventually, everybody else will see that that's a really successful sector of the economy and do the same thing."

Kassoy and his colleagues hoped that by certifying conscious companies, they could change the larger system of business. "I do think that we thought, and still do, that this is a systems-change model," he said. But in the MarketWorld way, they didn't take on the system directly. They simply sought to cultivate examples of a different way. Part of why they didn't do that systemic work, he said, was that they "had no real sense of how to get from here to there. And I think, in particular, all three of us, coming from the private sector, didn't have a great sense of, like, what really public policy is." He said the trio "had some vague notion that you prove something out and eventually government adopts it, was kind of the general idea."

In ten years, they had converted hundreds of companies to B Corps. But now, sitting in his living room, Kassoy said that B Lab was in the midst of a rethinking process, which was guided by his conviction that "what got us here is not going to get us where we're going." And where was it, exactly, they wanted to go? Toward that system change they had neglected. Kassoy said they knew they had done a better job of proving a model than changing how business itself works, and they wanted to switch gears.

This moment of rethinking was stirring up many questions, such as whether there should be a kind of "B Corps lite," a scoring system for companies that do not qualify as proper B Corps but would like a transparent rating of their practices. The thorniest questions, and the ones that seemed to anguish Kassoy, involved whether to stick to the MarketWorld mantra of "make good easier," or whether instead to seek to make those who commit harm pay a higher price—which meant changing the system of business for everyone, fighting in the arena of politics and law rather than the market, and elevating the stopping of bad business over the encouragement of good business. Kassoy was wrestling with whether to cling to the assumptions and dreams of MarketWorld and its win-win theory of change, or whether to pursue another genre of change that seemed to feel truer, if more elusive, to him.

For example, one's of B Lab's great victories had been the creation of a parallel corporate law, first enacted in Maryland and then adopted in other states, that allowed companies to embed a social mission into their work without fear of legal trouble such as shareholder complaints. It was important to give good companies this protection. Kassoy, though, still wondered about "the larger systemic question here about whether an opt-in system in the end can ever overcome the power of the incumbent interests." Was it more important to make it easier for Etsy to do good, or rather to make it harder for ExxonMobil to do harm? Was it possible to do both?

Kassoy felt drawn toward the systems work, even though he had devoted the last decade to the other approach. "I'm not sure everybody would say this, but I believe that there's a huge role for government regulation of business," he said. "We're not going to change everybody. We're not changing human greed. Businesses act badly." There were, in particular, "extractive industries where just the existence of the industry" means harm and social costs being dumped on humanity. "We're not getting rid of all of those things," he said.

The United States had millions of corporations and, after a decade of B Lab's evangelizing, just hundreds of B Corps. Kassoy saw now, more clearly than he did at the company's founding, that solving problems like inequality, greed, and pollution would require more than making good easier. He was not the only MarketWorlder coming around to the thought that their ways of operating might be inadequate to the actual work of changing the world, or even just one's own country. These MarketWorlders, though, often lacked an understanding of how actual change did work, or they felt, sometimes dubiously, that pursuing the other kind of change called upon skills they lacked. If government was the place you went to change systems, what could they as individuals do? They could petition the government. They could join movements fighting to change law and policy. But Kassoy, like many in MarketWorld, was daunted by this approach. He had the feeling that many in MarketWorld do that their grounding in the norms of business made them ill-equipped for the realm of politics, where win-lose was normal and where fights often had to be picked instead of mutually agreeable deals being struck. Conflict can scare the business type. "I am not a very effective activist," Kassoy said, "and I know a lot of people who are, of whom I'm very supportive, but I've never been very good at it. I can't tell you if that's lack of courage, lack of an understanding of how to—like, I think being a really good activist requires some amount of manipulation, and I'm not that good at that." It was peculiar, this idea of activism as manipulation; it sounded more like an excuse for not working on systems than a reason.

Sometimes Kassoy felt confident in his proposition that it was enough to show what a better capitalism looked like, and to leave the system-changing and harm-thwarting to others. System change, he said, was "not my highest and best use"—the corporate language unwittingly underscoring the point. It was not part of his skill set. In his mind, there was a way to justify his work-within-the-system approach by comparing it to the work of Dr. Martin Luther King Jr. "Martin needed Malcolm," he said. "I don't think that what we're doing can change capitalism by itself. But I do believe that what this does is it creates a model." On other days, Kassoy wasn't so sure about this logic. He kept coming back to regulation. "I'm a big-government kind of a person," he said. "I believe that there's a very strong role for the state. And I don't know how to make that happen."

Kassoy's ambivalence is what Jacob Hacker, the Yale political scientist, seems to have in mind when he speaks of political liberals who are philosophically committed to government, to the public solution of public problems, but who have absorbed, like second-hand smoke, the right's contempt for public action. While people on the right believe actively in the superiority of market solutions, liberals like Kassoy do so passively—passively in that they do not reject a public solution in theory, but pursue a private one in practice. "I have a constant debate with my father," Kassoy said, "who thinks the single most evil human being in the history of the planet was Ronald Reagan, because he single-handedly convinced us as a society the government's bad." He added, "If you think about Bill Clinton's success in the '90s, his Third Way was all about basically adopting a lot of that language. And so no one's really told us government is a good thing for a very long time." Saying this seemed to make Kassoy reflect on whether he had unwittingly become the latest link in this chain of liberals consolidating the war on government by proffering private solutions to public problems. "Now I'm not going to get a good night's sleep as I think about this," he said.

Whatever Kassoy's private doubts, B Corps were championed all over MarketWorld. The Aspen Institute had named not only Kassoy but all three cofounders of B Lab as Henry Crown Fellows. The Ford Foundation had given B Lab a grant. The founders were regularly praised by recognized "thought leaders" and often heard themselves called the same; two of the three of them had given a TED talk. B Corps certified by Kassoy's team were among the most admired companies at Summit at Sea. Their system for rating companies had been discussed at Davos. The Beeck Center for Social Impact & Innovation at Georgetown promoted B Lab's fellowship to train people on using "business as a force for good." A leading B Corp called Laureate Education had attracted George Soros and KKR as investors, and named Bill Clinton its "honorary chancellor"—a job that paid nearly $18 million over five years, according to the *Washington Post*. "You ought to look at these B Corporations," Clinton has said, and he elevated B Lab by featuring them one year on the main stage of CGI.

Kassoy wondered how much he and B Lab would have to change to pursue reform of the system itself—to get into that terrain of making bad harder. For starters, B Lab had a strict ethic of positivity. "We stand for something, not against anything" was one of its mantras. But real change can require being against things, and he knew that. Real change often demands sacrifice, and these days, Kassoy said, "Not that many people are really putting themselves at risk." Real change may compel trade-offs and the necessity of choosing your priorities. "I don't believe that everybody just trying to be more responsible leads to higher returns," he said. "There are trade-offs," he added, but "no one wants to tell that story." ?, *what does this look like.*

He sometimes looked at the little MarketWorld initiatives all around him that pursued change and avoided real change at the same time, and he wondered if it wasn't just a way of throwing scraps to keep the peace. When private equity firms quoted William Blake and spoke of changing the world, how genuine was it, and how much was it a bid, as Kassoy put it, "to make people feel like they've been heard and not have bloody revolution"?

Kassoy still believed deeply in what he and B Lab were doing. But he asked himself questions like, "At what point is it the right moment to say, 'Great, this is how all business must act'?" He said, "As big as what I think we're doing is, that would be taking a fundamental shot into the heart of capitalism." Some bright, burning force within Kassoy seemed to want to take that shot, to challenge the people he once worked with in finance, to change business for all so that everyone played by the same rules, to go after the worst first rather than make it easier for the already good to be good—to change the system, with the consent of its citizens, not just work around its decay. And yet that force could feel itself to be up against a hugely powerful and pervasive web of myths—MarketWorld. If the force throbbing within Kassoy, if change itself—genuine, from-the-root change—was to have a shot, many people would need to be freed of these myths and remember what change actually is.

O n the night when Kassoy sat wondering about his way of changing the world, his alma mater, Stanford, was hosting an event across the city that might have cost him even more sleep had he attended it. It was a panel discussion about a collection of essays titled *Philanthropy in Democratic Societies,* featuring two of its editors and two others representing the giving world. The host for the event was David Siegel, a philanthropist who had reportedly made $500 million in a single year, and who had opened the offices of his hedge fund, Two Sigma, to host the event, despite the book's rather critical take on philanthropists.

The people who came, some to hear big philanthropy get its comeuppance, first gathered in the hedge fund's airy kitchen, nibbling on miniature tacos the girth of a finger and sipping wine. Then the program began, and before long Chiara Cordelli, an Italian political philosopher at the University of Chicago who had coedited the collection and contributed an essay, found herself sitting two panel seats over from a philanthropist who embodied everything she challenged in her scholarly writings. He was Sanford Weill, a former chairman and chief executive of Citigroup and now an active donor whose name adorned a wide array of causes. Weill was the anti-Kassoy: a product of the system who had few doubts about it, who believed as fiercely as a person could believe in the importance of elite private saviors like him.

Weill hadn't been big on government doing things when he was building Citigroup and wanted to be free of regulation, and now he wasn't big on government doing things when it came to solving public problems. He thought, then and now, that problems were best left to people like Sanford Weill. That evening, Weill repeatedly said rich people like him had to step in and solve public problems because government was too broke, too incapable, wasn't up to the task. He said this even though he personally was one of the reasons the government from time to time lacked for resources. Weill had, after all, been named by *Time* one of "25 People to Blame for the Financial Crisis," because of his relentless push for a vision of banks as "all things to all customers," and his "persistent lobbying," ultimately successful, for the repeal of Glass-Steagall, a law dating back to the Great Depression that restricted investors' risk-taking. He had advocated for too-big-to-fail banks, and he had gotten his way, which had helped to bring about the largest financial crisis in decades, which had caused the government to spend tens of billions of dollars bailing Citi out. And now Sanford Weill bemoaned that the government had no money, and thus he had to chip in and help out. By the third or fourth time Weill said this, Cordelli had grown irritated enough to shoot back a reply: "The government is us."

Weill was unmoved by this and seemed immovable. Yet Cordelli's vision of what is really going on when elites try to change the world may be the bracing tonic that Kassoy—and other MarketWorlders harboring doubts—need to see their situations more clearly and perhaps alter their ways. More important, it may give the rest of us a sense of permission to seek a better world with or without their help.

The morning after the panel, Cordelli sat in a quiet, high-ceilinged room in the SoHo Grand Hotel, on a high-backed sofa in front of an unmanned DJ booth. She nursed coffee in a paper cup and, speaking in careful, methodical sentences, sought to unravel some of MarketWorld's self-justifications.

Take, for instance, the view that MarketWorld has a duty, and right, to address public problems—and, indeed, to take a lead in developing private solutions to them. This, for Cordelli, was like putting the accused in charge of the court system. The question that elites refuse to ask, she said, is: "Why are there in the world so many people that you need to help in the first place? You should ask yourself: Have your actions contributed at all to that? Have you caused, through your actions, any harm? And, if yes, the fact that now you are helping some people, however effectively, doesn't seem to be enough to compensate."

Cordelli was speaking of both the active committers of harm and the passive permitters of it. The committers are what she calls "the easy cases." She said, "If you have campaigned against inheritance tax, if you have directly tried to avoid paying taxes, if you supported and directly, voluntarily benefited from a system where there were low labor regulations and increased precarity," then, she argues, "you have directly contributed to a structure that foreseeably and avoidably harmed people." That is "direct complicity."

As for the people who don't help run Goldman Sachs or Purdue Pharma, who live decent lives and attempt to make the world slightly better through the market, Cordelli called them the harder cases. An economist might say the marginal contribution to the world made by someone like Kassoy was positive. Cordelli rejected this analysis. She saw in each of these types of efforts not a single moral act but two. Alongside the act of helping was a parallel act of acceptance.

These MarketWorlders, with their myriad private initiatives, were doing more than merely adding good to the world. They had benefited in the past, and often continued to benefit, from a system— a set of institutions and laws and norms—that dependably blocked many people from living full lives, and that had in the United States in recent decades increased rather than shrunk the ranks of those who had been shut out. These elites were, she said, like the owner of a painting who later finds out it had been stolen. Even if the theft was before the purchase, Cordelli said, "still, it seems that, if you know the person the painting has been stolen from, you have an obligation to return it to them. Maybe even to apologize, acknowledging that you have an object that is not your own, acknowledging that you have something that has been the fruit of that injustice."

As in Kassoy's case, the choice to solve a problem in one way is a choice not to solve it in another way. Had Kassoy pursued his thought of making it harder for companies to do bad things, involving himself with politics and the law and the system itself, success might have meant the loss of opportunity for the Kassoys of the future, and could even have come at a cost to his own earnings from his old life. That was no easy decision to make.

But that is a choice, Cordelli tells us. To do a modest bit of good while doing nothing about the larger system is to keep the painting. You are chewing on the fruit of an injustice. You may be working on a prison education program, but you are choosing not to prioritize the pursuit of wage and labor laws that would make people's lives more stable and perhaps keep some of them out of jail. You may be sponsoring a loan forgiveness initiative for law school students, but you are choosing not to prioritize seeking a tax code that would take more from you and cut their debts. Your management consulting firm may be writing reports about unlocking trillions of dollars' worth of women's potential, but it is choosing not to advise its clients to stop lobbying against the social programs that have been shown in other societies to help women achieve the equality fantasized about in consultants' reports.

Economistic reasoning dominates our age, and we may be tempted to focus on the first half of each of the above sentences— a marginal contribution you can see and touch—and to ignore the second half, involving a vaguer thing called complicity. But Cordelli was challenging elites to view what they allow to be done in their name, what they refuse to resist, as being as much of a moral action as the initiatives they actively promote.

Her argument is not that every bad thing that happens in the world is your fault if you fail to stop it. Her claim, rather, is that citizens of a democracy are collectively responsible for what their society foreseeably and persistently allows; that they have a special duty toward those it systematically fails; and that this burden falls most heavily on those most amply rewarded by the same, ultimately arbitrary set of arrangements. "If you are an elite who has campaigned for or supported the right policies, or let's suppose that you are not causally complicit in any direct sense," she said, "still, it seems to me that you might owe a responsibility or duty to return to others what they have been unfairly deprived of by your common institutions."

The winners bear responsibility for the state of those institutions, and for the effects they have on others' lives, for two reasons,

Cordelli said: "because you're worth nothing without society, and also because we would all be dominated by others without political institutions that protect our rights."

To take each of those in turn: She says you are worth nothing without society because there can be no hedge fund managers, nor violinists, nor technology entrepreneurs, in the absence of a civilizational infrastructure that we take for granted. "Your life, your talents, what you do could not be possible if they weren't for common institutions," Cordelli says. If the streets weren't safe or the stock markets weren't regulated, it would be harder to make use of one's talents. If banks weren't forced to offer a guarantee of guarding your money, making money would be pointless. Even if your children attended private school, public schools very likely trained some of their teachers, and publicly financed roads connected that island of a school to the grid of the society. Then there is the fact that absent a political system of shared institutions, anyone could dominate anyone. Every person with anything precious to protect would be at constant risk of plunder by everybody else. To live in a society without laws and shared institutions that applied equally to all would be, Cordelli says, to live "dependent on the arbitrary will of another. It would be like a form of servitude."

Think of the person who seeks to "change the world" by doing what can be done within a bad system, but who is relatively silent about that system. Think of the person who runs an impact investing fund aimed at helping the poor, but is unwilling to make the connection, in his own head or out loud, between poverty and the business practices of the financiers on his advisory board. Think of a hundred variations of this example. Such a person, for Cordelli, is putting himself in the difficult moral position of the kindhearted slave master.

"For me, it is equivalent to have a master who denies people the right to freedom, and then, however, justifies that by saying, 'I'm a benevolent master,'" she said. "So I actually support slavery, but once I have the slave, I really treat them well, and, actually, they live under great conditions."

One can counter that "if you have slavery, of course, it's better to be a benevolent master than a non-benevolent master. That seems to be obvious," Cordelli said. Yet when it comes to looking back on a system like slavery, most people would agree that the only reasonable course of action back then would have been to refuse to buy a slave, refuse to participate in slavery, refuse to go along. It is when considering the present that things get murkier. A political and economic system that has shut half the nation out of growth and progress for a generation becomes understandable, becomes something to work around; the issue is said to be complicated. While some fear their stance will come to seem unreasonable one day, they choose acceptance. They seek to work through and with the culprits of injustice. They might even enlist them to advise or sit on the board of their justice-seeking project.

Sometimes that acceptance masks itself as incompetence or ignorance. Yes, someone like Laurie Tisch might say, in theory the system must be changed. But it is so hard. "Structural changes and systemic changes" are fine and good, Amy Cuddy says; the problem she confronts is: "Who do you talk to to make that happen?" Creating a voluntary pool of better-behaved capitalism on the side is easy, Andrew Kassoy says; changing the law for all businesses requires an activist's gifts, which he claims to lack, and honorable officeholders at all levels of politics—a profession that doesn't offer the lucrative rewards of MarketWorld.

Cordelli dismisses this fatalism about the system, this emotion of impotence regarding institutional change, as "absurd." It is absurd, she says, because citizens of MarketWorld "live their life through a sense of themselves as entrepreneurs, as agents of change." But this gung-ho attitude about bending the world to their will turns out to be rather temperamental. "When it comes to effecting change in a way that makes them feel good—when it comes to building a business, lobbying for certain things, effectively helping some people through philanthropy, then they are agents," Cordelli said. "They powerfully and intentionally can exercise change." However, she went on, "When it comes to paying more taxes, when it comes to trying to advocate for more just institutions, when it comes to actually trying to prevent injustices that are systemic or trying to advocate for less inequality and more redistribution, then they're paralyzed. There is nothing they can do.

"This is absurd in the sense that it's a concept of agency that doesn't make sense philosophically and doesn't make sense practically," she said. It is, first of all, not necessarily any harder to fight for a change in corporate law than to invent a parallel infrastructure of capitalism. It is not necessarily harder to seek more effective taxation of globetrotting plutocrats than to develop an elaborate annual conference getting them to give a little back. The MarketWorlders, Cordelli is reminding us, are selling themselves short. They do big, complex, elaborate things all the time; they solve hard problems. Their declared inability to contribute to solutions at the political and systemic level can ring hollow. Besides, the system under which MarketWorld has thrived in recent decades was not a naturally occurring phenomenon. It was engineered by man. MarketWorld had shown itself willing and able to engage in the arena of politics— to "change the system"—when it came to seeking lower taxes, freer trade, the repeal of laws like Glass-Steagall, debt reduction, scaled-back regulation, and many other policies that have made the present age so bountiful for its own citizens. Yet the reversal of some of the very things it had fought for was deemed too hard, too political, too vast to take on.

As harsh as her criticisms might sound to them, Cordelli is giving Kassoy and others in MarketWorld a way out. She is confessing, on their behalf, what some of them privately fear to be true: that they are debtors who need society's mercy and not saviors who need its followership. She is offering what MarketWorlders so adore: a solution. The solution is to return, against their instincts and even perhaps against their interests, to politics as the place we go to shape the world.

If Cordelli is right, the basic assumptions of MarketWorld are wrong. Doing what good you can loses some of its luster in her mode of calculation, in which what you accept matters as much as what you do. Businesspersons calling themselves "leaders" and naming themselves solvers of the most intractable social problems represent a worrisome way of erasing their role in causing them. Seen through Cordelli's lens, it is indeed strange that the people with the most to lose from social reform are so often placed on the board of it. And MarketWorld's private world-changing, for all the good it does, is also, for Cordelli, marred by its own "narcissism." "It seems to me that these days everyone wants to change the world by themselves," she said. "It's about them; it's about what they do. But there are other people around you, and you owe it to them to support institutions that can, in the name of everyone, including in their own name, secure certain conditions for a more decent life."

When a society helps people through its shared democratic institutions, it does so on behalf of all, and in a context of equality. Those institutions, representing those free and equal citizens, are making a collective choice of whom to help and how. Those who receive help are not only objects of the transaction, but also subjects of it—citizens with agency. When help is moved into the private sphere, no matter how efficient we are told it is, the context of the helping is a relationship of inequality: the giver and the taker, the helper and the helped, the donor and the recipient.

When a society solves a problem politically and systemically, it is expressing the sense of the whole; it is speaking on behalf of every citizen. It is saying what it believes through what it does. Cordelli argues that this right to speak for others is simply illegitimate when exercised by a powerful private citizen. "You are an individual," she said. "You can't speak in their name. I can maybe speak in the name of my child, but other people are not your children.

"This is what it means to be free and equal and independent individuals and, for better or for worse, share common institutions," she said. Our political institutions—our laws, our courts, our elected officials, our agencies, our rights, our police, our constitutions, our regulations, our taxes, our shared infrastructure: the million little pieces that uphold our civilization and that we own together—only these, Cordelli said, "can act and speak on behalf of everyone." She admitted, "They often don't do that." But that isn't the way out that MarketWorld so often made it out to be. "It's our job," Cordelli said, "to make them do that, rather than working to weaken and destroy those institutions by thinking that we can effectuate change by ourselves. Let's start working to create the conditions to make those institutions better."

ACKNOWLEDGMENTS

In the summer of 2015, I stood anxiously at a podium in Aspen, Colorado, wondering what happens when you tell a roomful of rich and powerful people that they are not the saviors they think they are.

Four years earlier, I had been named a Henry Crown Fellow of the Aspen Institute. You may recall it from these pages as the program that seeks to deploy a "new breed of leaders" against "the world's most intractable problems." I was a strange pick. The fellowship says of its prospective leaders that "all are proven entrepreneurs, mostly from the world of business." I was not, nor have I ever been, an entrepreneur, and writing, if it is a business, isn't a very good one. But I don't make a habit of turning down trips to Aspen, and the fellowship sounded pleasant—four one-week sessions with a group of twenty or so classmates, spread over two years, in which we would read important texts and debate them and discuss our lives and woes in secrecy, while pondering how to "make a difference."

At first, my experience of the fellowship was defined by this small group. I bonded with my classmates and exchanged my struggles with theirs and ended up being the officiant at one of their weddings. As I nestled into the Aspen Institute's universe, there were other, more dubious pleasures. I began to have friends with private jets; sometimes I flew in them. I mingled with the ultra-rich in antler-decorated mansions overlooking the Roaring Fork Valley. I brought my mother to the Aspen Ideas Festival, where we shared a hotel room and could not stop laughing about who would get the tiger-print bathrobe and who the leopard-themed one.

Even as I savored these luxuries and connections, I found something amiss about the Aspen Institute. Here were all these rich and powerful people coming together and speaking about giving back, and yet the people who seemed to reap most of the benefits of this coming-together were the helpers, not the helped. I began to wonder what was actually going on when the most fortunate don't merely seek to make a difference but also effectively claim ownership of "changing the world."

It was peculiar that many of our conversations at the Aspen Institute about democracy and the "good society" occurred in the Koch Building, named after a family that had done so much to undermine democracy and the efforts of ordinary people to "change the world." It was off-putting when the organizers of our fellowship reunion sprang a Goldman Sachs–sponsored lunch on us, in which the company's do-gooding was trumpeted and its role in causing the financial crisis went unexamined. It bothered me that the fellowship asked fellows to do virtuous side projects instead of doing their day jobs more honorably. The institute brought together people from powerful institutions like Facebook, the hedge fund Bridgewater Associates, and PepsiCo. Instead of asking them to make their firms less monopolistic, greedy, or harmful to children, it urged them to create side hustles to "change the world."

I began to feel like a casual participant in—and timid accomplice to, as well as a cowardly beneficiary of—a giant, sweet-lipped lie. Who exactly were we leaders of? What had given us the right to solve the world's problems as we saw fit? What interests and blind spots were we bringing to that problem-solving, given the criteria by which we had been selected? Why were we coming to Aspen? To change the system, or to be changed by it? To speak truth to power, like the writers we read in our seminars, or to help to make an unjust, unpalatable system go down a little more easily? Could the intractable problems we proposed to solve be solved in the way that we silently insisted—at minimal cost to elites, with minimal redistribution of power?

In my fifth year in the program, I was asked to give a talk to a few hundred of my fellow fellows at our summer reunion. This wasn't unusual. A mantra of the fellowship is to learn from one another rather than fly in outside speakers. At a given reunion, dozens of the fellows will speak in one way or another. As summer dawned and the gathering approached, the complicated feelings of the last few years swirled within me. My guilt and discomfort churned, until at last, half certain, I decided to write and deliver the speech that was the seed of this book.

"I want to suggest," I said that day from the podium, "that we may not always be the leaders we think we are." I described what I called the Aspen Consensus: "The winners of our age must be challenged to do more good. But never, ever tell them to do less harm."

Public speaking doesn't usually scare me, but that day it did. I didn't know what happens when you tell a group of people who consider themselves your friends that they are living a lie. But there I was. I finished the speech. People stood and roared, to my enduring surprise. Soon afterward, though, Madeleine Albright, the former U.S. secretary of state, came onstage and gently disparaged my speech. "*Que cojones*," another woman whispered to me. Her husband, though, started speaking ill of me behind my back. A billionaire came up and thanked me for voicing what has been the struggle of her life. Some in the leadership of the Aspen Institute began frantically asking who had allowed this outrage to occur. That evening at the bar, some cheered me, others glared at me icily, and a private-equity man told me I was an "asshole."

Later that evening, beside a fireplace, David Brooks, the *New York Times* columnist, asked if he could write about my talk. I hadn't planned for my words to leave the room, but I agreed. He wrote his column. People began demanding to see the speech. I posted it online. It stirred many pots and conversations. I hadn't planned to write a book on this topic, but the topic chose me. Thus I spent the next two years talking to and writing about people living this paradox of elite change-making that somehow seems to keep things the same.

I tell you this so that you know the book's origins, and so that I can give my first thanks—to the Aspen Institute, for embracing me and pulling back the curtain on elite-led social change. And I tell it because this backstory makes the following acknowledgment as plain as it deserves to be: the best way to know about a problem is to be part of it.

This book is the work of a critic, but it is also the work of an insider-outsider to that which it takes on. There is almost no problem probed in this book, no myth, no cloud of self-serving justification that I haven't found a way of being part of, whether because of naïveté, cynicism, rationalization, ignorance, or the necessity to make a living. I chose not to write about these things in a personal way because I didn't want the book to be about me. But let me say here, while I am doing some acknowledging, that I once worked as an analyst at McKinsey, that I have given not one but two TED talks, that I earn a chunk of my income giving speeches, that I was attending conferences claiming to "change the world" long before I came to see them as a charade. I have tried to navigate my life honestly and ethically, but I cannot separate myself from what I criticize. This is a critique of a system of which I am absolutely, undeniably a part.

For a long time, as I wrote this book, I grappled with the strangeness of indicting the practices and beliefs of a group of people among whom I have many friends. I felt an instantaneous recognition when I came upon an old phrase from the poet Czesław Miłosz. In 1953, he published a book called *The Captive Mind,* about his dismay at so many of his fellow Polish thinkers' succumbing, one rationalization and excuse at a time, to the hypocrisies and repressions of Stalinism. He described his book as "a debate with those of my friends who were yielding, little by little, to the magic influence of the New Faith." That helped me greatly. For my book, too, is, among other things, a debate with my friends. It is a letter, written with love and concern, to people whom I see yielding to a new New Faith, many of whom I know to be decent. Of course, it is also a letter to the public, urging them to reclaim world-changing from those who have co-opted it.

Because it is a debate with my friends, some of those I have written about are, unusually for me, people I knew socially before entering into the relationship of journalist and subject: Sean Hinton, Amy Cuddy, Sonal Shah, Andrew Kassoy, Laurie Tisch. I am grateful that they were willing to wrestle with these issues with me, even though my views were clear to them. I am no less grateful to all those other subjects whom I did not know but who answered my emails and calls anyway, and took me up on sharing their stories and beliefs about making change. In a small handful of cases I have changed names to protect privacy.

I am indebted to two professors. As I read Thomas Piketty's masterpiece, *Capital in the Twenty-First Century,* I came upon a line that brought the purpose of my own book into focus. "Whether such extreme inequality is or is not sustainable," Piketty writes, "depends not only on the effectiveness of the repressive apparatus but also, and perhaps primarily, on the effectiveness of the apparatus of justification." That day I decided my book would be an inquiry into the apparatus of justification. And Michael Sandel, who taught me at Harvard, was perhaps the first to plant in me the thought that money had transcended being currency to become our very culture, conquering our imaginations and infiltrating domains that had nothing to do with it.

I want to salute those generous people who gave of their time to read chapters or even the whole manuscript: Richard Sherwin, Nicholas Negroponte, Joshua Cooper Ramo, Rukmini Giridharadas, Tom Ferguson, Hilary Cohen, and Casey Gerald. Thanks, too, to Zackary Canepari for lending me his cabin in the woods. Then there is my heroic wife, Priya Parker. She is the first to know how the writing is going, because, after all these years, she still insists on hearing every day's harvest out loud. My wise and ever-supportive parents, Shyam and Nandini, and a flotilla of friends too numerous to name helped in their own vital ways: lending advice, shoulders, and diversions when the writing grew hard, as it always does—and providing rapid text-message title feedback. And, once again, I was blessed with the talents of Vrinda Condillac, a masterful editor and a brilliant, effervescent friend, who sat beside me and went through the manuscript paragraph by paragraph for most of two weeks.

My wonderful agent, Lynn Nesbit, is one of those rare people who deserve their legendary status. There is no one better at shepherding books into the world, and at dealing with all the obstacles that come in their way. There is no one more reassuring to a writer, no one better at taking the long view, and, if there are still a few who, like Lynn, use their phones to gab and not just type, no one gabs better.

Lynn led me to Alfred A. Knopf, but it was also a kind of homecoming. I first met my editor on this book, Jonathan Segal, a decade or so ago when I was writing about India. He didn't end up acquiring that book, but he profoundly shaped it simply through his comments on the proposal. We found each other again with *Winners Take All*. Jon is smart, dedicated, passionate about books, and hard to please. When putting his penciled edits into the computer, I had the feeling of watching a master surgeon. At first, your eye focuses on the cutting. But then you notice the body he is bringing to health by removing what must be removed and transplanting and injecting and suturing. This book wouldn't exist without his eyes, hands, and faith. I am also grateful to Knopf's brave leader, Sonny Mehta, for his championing of books, and to Jessica Purcell, Paul Bogaards, Sam Aber, Julia Ringo, Kim Thornton Ingenito, and the rest of the team.

This book is dedicated to my children, Orion and Zora, and to yours, who deserve the new age that is coming.

A NOTE ON SOURCES

This is a work of reportage. In general, the people I write about and quote at length are people I have interviewed, with some exceptions indicated in the text. Similarly, the scenes I describe in detail are scenes that I have witnessed or attempted to reconstruct from the testimonies of people who were there. Where I have relied heavily on books, I have cited them directly in the text wherever possible. Thus what follows is a list of substantial sources that I did not cite in the text, to avoid cluttering the narrative and slowing down the reader. Not everything is covered. Where in the book there are small quotations easily searched on the Internet or facts of self-evident origin, I have not necessarily included them.

PROLOGUE

On American scientists' leading the world in biomedical research, see "Globalization and Changing Trends of Biomedical Research Output," by Marisa L. Conte, Jing Liu, Santiago Schnell, and M. Bishr Omary (*JCI Insight*, June 2017). On the average American's health remaining "worse and slower-improving than that of peers in other rich countries," see "U.S. Health in International Perspective: Shorter Lives, Poorer Health," by the Institute of Medicine and the National Research Council (Washington, DC: National Academies Press, 2013). On American life expectancy declining, see "Mortality in the United States," by Jiaquan Xu et al. (National Center for Health Statistics data brief no. 267, December 2016). On the decline in the average twelfth grader's reading level, see "The Condition of Education 2017," by Joel McFarland et al. (National Center for Education Statistics, 2017). On the incidence of obesity and related conditions, see

"Early Release of Selected Estimates Based on Data from the 2015 National Health Interview Survey," by B. W. Ward, T. C. Clarke, C. N. Nugent, and J. S. Schiller (National Center for Health Statistics, May 2016); and various resources at http://stateofobesity.org. On the drop in young entrepreneurship, see "Endangered Species: Young U.S. Entrepreneurs," by Ruth Simon and Caelainn Barr (*Wall Street Journal*, January 2, 2015). On Google Books, see "Torching the Modern-Day Library of Alexandria," by James Somers (*Atlantic*, April 2017). On American literacy, see "The U.S. Illiteracy Rate Hasn't Changed in 10 Years" (*Huffington Post*, September 6, 2013); and data from the National Center for Education Statistics. On the reading of literature, see "The Long, Steady Decline of Literary Reading," by Christopher Ingraham (*Washington Post*, September 7, 2016). On trust in government, see "Public Trust in Government Remains Near Historic Lows as Partisan Attitudes Shift" (Pew Research Center, May 3, 2017).

On the uneven spread of the "fruits of change," see "Distributional National Accounts: Methods and Estimates for the United States," by Thomas Piketty, Emmanuel Saez, and Gabriel Zucman (National Bureau of Economic Research Working Paper No. 22945, December 2016). On the changing realities of social mobility and the "opportunity to get ahead," see "The Fading American Dream: Trends in Absolute Mobility Since 1940," by Raj Chetty et al. (National Bureau of Economic Research Working Paper No. 22910, December 2016). On the rich/poor life expectancy gap, see "The Association Between Income and Life Expectancy in the United States, 2001–2014," by Raj Chetty et al. (*Journal of the American Medical Association*, April 26, 2016). On the billionaire growth rate versus others' and the wealth of the richest 10 percent, see "How Business Titans, Pop Stars and Royals Hide Their Wealth," by Scott Shane, Spencer Woodman, and Michael Forsythe (*New York Times*, November 7, 2017).

CHAPTER 1: BUT HOW IS THE WORLD CHANGED?

The further data from Piketty et al. is from the same "Distributional National Accounts" paper cited above. On Bill Clinton's time at Georgetown, see *On the Make: The Rise of Bill Clinton*, by Meredith L. Oakley (New York: Regnery, 1994). The David Harvey quotes on neoliberalism are from his book *A Brief History of Neoliberalism* (Oxford: Oxford University Press, 2007). For Yascha Mounk's ideas on the shifting meaning of "responsibility," see

The Age of Responsibility: Luck, Choice, and the Welfare State (Cambridge, MA: Harvard University Press, 2017). For Jonathan Haidt's conversation with Krista Tippett, see "Capitalism and Moral Evolution: A Civil Provocation," an episode of the radio show and podcast *On Being* (June 2, 2016).

CHAPTER 2: WIN-WIN

For the African Development Bank's take on so-called vulture funds, see its website: www.afdb.org/en/topics-and-sectors/initiatives-partnerships/african-legal-support-facility/vulture-funds-in-the-sovereign-debt-context (accessed September 2017). For more of the Economic Policy Institute's work on wage stagnation and rising productivity, see "Understanding the Historic Divergence Between Productivity and a Typical Worker's Pay," by Josh Bivens and Lawrence Mishel (EPI Briefing Paper No. 406, September 2015). The first Adam Smith quote comes from *The Wealth of Nations*, book I, chapter 2; the second, from *The Theory of Moral Sentiments*, part IV, chapter 1. Michael Porter's quote on the power of business to solve problems comes from his essay "Creating Shared Value," coauthored with Mark R. Kramer (*Harvard Business Review*, January–February 2011). Craig Shapiro's writings and Venn diagram come from the website of his Collaborative Fund: www.collaborativefund.com/about (accessed September 2017).

CHAPTER 3: REBEL-KINGS IN WORRISOME BERETS

Blair Miller's quote comes from an interview series called "Tastemakers," published by the New York clothing boutique Otte (no longer available online). Danah Boyd's critique of the tech barons is from her essay "It's Not Cyberspace Anymore" (*Points* blog on Medium, February 2016).

On the campaign against discrimination on Airbnb, see "Airbnb Has a Discrimination Problem. Ask Anyone Who's Tried to #Airbnbwhileblack," by Aja Romano (*Vox*, May 6, 2016). Airbnb's report in response to the accusations is titled "Airbnb's Work to Fight Discrimination and Build Inclusion," by Laura W. Murphy (September 8, 2016): http://blog.atairbnb.com/wp-content/uploads/2016/09/REPORT_Airbnbs-Work-to-Fight-Discrimination-and-Build-Inclusion.pdf?3c10be (accessed September 2017). The California Department of Fair Employment and Housing's allegations against Airbnb are contained here: www.dfeh.ca.gov/wp-content/uploads/sites/32/2017/06/04-19-17-Airbnb-DFEH-Agreement-Signed-DFEH-1-1

.pdf (accessed September 2017). Airbnb's response to California's charges is also contained in the above document.

For Judge Chen's ruling on Uber, see his "Order Denying Defendant Uber Technologies, Inc.'s Motion for Summary Judgment" in *O'Connor v. Uber,* Case No. C-13-3826 EMC, United States District Court for the Northern District of California, Docket No. 211. For Judge Chhabria's ruling on Lyft, see his "Order Denying Cross-motions for Summary Judgment" in *Cotter v. Lyft,* Case No. 13-cv-04065-VC, United States District Court for the Northern District of California, Dockets No. 69 and 74.

On Bill Gates's faith in technology's leveling powers, see his book *The Road Ahead* (New York: Viking, 1995). On Mark Zuckerberg and Priscilla Chan's faith in the Internet's powers, see their "Letter to Our Daughter" (Zuckerberg's Facebook page, December 2015).

David Heinemeier Hansson's critique of the Silicon Valley ethic comes from his essay "Reconsider" (*Signal v. Noise* blog on Medium, November 5, 2015). Maciej Ceglowski's critique is quoted in "California Capitalism Is Starting to Look a Lot Like Polish Communism," published on *Quartz* (September 24, 2015), or in its original form here: http://idlewords.com /talks/what_happens_next_will_amaze_you.htm. The Hobbes quotes come from his *Leviathan,* book I, chapter 13.

CHAPTER 4: THE CRITIC AND THE THOUGHT LEADER

Amy Cuddy's research papers can be found on her Google Scholar page: https://scholar.google.com/citations?user=1kdjewoAAAAJ. Her paper on men and perceptions of independence and interdependence is "Men as Cultural Ideals: How Culture Shapes Gender Stereotypes" (Harvard Business School Working Paper 10-097, 2010). Andrew Zolli's essay is "Learning to Bounce Back" (*New York Times,* November 2, 2012).

Regarding the statistics on job security: The tenure data come from "Higher Education at a Crossroads," a report by the American Association of University Professors (March–April 2016): www.aaup.org/sites/default /files/2015-16EconomicStatusReport.pdf (accessed September 2017). The newsroom data come from "Newsonomics: The Halving of America's Daily Newsrooms," by Ken Doctor (*Nieman Lab,* July 28, 2015).

The Adam Grant quotes are from his book *Originals: How Non-Conformists Move the World* (New York: Viking, 2016). The quotes from

Brené Brown come from "The Power of Vulnerability," her talk at TEDx-Houston (June 2010). Carol Hanisch's quote comes from her 1969 essay "The Personal Is Political," available at her website: www.carolhanisch.org/CHwritings/PIP.html (accessed September 2017). Malcolm Gladwell's discussion of the ethical quandary of paid speaking can be found in a "Disclosure Statement" on his website: http://gladwell.com/disclosure-statement (accessed September 2017). The Stephen Marche criticism of Niall Ferguson is from "The Real Problem with Niall Ferguson's Letter to the 1%" (*Esquire*, August 2012). Gautam Mukunda's observation is originally from his essay "The Price of Wall Street's Power" (*Harvard Business Review*, June 2014).

For more on the "identifiable-victim effect," see "Helping *a* Victim or Helping *the* Victim: Altruism and Identifiability," by Deborah Small and George Loewenstein (*Journal of Risk and Uncertainty*, January 2003). Jonathan Haidt's criticism of people who expect "way too much" comes from the same *On Being* interview quoted above.

CHAPTER 5: ARSONISTS MAKE THE BEST FIREFIGHTERS

The Open Society Foundations' 2016 budget can be found online here: www.opensocietyfoundations.org/sites/default/files/open-society-foundations-2016-budget-overview-2016-01-21.pdf. Kavita Ramdas's criticism of the technocratic takeover of the nonprofit world is from her essay "Philanthrocapitalism Is Not Social Change Philanthropy" (*Stanford Social Innovation Review*, December 2011). The letter to the world's Bahá'ís is from the 2010 installment of the Universal House of Justice's annual Ridván Message, available here: http://universalhouseofjustice.bahai.org/ridvan-messages/20100421_001.

CHAPTER 6: GENEROSITY AND JUSTICE

The quotes from Darren Walker come, unless otherwise indicated, from my interviews with him. For a magazine profile of Walker and his remarkable life, see also "What Money Can Buy," by Larissa MacFarquhar (*New Yorker*, January 4, 2016). The late historian Peter Dobkin Hall's account of the origins of American philanthropy is from a book chapter he wrote, "A Historical Overview of Philanthropy, Voluntary Associations, and Nonprofit Organizations in the United States, 1600 to 2000"; the book is *The*

Nonprofit Sector: A Research Handbook, 2nd ed. (New Haven, CT: Yale University Press, 2006). Jonathan Levy's quotes are from his chapter in the *Philanthropy in Democratic Societies* book mentioned in the text. Walker's letter, "Toward a New Gospel of Wealth," can be found at the Ford Foundation website: www.fordfoundation.org/ideas/equals-change-blog/posts/toward-a-new-gospel-of-wealth (accessed September 2017).

The section on the Sacklers, Purdue Pharma, and the opioid epidemic is, unlike most of the book, a work of historical synthesis built entirely on the primary reporting of others. The publications are quoted in the text, but let me record my gratitude for the reporting of, among others, Bruce Weber and Barry Meier at the *New York Times,* Katherine Eban at *Fortune,* and David Armstrong for his sustained and heroic work at *STAT.* John Brownlee's quotes about Purdue come from congressional testimony he gave, in a session titled "Ensuring That Death and Serious Injury Are More Than a Business Cost: OxyContin and Defective Products" (Senate Judiciary Committee, July 31, 2007).

CHAPTER 7: ALL THAT WORKS IN THE MODERN WORLD

Niall Ferguson's quotes about the globalists are from his essay "Theresa May's Abbanomics and Brexit's New Class War" (*Boston Globe,* October 10, 2016). The Lawrence Summers quote is from his column "Voters Deserve Responsible Nationalism Not Reflex Globalism" (*Financial Times,* July 9, 2016). Jonathan Haidt's analysis is from "When and Why Nationalism Beats Globalism" (*American Interest,* July 10, 2016).

I interviewed Bill Clinton twice for this book. The first instance was in September 2016, via email. The second was in May 2017, a ninety-minute conversation conducted in person at his foundation's offices in New York.

The analysis by Aaron Horvath and Walter Powell about philanthropy being "contributory" or "disruptive" of democracy comes from their chapter in the *Philanthropy in Democratic Societies* book.

EPILOGUE: "OTHER PEOPLE ARE NOT YOUR CHILDREN"

The extensive quotes from Chiara Cordelli are from an interview with me. For more on her ideas, see her chapter in the *Philanthropy and Democratic Societies* book, which she also coedited.

INDEX

O